中国社会科学院语言研究所 主办
中国语言学会语音学分会 会刊
PAC Phonetic Association of China

第14辑

Chinese Journal of Phonetics

中国语音学报

中国社会科学出版社

图书在版编目（CIP）数据

中国语音学报．第14辑／中国社会科学院语言研究所主办．—北京：中国社会科学出版社，2020.12
ISBN 978-7-5203-8474-2

Ⅰ.①中… Ⅱ.①中… Ⅲ.①汉语—语音学—文集 Ⅳ.①H11-53

中国版本图书馆CIP数据核字(2021)第092680号

出 版 人　赵剑英
责任编辑　张　林
责任校对　王佳玉
责任印制　戴　宽

出　　版　中国社会科学出版社
社　　址　北京鼓楼西大街甲158号
邮　　编　100720
网　　址　http://www.csspw.cn
发 行 部　010-84083685
门 市 部　010-84029450
经　　销　新华书店及其他书店

印　　刷　北京君升印刷有限公司
装　　订　廊坊市广阳区广增装订厂
版　　次　2020年12月第1版
印　　次　2020年12月第1次印刷

开　　本　787×1092　1/16
印　　张　9.75
插　　页　2
字　　数　258千字
定　　价　58.00元

党建武	天津大学
丁红卫	上海交通大学
顾文涛	南京师范大学
呼　和	中国社会科学院民族学与人类学研究所
胡　方	中国社会科学院语言研究所
贾　媛	中国社会科学院语言研究所
孔江平	北京大学
李爱军	中国社会科学院语言研究所
李蕙心	香港城市大学
李敬阳	公安部物证鉴定中心情报信息技术处
李永宏	西北民族大学
凌震华	中国科学技术大学
刘俐李	南京师范大学
刘新中	暨南大学
路继伦	天津师范大学
马秋武	同济大学
冉启斌	南开大学
石　锋	南开大学，北京语言大学
陶建华	中国科学院自动化研究所
王洪君	北京大学
王英利	广东省公安厅刑事技术中心
王韫佳	北京大学
魏建国	天津大学
吴民华	香港大学
谢　磊	西北工业大学
熊子瑜	中国社会科学院语言研究所
许　毅	伦敦大学学院
颜永红	中国科学院声学研究所
杨玉芳	中国科学院心理研究所
翟红华	山东农业大学
张　华	同仁医院耳鼻喉科
张劲松	北京语言大学
郑　方	清华大学
郑秋豫	台湾中研院语言学研究所
朱维彬	北京交通大学
朱晓农	香港科技大学
祖漪清	安徽科大讯飞信息科技股份有限公司

编者按　言语听觉科学与语音学的交叉研究新视野

于　珏

语音学的三个分支：发音语音学、声学语音学及听觉语音学，分别对应有声语言言语链的三个重要环节：言语的产生、传播以及感知，一起构成交际双方的感知链和自我感知反馈链。言语链上的各个环节需要相互关联，共同协作，才能保证顺利的言语交际。然而，对于重度或极重度听障患者而言，由于听觉器官病变或损伤，无法构成完整的言语交互回路，从而制约了其语言能力的正常发展，影响其社会化进程。

我国是世界上听力残疾人数最多的国家，约有 2780 万人，其中儿童听障患者约 13.7 万人，且每年以 2 万—3 万人的速度增长，给家庭及社会造成沉重负担。目前，多通道人工耳蜗和气导/骨导助听器可以利用听障患者的残余听力，刺激其声音感知，从而促进听觉中枢的发育，改善听力、提高言语能力。然而，与人耳自然聆听相比，目前的人工听觉技术依然存在诸多局限，其核心技术一直未有突破性的进展，无法使人工听觉更智能、更真实。例如，多通道人工耳蜗虽被公认为能够替代受损耳蜗功能，使重度或极重度感音性耳聋患者恢复听觉，但是受限于植入电极深度、通道数目及言语处理器的编码技术，该装置还无法精确解析语音信号中的声学线索（尤其是音高线索），致使植入者无法充分地感知及习得言语的韵律特征及规律，影响日常言语交际。其次，我国的言语听觉科学还处于起步阶段，在临床康复中，大多直接借鉴国外的评估工具与干预经验，而实际上却无法完全解决中国听障患者的言语问题。近年来，针对中国听障儿童的言语评估工具正日趋完善，但对于语音部分的评估依然较为粗糙，常以清晰度、流畅度、自然度等主观评测为主，缺乏具体的语音量化标准。上述问题的解决都有赖于语音学的相关研究成果，以便为中国听觉障碍人群探索出一套符合中国语言特点的、系统的、科学的言语障碍干预策略，实现其“听音辨意，意通音达”的口语无障碍沟通。

本期《中国语音学报》特编辑了听障儿童语音加工障碍的综述和研究成果，集中了 6 篇有关听障儿童的非典型语音特征及干预个案研究，抛砖引玉，希望能有更多的同仁参与相关的研究，为进一步揭示汉语言语障碍人群的语音加工机制，实现对其言语障碍的有效评估及干预而努力。除此之外，本期还呈现了疫情防御新形势下“口罩模态”的语音交际，健听者及二语习得者的音段及超音段的产出与感知特点等多方面的研究。

语音学是一门相对独立且交叉性很强的学科，涉及的研究领域相当广泛。中国的言语听觉科学需要与语音学、听力学、康复医学、计算语言学等多学科交叉融合，才能深入地考察中国言语障碍人群的话语特征；而语音学也应该发挥自身的学科优势，逐步开启从韵律小单元迈向韵律大单元的研究新视野，逐步完善对中国言语障碍人群从音段特征到超音段特征的系统描写，为中国言语听觉康复事业提供新的研究范式和理论依据。

目　录

RHYTHM FORMANTS OF STORY READING IN STANDARD MANDARIN

GIBBON Dafydd

Abstract Rhythm Formant Theory (RFT), a modulation-theoretic approach to the physical modelling of speech rhythm, is described and applied in an exploratory analysis of the rhetorical rhythms of read-aloud Mandarin Chinese translations of the IPA benchmark text *The North Wind and the Sun*. Rhythm Formant Analysis (RFA), a methodology for empirically investigating Rhythm Formant Theory without prior annotation of the speech signal, is presented in some detail, with the aim of studying rhythm variation in larger units throughout longer texts, rather than restricting analysis to words, phrases and sentences. A test case of read-aloud narratives was investigated, with the null hypothesis that male and female readers do not differ in rhetorical reading strategies. RFA was used to generate vectors of low frequency (LF) variation in spectrograms, for analysis with hierarchical clustering methods. The clustering indicates that the null hypothesis was falsified and rhetorical differences between female and male speakers were tentatively confirmed. Ongoing work includes the analysis of linguistic factors underlying LF variation. In the conclusion, RFT is placed into a more general framework of a Speech Modulation Frequency Scale of modulation types.
Key Words Rhythm Formant Theory, Speech rhythm, Rhythm formant, Rhythm spectrogram, Modulation-theory

1. SPEECH RHYTHM

The goal of the present study is to demonstrate core aspects of the relation between rhythmic patterns in speech, in terms of amplitude modulation (related to sonority curves) and frequency modulation (related to tones, pitch accents, intonations), and from an empirical and descriptive rather than an intuitive and structural point of view.

There have been many linguistic and phonetic studies of the rhythmic patterns of speech in the past, in three main paradigms, in addition to rhetorical and pedagogical accounts:

(1) A phonological paradigm with taxonomic and generative sub-paradigms, in which rhythm is an abstract structure consisting of relations between stronger and weaker abstract stress values, sometimes expressed numerically (cf. Pike [38]; Jassem [25]; Abercrombie [1], [2]; Chomsky, Halle and Lukoff [8]; Chomsky and Halle [9]; Liberman and Prince [32]; Selkirk [42]).

(2) A linguistic-phonetic paradigm, in which abstract units such as voiced phone sequences or syllables are annotated with time-stamps and interval durations from the speech signal, using software tools. The annotations are used for deriving speech rate, pause patterns, degrees of isochrony (equal timing), using descriptive statistics for distinguishing between languages in terms of duration irregularities (cf. Lehiste [30]; Roach [40]; Jassem et al. [26]; Scott et al. [41]; Ramus et al. [39]; Low et al. [33]; Asu and Nolan [4]; Li and Yin [31]; Yu and Gibbon [47]).

(3) A modulation-theoretic paradigm in which rhythms are modelled as low frequency (LF) oscillations in the speech signal, with signal processing applications in both speech production and speech perception models (cf. Dogil and Braun [15]; Todd et al. [45];

Cummins and Port [12]; Cummins and Schmidthuber [11]; O' Dell and Nieminen [36]; Foote and Uchihashi [16]; Barbosa [5]; Galves et al. [17]; Lee and Todd [29]; Tilsen and Johnson [44]; He? mansky [23]; Ludusan et al. [34]; Barbosa and da Silva [6]; Inden et al. [24]; Tilsen and Arvaniti [43]; He and Dellwo [22]; Varnet et al. [46]; Gibbon [19]; Gibbon and Li [20]; Kallio et al. [27]; Ludusan and Wagner [35]).

The first two approaches are deductive, based on intuition-based linguistic categories, often in a search for correlations in the speech signal or in physiology. The phonological paradigm has shown how rhythms relate to language structure, but does not address the issue of physical empirical grounding. The linguistic-phonetic paradigm does address physical grounding, and has provided heuristics for distinguishing languages in terms of differences in timing irregularity (partial isochrony, timing similarity). But it has often been pointed out that this approach does not in fact describe rhythm in the usual sense of regular beats or oscillation. These approaches also fail to identify rhythm because their use of descriptive statistical methods introduces a methodological problem: these methods apply to sets of static data, not to the dynamic time series data of speech signals which characterise physical properties of rhythm. Time series data require different methods. The second paradigm has been critically discussed in by Dauer [13], Barry et al. [7], Gibbon [18], Gut [21], Arvaniti [3] and Kohler [28].

The modulation-theoretic paradigm, on the other hand, is inductive and provides a physical grounding which complements the other two paradigms. A related early account of rhythm as "waves" rather than partially isochronous units was given by Pike [37]. Physical utterances are the starting point in this paradigm. Utterances are analysed in terms of component modulation frequencies, mainly amplitude modulation (AM) in the spectral region below about 10Hz, leading to generalisations about rhythms as timing patterns at different frequencies. The present study extends this modulation-theoretic paradigm by (a) permitting analysis of long texts (rather than words and phrases), (b) including frequency modulation (FM) in the domain of investigation, (c) introducing the concept of *rhythm formant* (RF), as opposed to *phone formant* (PF) to interpret high magnitude LF spectral peaks, and (d) extending LF spectral analysis to the *low frequency rhythm spectrogram* in order to analyse rhythm variation through longer speech instances.

2. METHODOLOGY

2.1 Basics of rhythm formant analysis

The purpose of this and the following subsections is to introduce the *Rhythm Formant Analysis* (RFA) methodology with "clear case" data, for the purpose of understanding the *Rhythm Formant Theory* (RFT) of AM and FM information in the speech signal.

The LF amplitude modulation (LFAM) of the speech signal is related to the sonority curve, a complex epiphenomenon resulting from the coordinated sequencing of consonants and vowels and from the emergent distribution of high frequency (HF) *phone formants* in the speech signal spectrum, which are due to resonances in the articulatory tract.

The LF modulation of the fundamental frequency (F0) of the speech signal (LFFM) is the direct correlate of tones, pitch accents and intonation.

Figure 1 shows the amplitude and frequency modulation of a counting sequence from one to seven in Standard British English. The AM component is shown by outlining the positive amplitudes of the signal, shown in the upper half of Figure 1, i. e. the *ampli-*

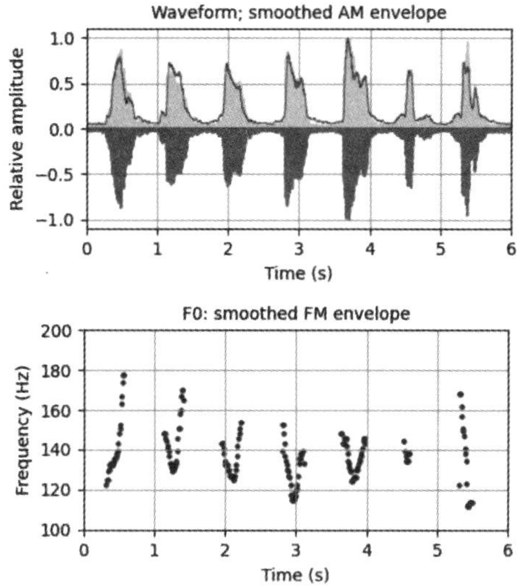

Figure 1 AM and FM envelopes for English counting one to seven (adult male speaker)

tude modulation envelope (*AM envelope*). The FM component is provided by the fundamental frequency estimation function (informally: "pitch track"), shown as the *frequency modulation envelope* (*FM envelope*) in the lower half of Figure 1. The FM envelope is extracted with the *Average Magnitude Difference Function*, which is similar to autocorrelation but uses window subtraction rather than multiplication.

The AM envelope corresponds roughly to the sonority curve of weak consonantal syllable margins which frame stronger vowel nuclei, resulting in an alternating or oscillating pattern. The sonority curve also delineates larger units than the syllable, for example phrases or "paragraph-sized" utterance segments with changing amplitudes.

The differences between the AM envelopes of each numeral in the sequence are rather small (except for "six", a short vowel flanked by voiceless consonants), and it is obvious where the rhythmic effect originates: the syllable-sized patterns are very similar and occur in similar time-slots.

Rhythms have frequencies. This obvious fact is ignored in many earlier analyses. The main frequency of the AM envelope of the numerals in this sequence can be calculated informally by observing that 7 numerals divided by 6 seconds yields a speech rate of 1.167 numerals per second, a frequency of 1.167Hz with an average unit duration or beat as the inverse of the frequency: $6/7 = 0.857$ s, 857 ms. The overall amplitude envelope pattern also contains lower frequencies from longer term patterns, as well as higher frequencies due to shorter syllable components.

The AM and FM envelopes have the same main frequency, due to alignment of the stress-pitch accents with the numerals, but the detailed pattern of the FM envelope is quite different, being determined by three main factors:

(1) Initial boundary tone, which involves a very high rising F0 in this sequence.

(2) Similar local fall-rise F0 patterns in the subsequent numerals (corresponding to the "head" of the intonation unit, in traditional terminology), with a stress-pitch accent sequence (SPAS) constraint on the head which creates expectations of up-coming structures ([14]). Each local F0 pattern contributes to higher frequency rhythms, with still higher frequencies determined by consonantal perturbations of the local F0 pattern at syllable margins.

(3) Final boundary tone, which starts higher and finishes lower than the previous local patterns, and contributes to a much lower phrasal frequency pattern.

The AM and FM envelopes represent modulations of the basic carrier signal which is generated either in the larynx or by obstruent "noise", and are demodulated in order to recover the rhythmic information generated in speech production for input to speech recognition and perception. Four assumptions are involved in the demodulation procedure:

(1) Rhythms can be discovered by spectral analysis of the AM and FM envelope

modulation by using low-pass filtering and the Fourier Transform, and visualised in the LF spectrum over the entire utterance.

(2) Spectral analyses of the AM envelope and the FM envelope are similar in revealing high magnitude LF spectral zones, interpreted as *rhythm formants*. The AM and FM frequency zones differ in detail, because of differences between syllable sonority patterns and pitch accent patterns.

(3) Languages with different prosodic typology show different pitch patterns. Specifically, lexical and morphological tone languages show more varied LFFM spectral structure than languages with no SPAS constraint, because lexical tones are arbitrary phonemes and not constrained to be similar.

(4) Variations in rhythm over time can be shown by frequency spectrograms of either AM or FM envelopes.

The claims #1 to #3 are discussed in the following subsections. The AM part of claim #4 is treated in Section 3 in the context of the distance-based clustering of reading aloud by Mandarin Chinese female and male readers.

2.2 Low frequency spectral analysis

The assumptions outlined in the previous subsection can be taken as predictions and investigated operationally by extracting AM and FM envelopes from the speech signal and applying a Fast Fourier Transform (FFT) to the envelopes to obtain the LF spectra. Figure 2 shows the LF spectra (1...5Hz) which result from applying the FFT with appropriate low-pass filtering to the AM and FM envelopes. The text boxes in the two graphs show the 5 highest magnitude frequencies in each spectrum.

Evidently, the AM and FM spectra agree closely even without correlation calculation: in each case there is an AM high magnitude frequency zone around 1.3Hz, peaking at 1.167Hz. This zone is a rhythm formant corresponding to the frequency of numerals in the counting sequence, which thus have an average duration of about 750ms. The result agrees roughly with the manual calculation.

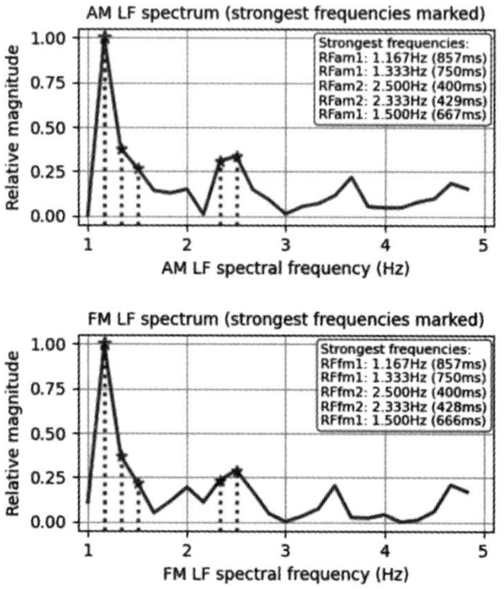

Figure 2 LF FFT spectra of AM (upper) and FM (lower) envelopes of the English counting sequence

A second rhythm formant occurs at around 2.42Hz, corresponding to an average period of 413ms. It is no accident that the frequency region of the second formant is twice that of the first formant: the AM and FM envelopes both show a binary syllable structure. The AM numeral envelopes have a secondary peak due to the voiced codas (or nasal syllable in "seven"). In the FM envelopes a binary structure also dominates due to the fall and rise components of the pitch contours.

The term "formant" is defined acoustically in exactly the same way for these LF rhythm formants (RF) as it is for HF phone formants (PF). In the speech production domain, the LF patterns are, of course, not resonances of the vocal tract, but neural resonances or oscillations which "conspire" to drive the muscle patterns of articulation. In the speech perception domain, the functions differ: perception of an LF resonance is rhythm, perception of an HF resonance is sound quality.

2.3 FM envelope: tone vs. stress-pitch

The prediction that FM envelope rhythm differs in tone and stress-pitch accent languages can be demonstrated by comparing the English counting sequence with a Mandarin counting sequence, in Pinyin transcription *yī èr sān sì wǔ liù qī*, with high, fall, high, fall, fall-rise (dipping), fall and high lexical tones (i. e. tones 1, 4, 1, 4, 3, 4, 1). The null hypothesis is that the two languages do not differ in relevant ways.

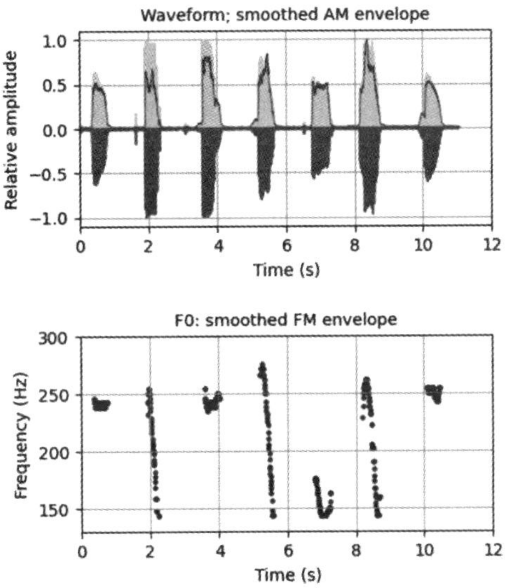

Figurc 3 AM and FM cnvclopcs for Mandarin counting scqucncc onc to scvcn (fcmalc)

An example of counting from 1 to 7 in Mandarin Chinese by a female subject is shown in Figure 3. Informal observation shows that average F0 is higher, as expected. The individually determined speech rate of the Mandarin speaker is also considerably slower than the speech rate of the English speaker: an informal count shows 7 numerals in just under 11 seconds, i. e. around 7/11 = 0.636 items/s, 0.636Hz, averaging 1.571s per numeral.

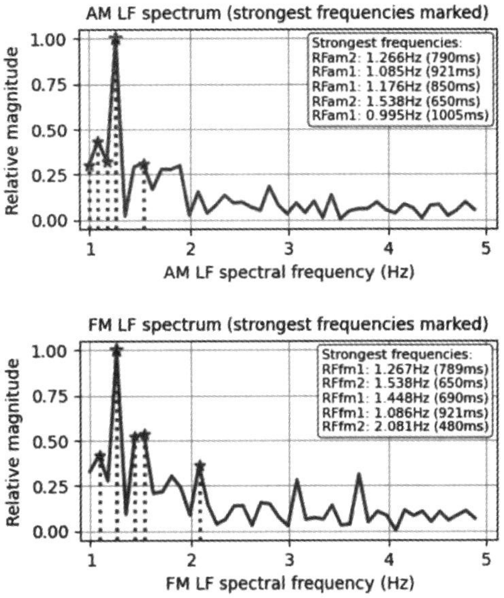

Figure 4 AM and FM LF spectra for Mandarin counting sequence one to seven (adult female)

The overall AM envelope pattern is similar to the English pattern, with expected lower LF formant frequencies and some differences related to the variation in Mandarin syllable structure. Measurements yield a somewhat variable first LF formant of about 1.085Hz and an average unit duration of about 921ms for both the AM envelope rhythm. Thcsc valucs arc cxpcctcd bccause of the slower tempo than in the English counting, and reflect the informal observation of differences in numeral rate and duration. A more precise measurement would need a higher spectral resolution than was possible with these recordings.

The phonotactic diversity of the Mandarin syllable structures is reflected in the different spectral patterns between 1.5Hz and 2Hz, due to the absence of the SPAS constraint.

In addition to the difference between the English and Mandarin spectral patterns, the variety of Mandarin syllable patterns and lexical tone patterns, with absence of the SPAS constraint, leads to differences between the Mandarin AM and FM spectra which are not observable for English: the English LFFM and LFAM rhythm formants (Figure 2) are relatively compact and resemble each other, while the Mandarin LFFM and LFAM rhythm formants (Figure 4) are more diffuse.

Although there are general similarities, the conspicuous differences do not support the null hypothesis of strong similarity between the rhythm formant analyses of the English and Mandarin counting sequences.

2.4 Data

One major empirical innovation of RFT and its RFA methodology is that in contrast to earlier approaches they permit the analysis of rhythm variation over entire narratives. The data used in the small-scale study in the following section consist of a read-aloud translated narrative in Pǔtōnghuà, Standard Mandarin Chinese. The narrative is the IPA benchmark fable, *The North Wind and the Sun*, spoken by 5 female and 5 male native speakers, from the Tongji University Yu corpus. The data were analysed in a preliminary study, and are further investigated here with hierarchical classification, a basic variety of unsupervised machine learning, using vectors derived from the RFA LF spectrogram.

Table 1 Durations of narratives

	Durations of narratives (seconds)					Mean
F	53.30	38.74	40.90	45.41	53.90	46.45
M	40.50	43.00	54.24	60.93	40.60	47.85

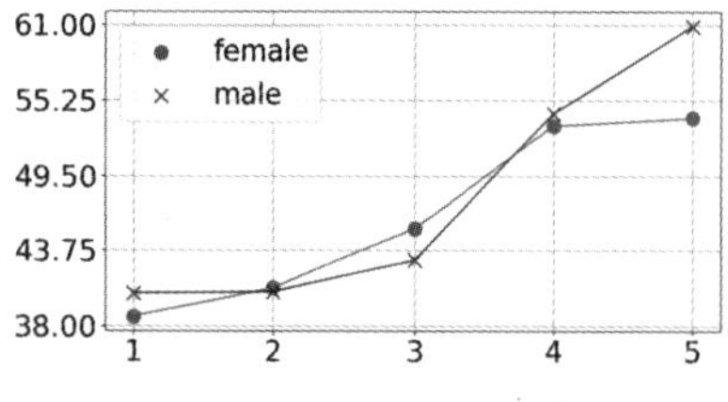

Figure 5 Distribution of recording durations of female and male Mandarin story readers

The narratives differ considerably in duration, from 38.74s to 60.93s, whereby the female and male narratives share roughly similar range and distributions (cf. Table 1 and Figure 5), with female readings on average very slightly faster.

It might therefore be predicted that on the basis of duration, and thus of utterance rate, or indeed of F0 height alone, a null hypothesis of no difference between female and male speakers can be confirmed. But a more interesting and potentially easily falsifiable null hypothesis is that a modulation-theoretic analysis will find no difference in rhythm between female and male readers.

To investigate this hypothesis an inductive search for hierarchical clusters is undertaken, rather than conventionally looking for flat clusters or sets of correlations. The criterion for clustering is least distance (or: least difference, similarity) between rhythm variation vectors over the LF spectrograms of the readings. The goodness of clustering criterion G is the sum of the largest male and female reader cluster sizes, divided by the size of the data set.

3 RESULTS

3.1 Envelope extraction

For the extraction of the AM envelope, the absolute Hilbert Transform is often cited (cf. [22]). However, in this study the waveform is rectified (converted to absolute values) and low-pass filtered, which achieves the same result (Figure 6).

3.2 Spectral analysis

Figure 7 shows the female (left) and male (right) results, each ordered alphabetically.

Visual examination of the spectra shows conspicuous differences between the spectral shapes and in the distribution of the highest magnitude frequencies. In the spectra of the narratives of female readers, the highest magnitude frequencies tend to cluster around the lower part of the LF spectrum, while in the spectra of the narratives of the male readers, the highest magnitude frequencies tend to be distributed more widely across the LF band. The bandwidth differences suggest that the female readers tend to have more regular rhythms, while the male readers tend to have more varied rhythms.

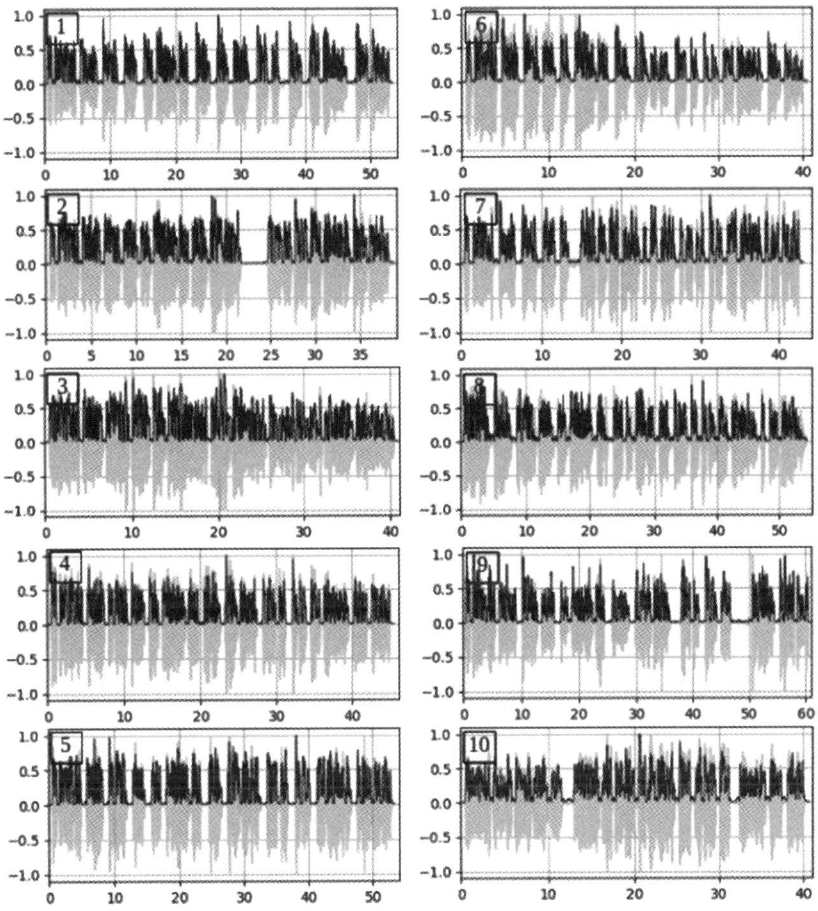

Figure 6　AM waveforms. F (left) and M (right), same order in all graphs

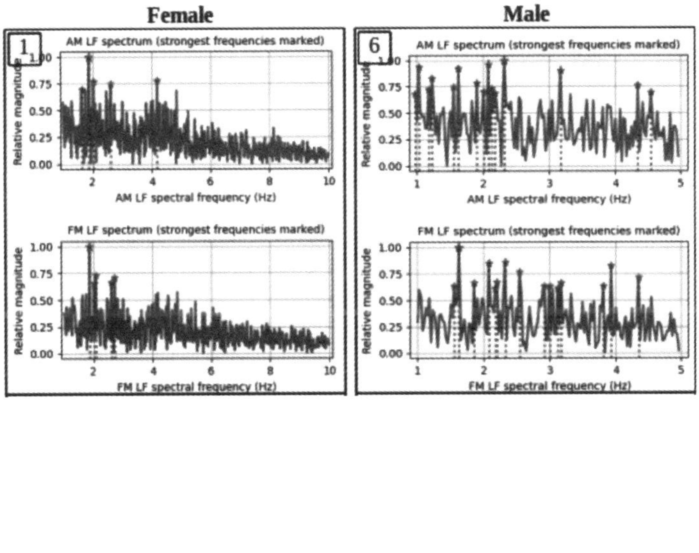

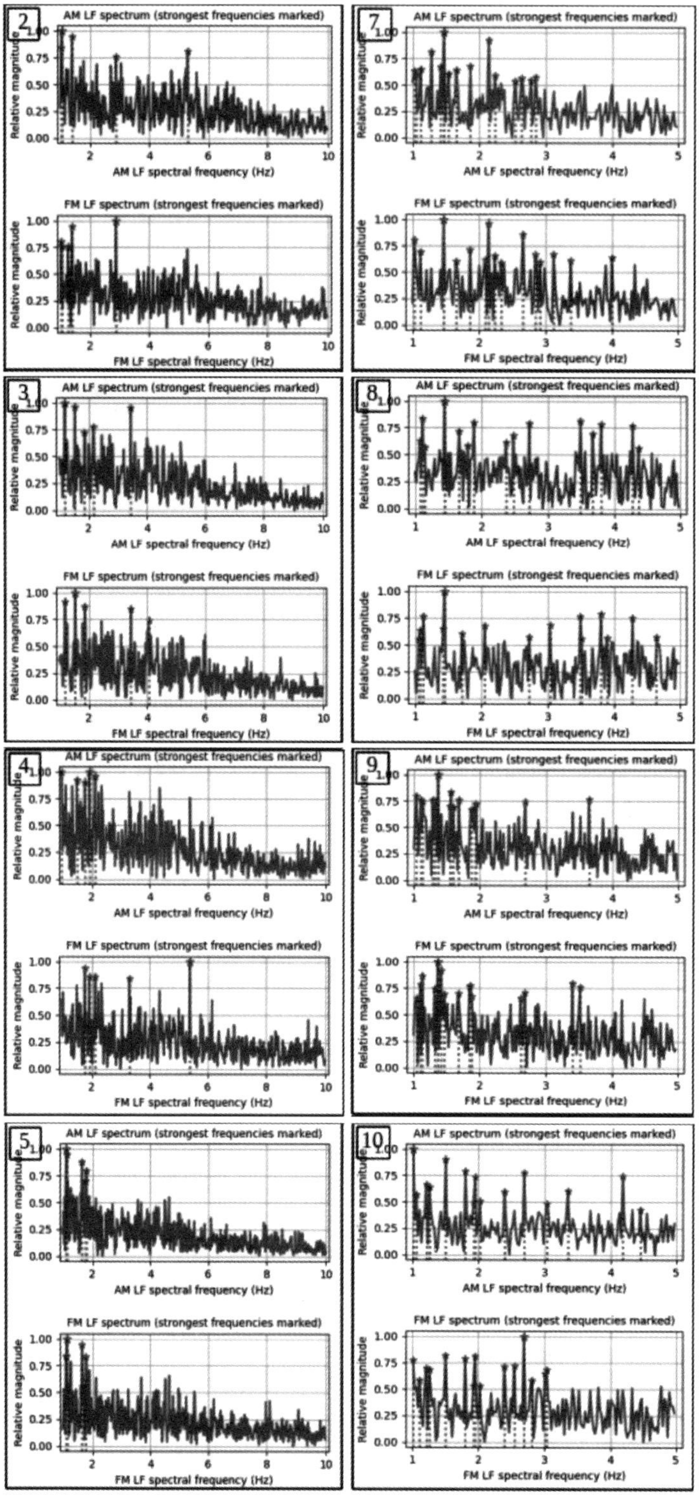

Figure 7　LFAM spectra, peak frequencies marked. F (left) and M (right), same order in all graphs

The purpose of presenting spectral analyses of all the readings is not to examine them in detail by "eyeballing", but to gain an impression of the "gestalt" of the spectrum in each case. The spectra are purely in the frequency domain and contain no information about time, and thus no information about temporal variation through the narration. Temporal information is added by the *rhythm spectrogram* analysis described in the following section.

3.3 Rhythm variation in time

Intuitively, one simple way of distinguishing male from female readings is to determine the height and range of F0 patterning. The present task is more interesting from a phonetic and linguistic perspective: to determine whether the temporal "rhetorical" variation of rhythm within the narrative aligns with the gender distinction. Other factors such as practice, social role, age, dialect, factors conditioning pitch height and range, utterance rate, etc. could be considered, but these are matters for future study.

To enable the study of rhythm variation, the next stage in the combined frequency and time domain analysis of rhythm is to generate *LF spectrograms* (cf. Figure 8). Again, the purpose of presenting all the spectrograms is not for detailed analysis, but to gain initial visual impressions with which general tendencies can be observed.

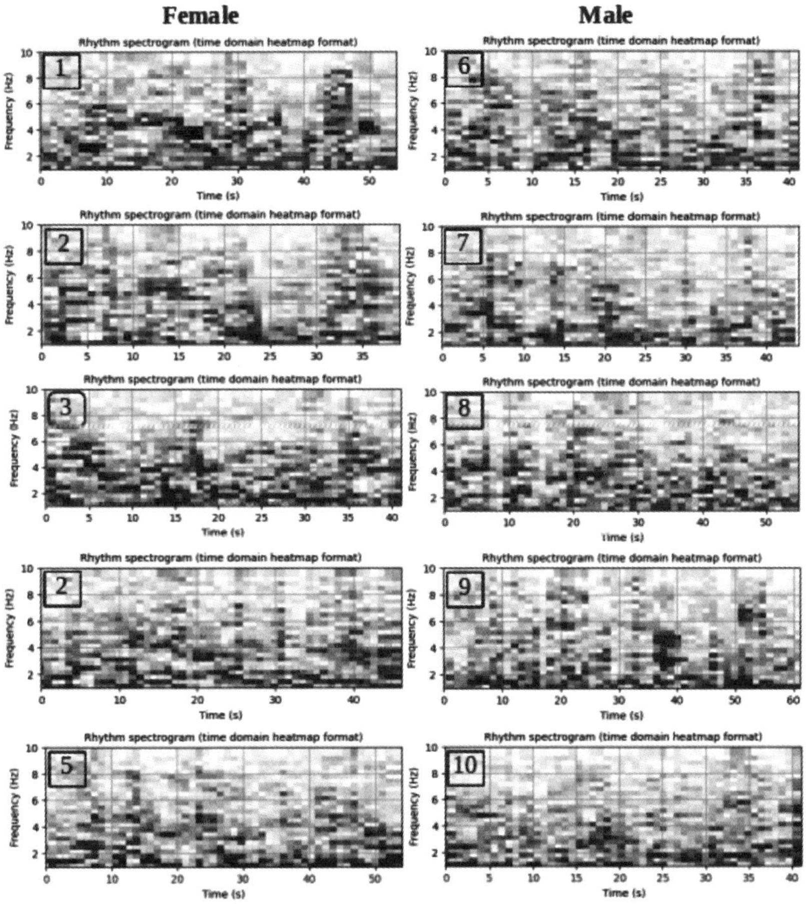

Figure 8 LFAM rhythm spectrograms (1Hz to 10Hz) in heatmap format. Same order in all graphs. Highest to lowest magnitude: dark to light colour

The spectrograms in these examples consist of the low frequency end of the vertically oriented spectra resulting from FFTs of overlapping windows, following standard spectrographic conventions. The episodic structure of the narrative readings is shown in the vertically oriented dark clusters showing simultaneous rhythms, contrasting with intervening stronger horizontal tendencies indicating more homogeneous rhythm patterns. Rhythms vary, but according to this criterion there are also coherent rhythmic stretches.

The vectors for comparison in hierarchical clustering are extracted from the highest magnitude points in each component spectrum of the spectrogram:

(1) It is assumed that the time domain factor of utterance rate will affect the rhythm analysis; however, isolation of this factor by time normalisation is a topic for future study.

(2) It is assumed that modulation frequencies in the AM envelope, the physical analogue of the abstract phonological "sonority curve", constitute the main physical property which contributes to speech rhythm.

(3) It is assumed that the combined frequency and time domain variation factor ΔF0 in the FM envelope is relevant for rhythm analysis, but that other frequency domain factors such as height and range are not. FM rhythm variation is not dealt with in this study.

(4) An FFT is applied in a 2s moving window with an overlap step parameter, in order to derive a 3 - dimensional spectrogram.

(5) A rhythm variation vector consisting of the highest magnitude frequency (HMF) in each window in the LF spectrogram is constructed as input for distance-based hierarchical clustering algorithms.

(6) The HMF vector is a vector of pairs of magnitude and frequency, which can be separated for further analysis into a magnitude vector and a frequency vector.

HMF vector analyses of both AM and FM envelopes can be made, but within the scope of the present study, analysis is restricted to AM results. Figure 9 shows AM frequency trajectories for readings by female readers (left half) and male readers (right half). The three highest magnitude frequencies are represented for each component spectrum in the spectrogram (darker means higher magnitude). Clearly, this can only be the beginning of the exploitation of the rhythm spectrogram as a source of information about rhetorical features of the reader's speech.

The readings are of slightly different lengths, but the graphs are visually scaled to show corresponding relative times across readings. In the following discussion, the graphs are numbered #1 to #5 (F set, left column) and #6 to #10 (M set, right column). A number of similarities are apparent. First, the F patterns #1 to #4 are impressionally similar, and one male pattern (#8 in consecutive numbering) is similar to the F patterns. One F pattern, #5, is distinctly different from the other F patterns, and its central spike has similarities with M patterns #7, #9 and #10. Male patterns #9 and #10 are similar to #6, though #6 is slightly different from the other two. On this basis it might be predicted that F reading #5 would tend to cluster with the M readings, and M reading #8 would tend to cluster with the F readings.

The spectral patterns and the HMF vectors are also influenced by pause patterns (cf. Figure 6), which are clearly somewhat different in each reading. It remains to be seen how these and the vectors relate to the narrative structure of the text. Analysis of text-linguistic and of sociophonetic determinants of the patterns is a task for later specialist text linguistic studies and sociolinguistic experiments. The present study is restricted to acoustic classification.

3.4 Classifying rhythm variation

The task of the hierarchical clustering module in the RFA approach is to determine whether the informal characterisation of differences between male and female readings stands up to algorithmic evaluation.

Given the HMF vector for each reader, whether based on AM or FM envelopes, similarities between the vectors can be determined by using distance metrics, and by hierarchically clustering the vectors and vector clusters based on their pairwise distances. Hierarchical clustering is preferred here over standard flat clustering, since it is more informative and provides a simple but plausible criterion for the goodness of clustering *G*.

For the distance calculation, six well-known distance metrics were compared: Manhattan Distance (also: Cityblock or Taxicab Distance), Canberra Distance (also: normalised Manhattan Distance), Euclidean Distance, Cosine Distance and Chebyshev Distance (also: Chessboard Distance). The Manhattan and Canberra "round the corner" metrics are intuitively more suitable for comparing somewhat irregular data, while the Euclidean "as the crow flies" metric takes shortcuts, and appears less suitable. The Chebyshev metric is intermediate between the two. Cosine Distance shows differences in direction or orientation, not actual distance. The Manhattan and Canberra metrics are assumed to be most relevant for the present task.

Four clustering methods are selected for applying the distance measures: average distance of cluster members (Average Clustering), furthest distance of cluster members (Complete Linkage, Farthest Point, Voorhees Clustering), distance between the closest cluster member (Single Clustering), and minimal variance (Ward Clustering). The evaluation criterion for goodness of clustering *G* is defined as the size of the largest homogeneous cluster of female readings (F) plus the size of the largest homogeneous cluster of male readings (M), divided by the size of the dataset, yielding a maximum of $G = 10/10 = 1.0$ in the present data set with perfect separation of F and M instances.

An earlier version of the classifier yielded a number of perfect partitions into five F and five M instances, with $G = 1$ (for example with the Chebyshev-Ward combination); in other cases a right-branching, effectively linear scale emerged with the F instances in one half and the M instances in the other (e.g. Manhattan-Average). However, with revised higher resolution spectrogram analysis the M/F distinction was slightly blurred, but still clear.

The two distance metrics which showed relevant results are the Manhattan (Cityblock) and Canberra metrics, as anticipated. Figure 10 shows sample clustering results, with goodness values $G = 1$, $G = 0.8$, $G = 0.6$, $G = 0.7$ (clockwise starting top left).

The clustering methods yielded varied results but shared some tendencies. For example, members of the M set tended to cluster together, while the F set members are more loosely linked at higher hierarchical ranks. In each case, one of the F set, #5, *wx*, intruded into the M linkage. Examination of the trajectory in Figure 9 reveals a possible reason: as already noted, the spike at about 26 s roughly matches peaks in this region in some M set members. Conversely, #8 in the M set tends to intrude into the F set: inspection shows a less "spiky" pattern than for the other members of the M set (cf. Figure 9).

Another point worth noting is the preservation of local clusters through each cluster type in some cases, e.g. #2 with #3, and #6 with #10. Further investigation is needed in order to understand the fine structure of the rhythm formant trajectories.

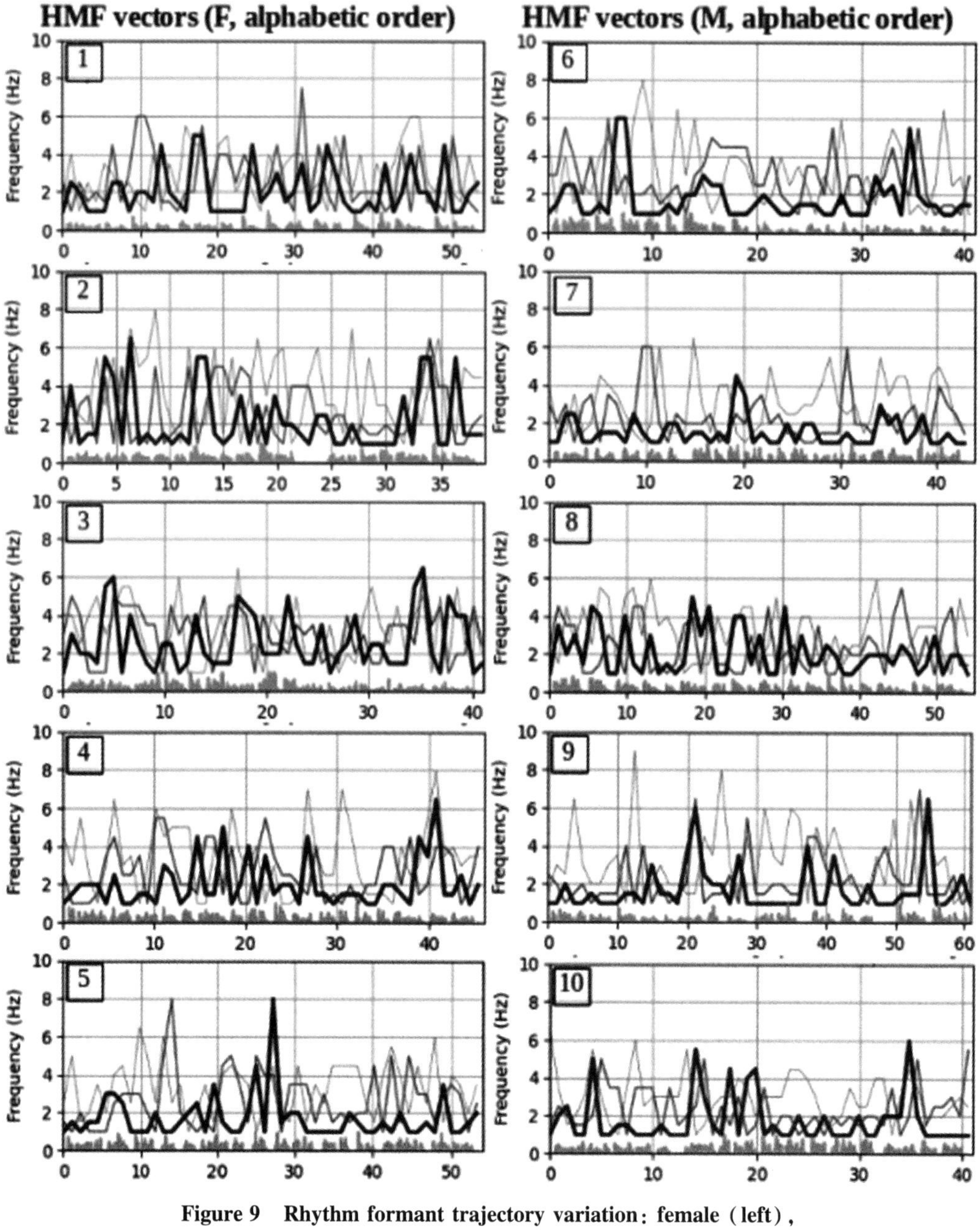

Figure 9 Rhythm formant trajectory variation: female (left), male (left), visually time-normalised. Same order in all graphs

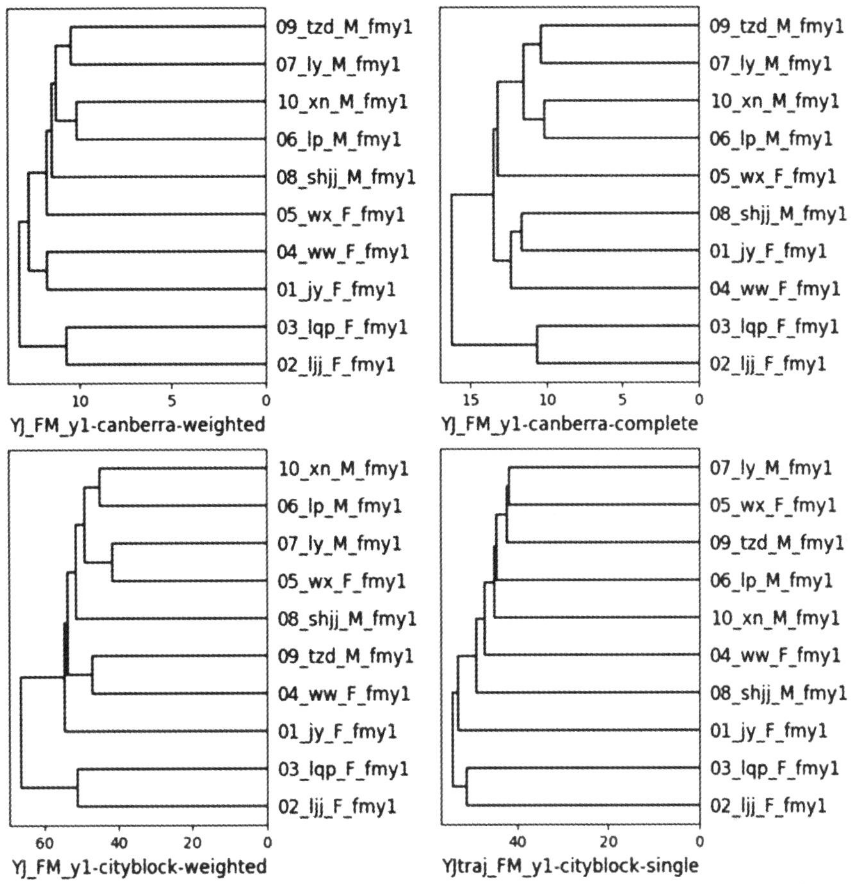

Figure 10 Distance based hierarchical cluster dendrograms for highest magnitude spectrogram frequencies (F set #1 to #5, M set #6 to #10, top to bottom)

Building on the present hierarchical clustering results, it will be interesting in more large-scale studies to examine possible reasons for the partition of female and male readings and for the cluster-internal hierarchies, for example individual styles, conventional gender styles, or physiological differences. Although the separation of the F and M categories is incomplete, it is clear enough to warrant further investigation on the basis of this tentative refutation of the null hypothesis that the M and F sets are indistinguishable.

4. SUMMARY AND OUTLOOK

A modern approach to the study of rhythm, Rhythm Formant Theory, with its Rhythm Formant Analysis methodology, was introduced in terms of modulation theory. RFA was applied to the speech signal in an exploratory analysis with data involving long-term narrative domains, rather than the word or phrase-sized utterances of previous approaches in this paradigm. After a brief account of paradigms of speech rhythm study in the introduction, the modulation-theoretic background was described, and the specific procedure of modulation-theoretic analysis of both amplitude modulation and frequency modulation of the speech signal was outlined.

Starting with the amplitude modulation (AM) envelope, related to the phonological "sonority curve", and also the frequency modulation (FM) envelope, the "pitch" track, low frequency (LF) spectral analysis was motivated and described in a small-scale study of rhythmic variation in narrative readings by ten Mandarin native speakers. A new conceptual orientation was introduced, with the *rhythm formant* and the *rhythm spectrogram* derived from AM or FM envelopes, and the *highest magnitude frequency vector* (HMF vector) through the spectrogram.

The HMF vectors from each reading were subjected to a hierarchical cluster analysis with several distance metrics and clustering methods, which resulted in the tentative falsification of the null hypothesis that there is no difference between the rhythmic patterns used by female and male readers.

Concentration on the frequency property of rhythm in the speech signal involves a different "mindset" from the traditional approaches which were concerned with manual measurement of duration irregularities of phonologically defined units, missing the resonant or oscillatory property of rhythm frequency.

Taking one more step, the frequency oriented approach to rhythm studies which underlies Rhythm Formant Theory and its methodology, Rhythm Formant Analysis, can be put into a general modulation-theoretic framework of timing patterns, derived originally from Cowell's classic theory of harmonic relations in musicology [10], and centring on a logarithmic *Speech Modulation Frequency* (*SMF*) *Scale* (Figure 11).

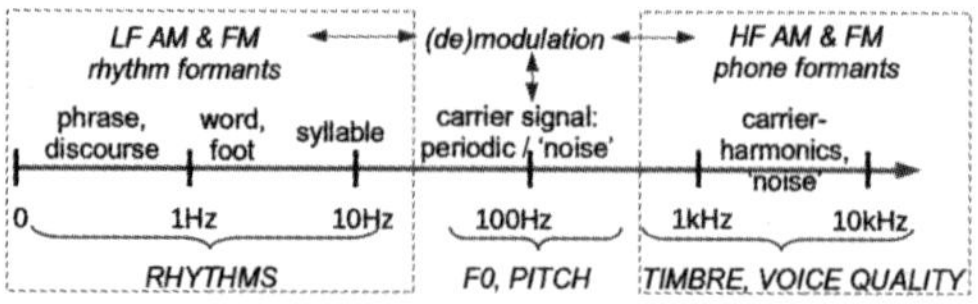

Figure 11: Modulation-theoretic frequency scale of carrier and formant types

This general framework of frequency bands offers a coherently structured model of the "carrier signals" and "modulation signals" in speech communication, and provides motivation and orientation for further development of large-scale, machine-learning supported modulation-theoretic studies of speech and language prosody.

5. ACKNOWLEDGMENTS

Debts of gratitude are owed to the referees for insightful comments; to Yu Jue, Liu Huangmei, Ma Qiuwu, Gong Qi, Li Peng and Lin Xuewei for data and discussions on many aspects of Chinese; to Doris Bleiching, Laura Dilley, Alexandra Gibbon, Sascha Griffiths, Ulrike Gut, Rosemarie Tracy and Ratree Wayland for technical and practical discussions and much encouragement; to the late Grzegorz Dogil and the late Wiktor Jassem for their pioneering work and for many discussions on methods and applications of envelope extraction and spectral analysis.

REFERENCES

[1] Abercrombie, D. 1965. *Studies in Phonetics and Linguistics*. London: OUP.

[2] Abercrombie, D. 1967. *Elements of General Phonetics*. Edinburgh: Edinburgh University Press.

[3] Arvaniti, A. 2009. Rhythm, timing and the timing of rhythm. *Phonetica* 66(1-2), 46-63.

[4] Asu, E. L., Nolan, F. 2006. Estonian and English rhythm: A two-dimensional quantification based on syllables and feet. *Proc. Speech Prosody* 3.

[5] Barbosa, P. A. 2002. Explaining cross-linguistic rhythmic variability via a coupled-oscillator model for rhythm production. *Proc. Speech Prosody* 1, 163-166.

[6] Barbosa, P. A., da Silva, W. 2012. A new methodology for comparing speech rhythm structure be-

tween utterances: Beyond typological approaches. *Proc. Int. Conf. on Computational Processing of the Portuguese Language*, 1 – 9.

[7] Barry, W. J., Andreeva, B., Russo, M., Dimitrova, S., Kostadinova, T. 2003. Do rhythm measures tell us anything about language type? *Proc. 15th ICPhS* Barcelona, 2693 – 2696.

[8] Chomsky, N., Halle, M., Lukoff, F. 1956. On accent and juncture in English. In: Halle, M., Lunt, H., Maclean, H. (eds), *For Roman Jakobson. Essays on the Occasion of his Sixtieth Birthday, 11th October 1956*. Den Haag: Mouton, 65 – 80.

[9] Chomsky, N., Halle, M. 1968. *The Sound Pattern of English*. New York: Harper & Row.

[10] Cowell, H. 1930. *New Musical Resources*. New York: Alfred A. Knopf Inc.

[11] Cummins, F., Gers, F., Schmidhuber, J. 1999. Language identification from prosody without explicit features. *Proc. Eurospeech*, 371 – 374.

[12] Cummins, F., Port, R. 1998. Rhythmic constraints on stress timing in English. *Journal of Phonetics* 26, 145 – 171.

[13] Dauer, R. M. 1983. Stress-timing and syllable-timing reanalyzed. *Journal of Phonetics* 11, 51 – 62.

[14] Dilley, L. C. 1997. *The Phonetics and Phonology of Tonal Systems*. Doctoral Dissertation, Massachusetts Institute of Technology.

[15] Dogil, G., Braun, G. 1988. *The PIVOT Model of Speech Parsing*. Verlag der Österreichischen Akademie der Wissenschaften, Philosophisch-Historische Klasse.

[16] Foote, J., Uchihashi, S. 2001. The beat spectrum: A new approach to rhythm analysis. *Proc. IEEE International Conference on Multimedia and Expo*, Tokyo.

[17] Galves, A., Garcia, J., Duarte, D., Galves, C. 2002. Sonority as a basis for rhythmic class discrimination. *Proc. Speech Prosody* 1, Aix-en-Provence, France, 323 – 326.

[18] Gibbon, D. 2006. Time types and time trees: Prosodic mining and alignment of temporally annotated data. In Sudhoff, S., Lenertova, D., Meyer, R., Pappert, S., Augurzky, P., Mleinek, I., Richter, N., Schließer, J. (eds.), *Methods in Empirical Prosody Research*. Berlin: Walter de Gruyter, 281 – 209.

[19] Gibbon, D. 2018. The future of prosody: It's about time. *Proc. Speech Prosody* 9.

[20] Gibbon, D., Li, P. 2019. Quantifying and correlating rhythm formants in speech. *Proc. 3rd International Symposium on Linguistic Patterns in Spontaneous Speech*, Taipei.

[21] Gut, U. 2012. Rhythm in L2 speech. In Gibbon, D., Hirst, D., Campbell, N. (eds.), *Rhythm, Melody and Harmony in Speech. Studies in Honour of Wiktor Jassem. Special Edition of Speech and Language Technology* 14/15. Poznań: Polish Phonetics Society, 83 – 94.

[22] He, L., Dellwo, V. 2016. A Praat-based algorithm to extract the amplitude envelope and temporal fine structure using the hilbert transform. *Proc. Interspeech*, San Francisco, 530 – 534.

[23] Hemanský, H. 2010. History of modulation spectrum in ASR. *Proc. International Conference on Acoustics, Speech and Signal Processing (ICASSP)*.

[24] Inden, B., Malisz, Z., Wagner, P., Wachsmuth, I. 2012. Rapid entrainment to spontaneous speech: A comparison of oscillator models. *Proc. 34th Annual Conference of the Cognitive Science Society*. Austin, TX: Cognitive Science Society, 1721 – 1726.

[25] Jassem, W. 1952. *Intonation of Conversational English (Educated Southern British)*. Wrocław: Wrocławskie Towarzystwo Naukowe.

[26] Jassem, W., Hill, D. R., Witten, I. H. 1984. Isochrony in English Speech: Its statistical validity and linguistic relevance. In Gibbon, D., Richter, H. (eds.). *Intonation, Accent and Rhythm. Studies in Discourse Phonology*. Berlin: Walther de Gruyter, 203 – 225.

[27] Kallio, H., Suni, A., Šimko, J., Vainio, M. 2020. Analyzing second language proficiency using wavelet-based prominence estimates. *Journal of Phonetics* 80, 1 – 12.

[28] Kohler, K. 2009. Editorial: Whither speech rhythm research? *Phonetica* 66, 5 – 14.

[29] Lee, C. S., Todd, N. P. M. 2004. Towards an auditory account of speech rhythm: Application of a model of the auditory "primal sketch" to two multi-language corpora. *Cognition* 93(3), 225 – 254.

[30] Lehiste, I. 1970. *Suprasegmentals*. Cambridge, MA: MIT Press.

[31] Li, A., Yin, Z. 2006. A rhythmic analysis on Chinese EFL speech. *Proc. Speech Prosody* 3, Dresden, Germany.

[32] Liberman, M. Y., Prince, A. 1977. On stress and linguistic rhythm. *Linguistic Inquiry* 8, 249 – 336.

[33] Low, E. L. , Grabe, E. , Nolan, F. 2000. Quantitative characterisations of speech rhythm: "Syllable-timing" in Singapore English. *Language and Speech* 43, 377 – 401.

[34] Ludusan, B. , Origlia, A. , Cutugno, F. 2011. On the use of the rhythmogram for automatic syllabic prominence detection. *Proc. Interspeech*, 2413 – 2416.

[35] Ludusan, B. , Wagner, P. 2020. Speech, laughter and everything in between: A modulation spectrum-based analysis. *Proc. Speech Prosody* 10, Tokyo, Japan, 995 – 999.

[36] O' Dell, M. L. , Nieminen, T. 1999. Coupled oscillator model of speech rhythm. *Proc. 14th International Congress of Phonetic Sciences*, San Francisco, 1075 – 1078.

[37] Pike K. L. 1962. Practical phonetics of rhythm waves. *Phonetica* 8, 9 – 30.

[38] Pike, K. L. 1945. *The Intonation of American English*. Ann Arbor: University of Michigan Press.

[39] Ramus, F. , Nespor, M. , Mehler, J. 1999. Correlates of linguistic rhythm in the speech signal. *Cognition* 73, 265 – 292.

[40] Roach, P. 1982. On the distinction between "stress-timed" and "syllable-timed" languages. In Crystal, D. (ed.), *Linguistic Controversies: Essays in Linguistic Theory and Practice*. London: Edward Arnold, 73 – 79.

[41] Scott, D. R. , Isard, S. D. , de Boysson-Bardies, B. 1985. Perceptual isochrony in English and French. *Journal of Phonetics* 13, 155 – 162.

[42] Selkirk, E. 1984. *Phonology and Syntax: The Relation between Sound and Structure*. Cambridge, MA: The MIT Press.

[43] Tilsen, S. , Arvaniti, A. 2013. Speech rhythm analysis with decomposition of the amplitude envelope: Characterizing rhythmic patterns within and across languages. *Journal of the Acoustical Society of America* 134, 628 – 639.

[44] Tilsen, S. , Johnson, K. 2008. Low-frequency Fourier analysis of speech rhythm. *Journal of the Acoustical Society of America* 124(2), EL34 – EL39.

[45] Todd, N. P. M. , Brown, G. J. 1994. A computational model of prosody perception. *Proc. International Conference on Spoken Language Processing (ICLSP – 94)*, 127 – 130.

[46] Varnet, L. , Ortiz-Barajas, M. C. , Erra, R. G. , Gervain, J. , Lorenzi, C. 2017. A cross-linguistic study of speech modulation spectra. *Journal of the Acoustical Society of America* 142(4), 1976 – 1989.

[47] Yu, J. , Gibbon, D. , Klessa, K. 2014. Computational annotation-mining of syllable durations in speech varieties. *Speech Prosody* 7.

Dafydd Gibbon He is emeritus professor of Linguistics at Bielefeld University, Germany. His main research interests cover computational linguistics, prosody, the documentation of under-resourced languages, and standards and resources for speech technology.
Email: gibbon@ uni – bielefeld. de

LIFESPAN CHANGE OF VOICE IN MANDARIN CHINESE SPEAKERS

WU Xiyu, KONG Jiangping

Abstract The purpose of this study was to investigate to what extent age and gender would affect the voice parameters of native Mandarin Chinese speakers. Participants were required to produce sustained vowel /a/ with comfortable pitch and loudness. From the speech samples, 34 voice parameters were extracted by using Multi-Dimensional Voice Program (MDVP). The parameters were divided into several groups according to their correlation coefficients. Groups related to F0, to short-term perturbation of period and amplitude, to long-term variation of period and amplitude, to spectrum and to duration were found to be affected by age and gender. In each of them, one of the most important parameters was selected to represent the variation tendency with gender and age. Therefore, to estimate the degree of a voice deviation from normal, the factors of age and gender should be considered. The mean and variance of the parameters were given in this paper, and were compared according to their gender and age. Finally, a normative voice database was constructed for the reference of dysphonia diagnosis for Chinese.
Key Words Voice-Lifespan, MDVP, F0, Jitter, Shimmer

1. INTRODUCTION

In order to assess the deviation degree of a disordered voice from normal, it is necessary to construct a normative voice database. As we know, the physiological tissue of larynx varies across the whole lifespan. This may affect the characteristics of produced voice. With the growth of age, the descent of hyoid and larynx happens in the first nine years of human life [1]. The change of the physiological structure affects the generated speech sounds. During the adolescence, with the effects of hormone, the change of thyroid bone and the vocal folds is different greatly between male and female, which results in the gender distinction of voice parameters from this period [2]. After 50, because of the change of hormone, the decrease mass of the folders results in the change of F0 [3]. The structure of vocal folders such as the cover, lamina propria, and muscle of elderly people becomes vestigial, which results in the change of produced voice [4].

From the perspective of speech perception, listeners can easily identify the sex of a speaker even if the speaker is only four years old [5]. The age of a speaker can be ordered chronologically according to his/her speech within several years [6]. The results of these studies imply that parameters of voice are affected by gender and age. Therefore, it is necessary to construct a normative database considering the factors of age and gender.

There are two main methods to investigate how age and gender affect voice parameters across the life span: the longitudinal study and the cross-sectional study. In the longitudinal studies, the voice parameters are extracted from the same subject as the age of the subject increases. Kasuya et al. explored the longitudinal change of voice parameters of the sustained vowel /a/ based on the speech recorded over a period ranging from 10 to 18 years for 20 males and 30 females [7]. Reubold et al. analyzed the voice data of two speakers in successive 50 years period [8]. However, it is difficult to trace massive people for a long time, such as the whole lifespan, therefore, conclusions based on limited subjects may not reflect the tendency of the whole population.

Different from the longitudinal study, using the cross-sectional study we can record voice from massive speakers with different ages in a short term. If the number of speakers is large enough, the change of voice parameters can accurately reflect the tendency in the lifespan. Several cross-sectional studies have been carried out to investigate the effect of age and gender on the voice parameters. Awan studied the effect of aging on voice parameters of female native speaker of American English, where the subjects were divided into five groups according to their age [9]. In his study, the youngest subject was 18 years old. Unfortunately, the data did not include children and adolescents, when the anatomical structure of larynx changes dramatically. It should be noted that Awan's study [9] is short of data of male speakers, which would have a different tendency from female. Stathopoulos et al. investigated the effect of age on voice parameters including fundamental frequency, sound pressure level and signal-to-noise ratio from 4 to 93 years of age, but the perturbation parameters were not included, which are very important in assessing the quality of voice [3] . Goy et al. constructed a normative voice database of adults for two age groups: younger and older, where the parameters include F0, and perturbation parameters, yet the classification was a little bit rough [10].

So far, there is no systematic exploration of how age and gender affect the voice parameters of native speakers of Mandarin Chinese. Here, we target Mandarin Chinese because: (1) The larynx muscle and cartilage of East Asians maybe somewhat different from those of westemers, which may result in different rules of voice characteristics. (2) Different characteristics of mother languages shape different habit of phonation. In this study, we constructed a voice database from a large number of participants across almost the whole lifespan.

Based on the database, we investigated the effects of age and gender on voice parameters, and gave a normative voice data as a reference for dysphonia diagnosis. There are more voice parameters in this study than in the previous ones, and the relationships of the parameters were explored systematically by a correlation coefficient matrix. According to the matrix, the important parameters were selected to evaluate the voice.

2. METHOD

2.1 Participants

All the participants were citizens of Beijing, China, and their mother language was Mandarin Chinese. In total, about 800 people (400 females and 400 males) were enrolled and divided into 8 age groups (AG). The number of participants and the intervals of their age are shown in Table 1.

All the participants signed the informed consent document before voice recording and were allowed to unconditionally withdraw from the experiment. Each participant was paid 30 RMB, or received a present with the equivalent value. Participants were healthy and had no hearing impairments. Most of them have no smoking history, except for some aging participants who smoke occasionally without producing obvious effect on their voice. If a participant felt his/her their voice was different from the normal condition during the experiment, his/her voice would not be recorded.

Table 1 Age ranges and number of participants of each group

Age group (AG)	1	2	3	4	5	6	7	8
Interval of age (year)	3—6	7—10	11—15	16—18	19—30	31—45	46—60	Above 60
Number of participants (female, male)	53, 49	47, 51	49, 35	53, 32	52, 51	51, 49	51, 49	46, 49

2.2 Data collection

Factors that affect the voice parameters include not only the age and gender but also the emotional state [11], semantic information of a sentence [12], and so on. To exclude the other factors except age and gender as much as possible, the sustained vowel /a/ was recorded for each subject. Another advantage of using the sustained vowel is that to assess the voice quality a patient is required to produce only a sustained vowel, which is very convenient. It is more robust to extract parameters from a sustained vowel than from a sentence, which can promote the effectiveness of assessment. In this study, participants were asked to produce the sustained vowel /a/ twice in comfortable pitch and loudness, with the duration of each being no less than one second.

In the recording, the following devices were used: microphone (SHURE BETA 54 Headworn); sound card (Creative Sound Blaster X - Fi Surround 5.1 Pro); and ThinkPad X1 Carbon laptop. Software of Cool Edit Pro 2.0 was used to monitor the amplitude of recorded sounds in real time to maintain the amplitude less than 80% of the maximum quantification. The quantify precision was 16 bits, and the sampling rate was 44.1 kHz, which was high enough for calculating the perturbational parameters.

2.3 Acoustic measures

There are many parameters that can be extracted from a sustained vowel. In this study, all the parameters were calculated by Multi-Dimensional Voice Program (MDVP, Model 5105, Kay Elemetrics Corp, 2003, Version 2.6.2) [13].

3. DATA ANALYSIS

For each vowel sample, 34 kinds of parameters in total were extracted. The definitions and explanations of the parameters are given in APPENDIX I. Ten parameters with no values for most of the speech samples, such as, Fftr, Fatr, FTRI, ATRI, DVB, DSH, DUV, NVB, NSH, and NUV, were excluded in this study.

It is not necessary to analyze all the parameters one by one, because not all of them are independent. The first step is to classify the parameters into several groups according to their definitions and correlation coefficients. According to a careful consideration, the parameters were divided into six categories. (1) Parameters related to fundamental frequency, including F0, MF0, T0, Fhi, Flo, STD and PFR; (2) Short-term perturbation of period, including Jita, Jitt RAP and PPQ; (3) Short-term perturbation of amplitude, including ShdB, Shim and APQ; (4) Long-term period variation, including SPPQ, vF0, vAm and SAPQ; 5) Spectrum related parameters, including NHR, VTI and SPI; (6) Duration related parameters, including TSAM, SEG and PER.

In each category, the correlation coefficients of the parameters were divided into groups according to their correlation coefficients. If the correlation coefficients of each other were high enough, and the parameters had similar meanings for sustained vowels, then they were classified into a group and one of the parameters was designated to represent the group. If a parameter was affected by age, the boxplots were given, otherwise the mean and standard deviation of the parameter were given. For the mean and standard deviation of each parameter, please refer to APPENDIX Ⅱ.

Because most of the parameters were significantly different between male and female, all of them were analyzed by gender. In the following, the data was analyzed based on the six categories.

3.1 Fundamental frequency related

There are seven parameters in this category. Table 2 shows the correlation coefficients of parameters in this category. According to this table, the parameters can be divided into two groups according to their correlation coefficients: (1) F0, MF0, T0, Fhi and Flo; (2) STD and PFR. The minimum correlation coefficients in these two groups are 0.876 and 0.789, respectively. The parameters F0 and STD were selected to represent each of the groups, respectively.

3.1.1 Fundamental frequency

The anatomical structure of larynx changes throughout the lifespan, and the most important parameter to identify the age is fundamental frequency. The result of F0 is shown in Fig. 1. As one can see from AG1 to AG3 (below 15 years old), the F0 decreases steadily for both males and females. This is because of the increased length and mass of the vocal folds in these periods [14]. From AG3 to AG4, the F0 decreases sharper for males because AG4 is at the period of puberty; as for females, F0 also decreases steadily. From AG4 to AG5, F0 increases for both males and females, but more significantly for males than females. From AG5 to AG7, F0 of both genders decreases. From AG7 to AG8, F0 does not change in females yet increases significantly in males. According to the analysis we can see that the relationship between age and F0 is nonlinear for both sexes, similar to the results of Stathopoulos et al. [3]. A small difference from Stathopoulos et al.'s study is that above 60 years old, the F0 of female does not change in our study but increase in their study. The main reason is that, in our study the age of most of the participants in AG8 is between 60 to 70; if the age continues to increase the F0 may increase in our study. The F0 of males increases more than females in elder people in our study which is the same as Stathopoulos's results [3].

In this study, we can see that there are three main different tendencies between males and females: (1) From AG4 to AG5, F0 decreases much more greatly in males than in females because this period is the voice mutation period. (2) From AG7 to AG8, F0 increases greatly in males but does not change in females. The two differences can be explained by male hormones. (3) The F0 decrease in males is not as significant as females from AG5 to AG6 because in this period the change of menopausal hormone of females results in thickened or edematous vocal folds.

Table 2 Correlation coefficients of fundamental related parameters

	F0	MF0	T0	Fhi	Flo	STD	PFR
F0	1.000	1.000	-0.938	0.956	0.960	0.334	0.214
MF0	1.000	1.000	-0.938	0.954	0.963	0.319	0.204
T0	-0.938	-0.938	1.000	-0.895	-0.907	-0.296	-0.204
Fhi	0.956	0.954	-0.895	1.000	0.876	0.457	0.429
Flo	0.960	0.963	-0.907	0.876	1.000	0.124	-0.031
STD	0.334	0.319	-0.296	0.457	0.124	1.000	0.789
PFR	0.214	0.204	-0.204	0.429	-0.031	0.789	1.000

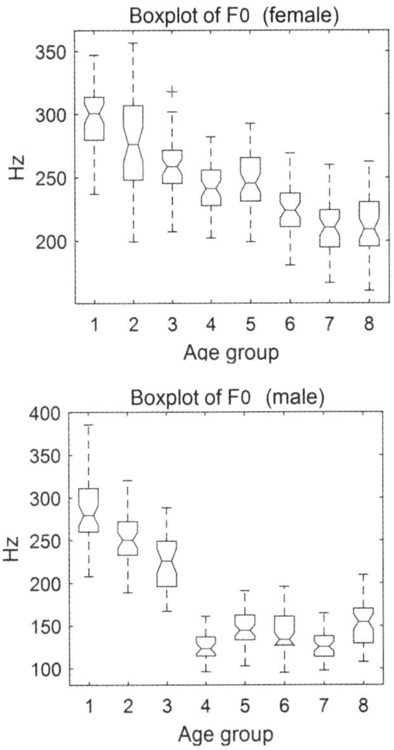

Figure 1 The change of F0 with age

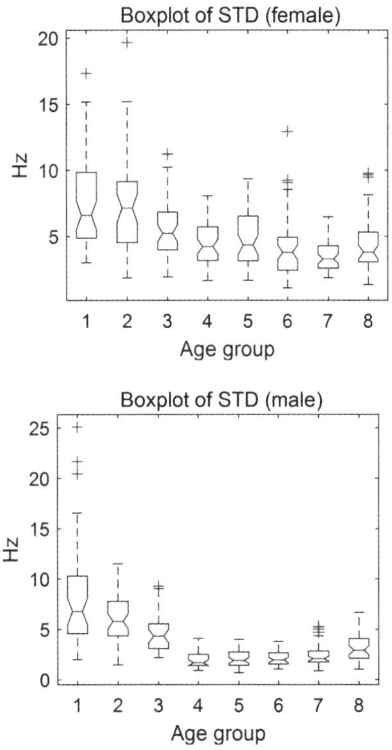

Figure 2 The change of STD with age

3.1.2 Deviation of F0

There are two parameters reflecting the deviation of F0: STD and PFR. STD is the standard deviation of F0 in the sustained vowel, and PFR is the range between the highest (Fhi) and the lowest (Flo) F0 in semitones.

These two parameters were used to describe the stability of F0 in a sustained vowel and the parameter is affected by age. The correlation coefficient of these two parameters is 0.789 (Table 2). Therefore, STD was used to represent the group in this paper. The Boxplot of STD is shown in Fig. 2. The STD of males and females have similar tendencies, which is first decreasing and then increasing. The parameter demonstrates a U-shaped pattern as a function of age. The result shows that the STD for both children and elders increases, which means that motor control ability is not strong in these periods comparing to young adults [15, 16].

3.2 Variation between periods

Sustained vowel are a kind of quasi-periodic signal, in which the amplitude and period are different from period to period. The parameters depicting variation of period can be divided into two categories: short-term and long-term.

3.2.1 Short-term perturbation of period

There are four parameters used to depict short-term period perturbation (jitter): Jita, Jitt, RAP and PPQ.

The correlation coefficients of the first group are shown in Table 3. From this table one can see that the four parameters have strong correlations. The Jitt was used to represent the group because it has the highest coefficient with the other three parameters. The calculation method of Jitt is shown in function (1), where $i = 1, 2, 3 \cdots N$, and N is the number of periods.

$$Jitt = \frac{\frac{1}{N-1}\sum_{i=1}^{N-1}|T_0^{(i)} - T_0^{(i+1)}|}{\frac{1}{N}\sum_{i=1}^{N}T_0^{(i)}} \quad (1)$$

The parameters in this group are significantly affected by age. Fig. 3 shows the change of the Jitt affected by age. From this figure one can see from AG1 to AG4 the Jitt decreases, and from AG4 to AG5 it increases a little bit, from AG5 to AG7 it continues to decrease, and from AG7 to AG8 it increases. Both males and females have similar tendencies.

Table 3 Correlation coefficients of short-term perturbation of period

	Jita	Jitt	RAP	PPQ
Jita	1.000	0.879	0.871	0.868
Jitt	0.879	1.000	0.996	0.982
RAP	0.871	0.996	1.000	0.980
PPQ	0.868	0.982	0.980	1.000

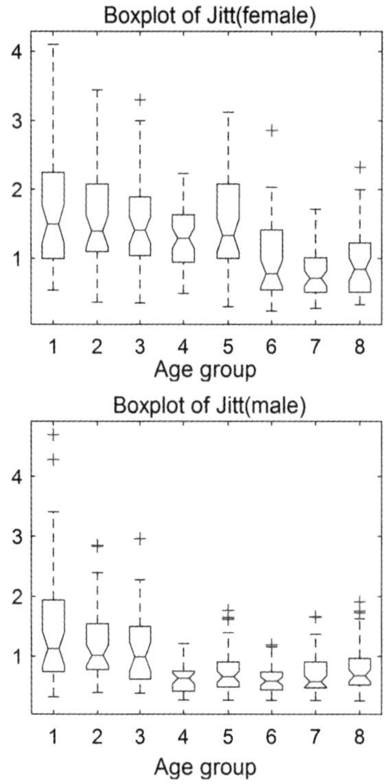

Figure 3 The change of Jitt with age

3.2.2 Short-term Perturbation of amplitude

The short-term perturbation of amplitude (shimmer) includes three parameters: ShdB, Shim and APQ. The correlation coefficients of these parameters are shown in Table 4. From this table one can see that the three parameters have strong correlations. The ShdB was used to represent the group. The calculation method of ShdB is shown in formula (2), where i = 1, 2, 3…N, and N is the number of periods, A is the maximum amplitude of the ith period.

$$ShdB = \frac{1}{N-1}\sum_{i=1}^{N-1}|20\log(A^{(i+1)}/A^{(i)})| \quad (2)$$

The boxplot of ShdB is shown in Fig. 4. According to this figure, from AG1 to AG6 the tendency of ShdB is similar as Jitt, but from AG6 to AG8 the tendency is opposite to Jitt. The basic tendency of ShdB is decreasing first and then increasing a little bit. The minimum standard deviation of ShdB is in AG4, where the young adults converge and the individual difference is small in this period.

Table 4 Correlation coefficients of short-term perturbation of amplitude

	ShdB	Shim	APQ
ShdB	1.000	0.989	0.924
Shim	0.989	1.000	0.935
APQ	0.924	0.935	1.000

3.2.3 Long-term period variation

There are four parameters used to represent long-term period variation: SPPQ, vF0, SAPQ and vAm. The SPPQ and vF0 depict the long-term variation of period, and SAPQ and vAm depict the long-term variation of amplitude. The correlation coefficients of four parameters are shown in Table 5. The coefficient between sPPQ and vF0 is 0.759, but SAPQ and vAm have low correlations with the other parameters.

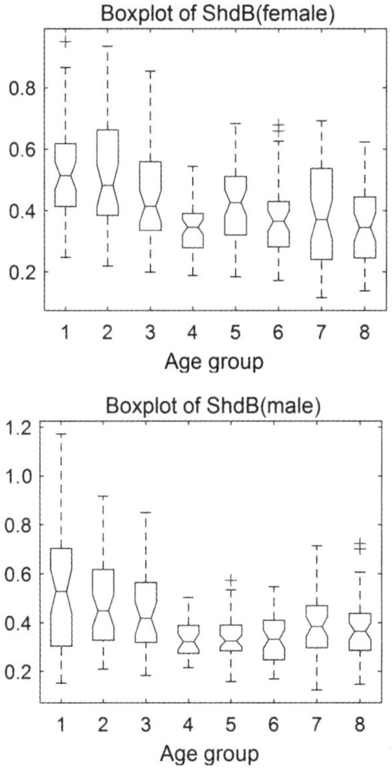

Figure 4 The change of ShdB with age

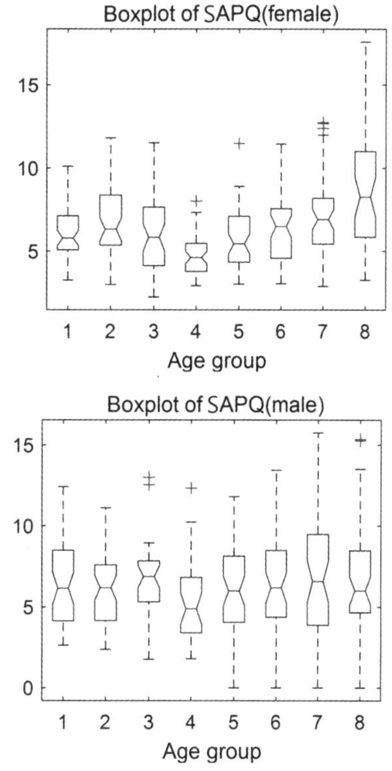

Figure 5 Change of SAPQ with age

Table 5 Correlation coefficients of long-term period variation

	SPPQ	vF0	SAPQ	vAM
SPPQ	1. 000	0. 759	0. 345	0. 198
vF0	0. 759	1. 000	0. 210	0. 181
SAPQ	0. 345	0. 210	1. 000	0. 330
vAM	0. 198	0. 181	0. 330	1. 000

The age has no significant effect on SPPQ, vF0 or vAm, the analysis of these parameters based on age is thus unnecessary; therefore the mean and standard deviation in all ages of these parameters were given, as in Appendix Ⅱ.

The SAPQ is affected by age significantly for females but has no significant effect in males. The boxplot of SAPQ is shown in Fig. 5. From this figure, one can see that in females from AG1 to AG2 the SAPQ increases and from AG2 to AG4 the SAPQ decreases, while from AG4 to AG8, the SAPQ increases. The general tendency is first decreasing and then increasing. The minimum individual difference is in young adult.

3.3 Spectrum related parameters

The spectrum related parameters are extracted according to spectral characteristics of the voice signals, which are calculated according to the ratio of energy in different frequencies. There are three parameters in this category: VTI, NHR and SPI. The correlation coefficients of the three parameters are shown in Table 6. From this table, we can see that the three parameters are independent from each other. The three parameters are all affected by age for both males and females.

Table 6 Correlation coefficients of spectrum related parameters

	NHR	VTI	SPI
NHR	1.000	0.381	-0.119
VTI	0.381	1.000	-0.452
SPI	-0.119	-0.452	1.000

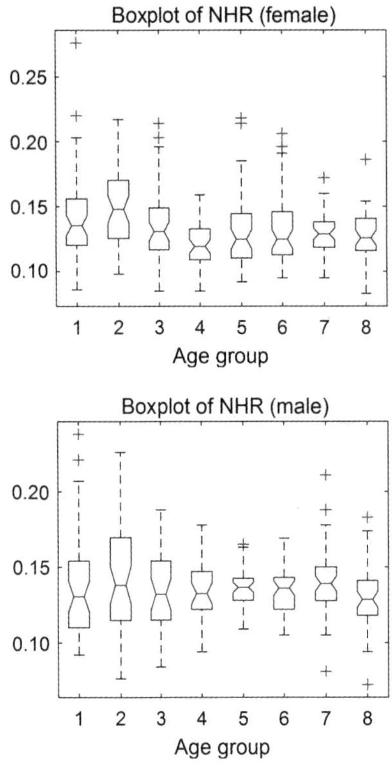

Figure 6 The change of NHR with age

NHR is used to represent noise-to-harmonics ratio, which is one of the most important parameters in predicting perceptual qualities such as breathiness or dysphonia severity [17, 18]. The boxplot of NHR is shown in Fig. 6. From this figure, one can see that the NHR increases from AG1 to AG2, decreases from AG2 to AG4, increases from AG4 to AG7, but decreases from AG7 to AG8. It has a similar tendency for males and females. In H. Goy et al.'s study, they constructed a normative database of NHR for younger and older adults [10]. However, according to Fig. 8 the means and standard deviations are different when age changes. Therefore, it will be more precise by using the normative database with different age groups in our study.

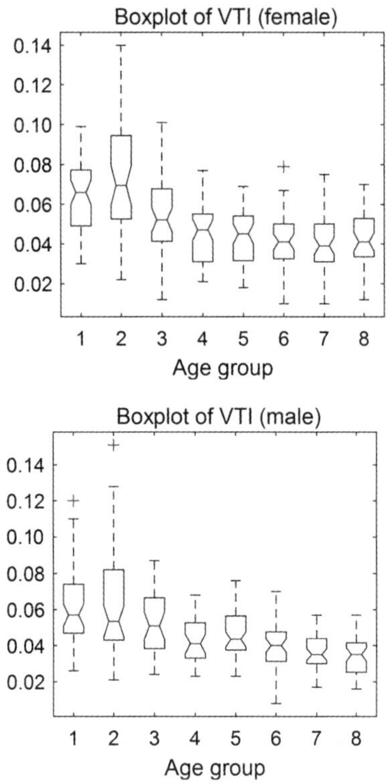

Figure 7 The change of VTI with age

The parameter VTI (Voice Turbulence Index) measures the relative energy level of high-frequency in harmonic spectral energy (2800 - 5800Hz) to the spectral of harmonic energy (70 - 4500Hz), which is usually used to explain the degree of glottal closure [13]. The boxplot of VTI is shown in Fig. 7. The tendency of VTI is that from AG1 to AG2 it increases in females but decreases in males. From AG2 to AG4, it decreases in both males and females. From AG4 to AG5, it does not change in females but increases in males. From AG5 to AG7 it decreases and from AG7 to AG8 it increases, for both males and females. In the age period from seven years old to ten years old, it has the maximum individual difference.

The parameter SPI is the average ratio of the lower-frequency (ranging from 70Hz to 1600Hz) to higher-frequency (ranging from 1600Hz to 4500Hz) harmonic energy. If SPI is elevated, the voice will be perceived as soft. The boxplot of SPI is shown in Fig. 8. The tendency of SPI shows great differences between males and females. In females from AG1 to AG6, the SPI increases, and from AG6 to AG8 it decreases and then increases. In males, the SPI increases from AG1 to AG4, from AG4 to AG8, it first decreases till AG6 and then increases. In the age period from three years old to six years old, it has the minimum mean value and individual difference.

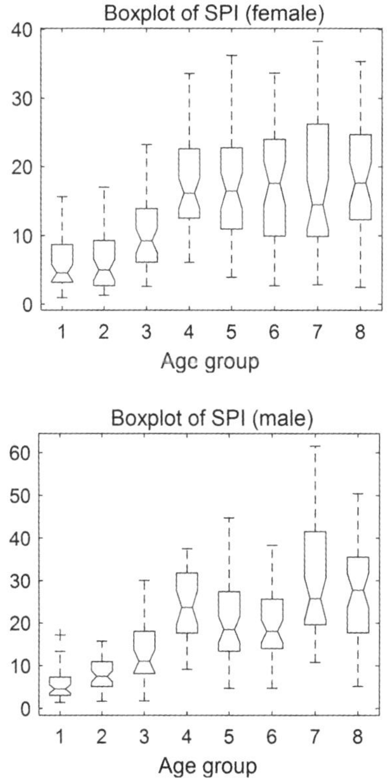

Figure 8 The change of SPI with age

3.4 Duration related parameters

There are three parameters related to the duration of sustained vowels. The correlation coefficients of the parameters are shown in Table 7. They have strong correlations and the parameter SEG was used to represent the group. The parameters are affected by age significantly, and the boxplot of SEG is shown in Fig. 9. According to the figure, one can see that in puberty, speakers tend to produce the sustained vowel with shorter duration, and the individual difference is relatively smaller.

Table 7 Correlation coefficients of duration related parameters

	TSAM	SEG	PER
TSAM	1	1	0.734
SEG	1	1	0.733
PER	0.734	0.733	1

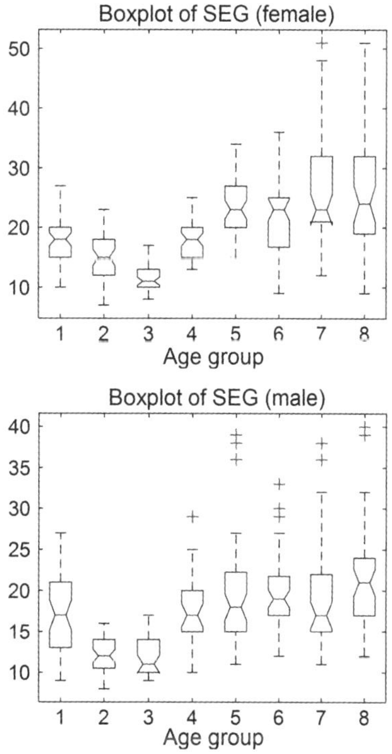

Figure 9 The change of SEG with age

4. DISCUSSION AND CONCLUSION

In this study, we have analyzed the voice parameters of the sustained vowel /a/ across almost the whole lifespan. As a result, most of the parameters have demonstrated U-shaped curves, which confirms the study of Stathopoulos et al. [3].

A voice database constructed based on a large number of speakers is very important for evaluation and treatment in voice pathology. In this study, we constructed a normative voice database of Mandarin Chinese speakers from the sustained vowel /a/. Parameters are categorized according to their definitions and correlation coefficients. According to the analyses, we understand the correlativity of the parameters in sustained vowels. We found that most of the parameters are affected by age significantly, which means that to evaluate a speech sound based on its age will be more precise. To assess speech sound we can refer to the database shown in APPENDIX Ⅱ.

So far, the speech sounds used to construct the normative voice database are normal speech sounds. In the future, we will record disorder voices to verify our normative database and explore which parameter can be used to evaluate the subcategory of disorder voice.

5. ACKNOWLEDGEMENTS

This work was supported by the National Social Science Foundation of China (No. 18BYY189) and Major projects of Ministry of Education of China (No. 17JJD740001).

REFERENCES

[1] Lieberman, D. E., McCarthy, R. C., Hiiemae, K. M., Palmer, J. B. 2001. Ontogeny of postnatal hyoid and larynx descent in humans. *Archives of Oral Biology* 46, 117 - 128.

[2] Stathopoulos, E. T. Sapienza, C. M. 1997. Developmental changes in laryngeal and respiratory function with variations in sound pressure level. *Journal of Speech, Language, and Hearing Research* 40(3), 595 - 614.

[3] Stathopoulos, E. T., Huber, J. E., Sussmana, J. 2011. Changes in acoustic characteristics of the voice across the life span: Measures from individuals 4 - 93 years of age. *Journal of Speech, Language, and Hearing Research* 54, 1011 - 1021.

[4] Hirano, M., Kurita, S., Nakashima, T. 1983. Growth, development, and aging of the human vocal folds. In Abbs, D. B. J. (ed.), *Vocal fold physiology: Contemporary research and clinical issues*. San Diego, CA: College - Hill Press, 22 - 43.

[5] Ingrisano, D., Weismer, G., Schuckers, G. H. 1980. Sex identification of preschool children's voices. *Folia Phoniatrica* 32, 61.

[6] Linville, S. E., Fisher, H. B. 1985. Acoustic characteristics of perceived versus actual vocal age in controlled phonation by adult females. *The Journal of the Acoustical Society of America* 78, 40 - 48.

[7] Kasuya, H., Yoshida, H., Ebihara, S., Mori, H. 2010. Longitudinal changes of selected voice source parameters. *INTERSPEECH 2010*, September, Makuhari, Chiba, Japan, 26 - 30.

[8] Reubold, U., Harrington, J., Kleber, F. 2010. Vocal aging effects on F0 and the first formant: A longitudinal analysis in adult speakers. *Speech Communication* 52, 638 - 651.

[9] Awan, S. N. 2006. The aging female voice: Acoustic and respiratory data. *Clinical Linguistics & Phonetics* 20(2 - 3), 171 - 180.

[10] Goy, H., Fernandes, D. N., Pichora - Fuller, M. K., Lieshout, P. V. 2013. Normative voice data for younger and older adults. *Journal of Voice* 27, 545 - 555.

[11] Campbell, N. 2004. Databases of expressive speech. *Journal of Chinese Language and Computing* 14 (4), 295 - 304.

[12] Beckman, M. E., Venditti, J. J. 2010. Tone and intonation. In: Hardcastle, W. J., Gibbon, F., Laver, J. (eds.), *Handbook of Phonetic Sciences* (second ed). Blackwell, 603 - 652.

[13] Software Instruction Manual of Multi - Dimensional Voice Program (MDVP). Model 5105. Kay Elemetrics Corp. 2 Bridgewater Lane Lincoln Park, NJ 07035 - 1488 USA.

[14] Stathopoulos, E. T. 2000. A review of the development of the child voice: An anatomical and

functional perspective. In White, P. (ed.), *Child Voice*.
[15] Ramig, L. A., Ringel, R. L. 1983. Effects of physiological aging on selected acoustic characteristics of voice. *Journal of Speech, Language, and Hearing Research* 26, 22 – 30.
[16] Walsh, B., Smith, A. 2002. Articulatory movements in adolescents: Evidence for protracted development of speech motor control processes. *Journal of Speech, Language, and Hearing Research* 45, 1119 – 1133.
[17] Childers D. G., Lee C. K. 1991. Vocal quality factors: Analysis, synthesis, and perception. *The Journal of the Acoustical Society of America* 90, 2394 – 2410.
[18] Wolfe V., Fitch J., Martin D. 1997. Acoustic measures of dysphonic severity across and within voice types. *Folia Phoniatr Logop* 49, 292 – 299.

WU Xiyu PhD He is an assistant professor of Department of Chinese Language and Literature, and Center for Chinese Linguistics, Peking University. His research interests include speech production and perception.
E-mail: xiyuwu@ pku. edu. cn

KONG Jiangping PhD He is a professor of Department of Chinese Language and Literature, and Center for Chinese Linguistics, Peking University. His research interests include speech production and perception. He is the correspondent author of this paper.
E-mail: jpkong@ pku. edu. cn

APPENDIX Ⅰ

Definition of Parameters

F0 (Hz): Average Fundamental Frequency
T0 (ms): Average Pitch Period
Fhi (Hz): Highest Fundamental Frequency
Flo (Hz): Lowest Fundamental Frequency
STD (Hz): Standard Deviation Frequency
PFR: Phonatory F0-range in semitones
Fftr (Hz): F0-Tremor Frequency
Fatr (Hz): Amplitude Tremor Frequency
Tsam (s): Length of Analyzed Sample
Jita (us): Absolute Jitter
Jitt (%): Jitter percent
RAP (%): Relative Average Perturbation
PPQ (%): Pitch Perturbation Quotient
sPPQ (%): Smoothed Pitch Perturbation Quotient
vF0 (%): Fundamental Frequency Variation
ShdB (dB): Shimmer in dB
Shim (%): Shimmer in Percent
APQ (%): Amplitude Perturbation Quotient
sAPQ (%): Smoothed Amplitude Perturbation Quotient
vAm (%): Peak-to-Peak amplitude variation
NHR: Noise to Harmonic Ratio
VTI: Voice Turbulence Index
SPI: Soft Phonation Index
FTRI (%): F0-Tremor Intensity Index
ATRI (%): Amplitude Tremor Intensity Index
DVB (%): Degree of Voice Breaks
DSH (%): Degree of Sub-harmonics
DUV (%): Degree of Voiceless
NVB: Number of Voice Breaks
NSH: Number of Sub-harmonic Segments
NUV: Number of Unvoiced Segments
SEG: Number of Segments Computed
PER: Total Number Detected Pitch Periods

APPENDIX Ⅱ　　　Mean and Standard Deviation of Parameters

Age Group	Gender	F0		MF0		T0		Fhi		Flo		STD	
		Mean	STD	Mean	STD	Mean	STD	Mean	STD	Mean	STD	Mean	STD
1	Female	295.477	25.814	295.017	26.075	3.390	0.337	326.666	42.858	271.592	26.387	7.512	3.395
	Male	286.093	40.931	285.528	41.324	3.520	0.506	319.015	55.107	265.451	43.179	8.071	5.153
2	Female	278.164	40.124	279.577	38.635	3.645	0.509	305.699	49.918	248.540	40.607	7.466	3.712
	Male	254.348	30.166	254.149	30.168	3.876	0.510	278.682	38.948	236.107	34.449	6.167	2.623
3	Female	257.656	22.348	257.449	22.328	3.855	0.356	274.731	30.730	233.676	30.850	5.627	2.407
	Male	224.152	33.569	224.007	33.586	4.519	0.742	236.730	43.070	209.919	36.524	4.593	1.945
4	Female	242.053	20.466	241.956	20.474	4.147	0.365	259.105	24.362	225.550	24.137	4.420	1.628
	Male	127.998	18.012	127.948	18.017	7.626	1.225	132.983	18.427	123.537	18.589	2.091	0.955
5	Female	247.534	23.159	247.230	22.920	4.045	0.372	270.479	30.912	224.739	27.445	4.898	2.150
	Male	145.644	22.852	145.603	22.844	6.990	1.117	152.122	23.892	140.305	20.345	2.160	0.904
6	Female	223.908	21.495	223.423	22.249	4.496	0.437	238.697	25.396	212.625	24.705	4.143	2.385
	Male	140.913	24.259	140.879	24.258	7.182	1.249	145.890	24.603	134.507	23.074	2.145	0.745
7	Female	211.262	21.767	211.179	21.768	4.760	0.470	222.522	25.882	198.303	23.828	3.479	1.182
	Male	127.202	16.950	127.129	16.937	7.951	0.984	132.491	17.851	119.252	13.611	2.504	1.263
8	Female	211.088	25.309	210.949	25.309	4.811	0.604	223.318	31.712	197.035	26.787	4.424	2.107
	Male	153.322	27.592	153.217	27.575	6.743	1.250	160.866	28.341	141.909	22.770	3.154	1.349

Age Group	Gender	PFR		APQ		Jita		Jitt		RAP		PPQ		sAPQ	
		Mean	STD	Mean	STD	Mean	STD	Mean	STD	Mean	STD	Mean	STD	Mean	STD
1	Female	4.041	2.081	4.210	1.288	57.504	26.344	1.706	0.820	1.023	0.504	0.988	0.487	6.037	1.778
	Male	4.128	2.643	4.193	1.858	52.765	39.431	1.459	1.041	0.915	0.673	0.967	0.790	6.369	2.663
2	Female	4.756	2.586	4.267	1.695	58.082	27.652	1.545	0.671	0.891	0.401	0.847	0.364	6.782	2.214
	Male	3.604	1.621	3.808	1.526	45.901	23.896	1.235	0.622	0.697	0.348	0.706	0.355	6.084	2.225
3	Female	3.362	1.661	3.515	1.348	60.026	27.191	1.537	0.667	0.885	0.366	0.862	0.404	5.738	2.123
	Male	3.094	1.376	3.646	1.505	53.444	28.216	1.144	0.589	0.659	0.354	0.638	0.304	6.673	2.344
4	Female	3.462	1.379	2.767	0.675	52.433	18.502	1.306	0.450	0.778	0.276	0.741	0.248	4.745	1.156
	Male	2.355	0.839	3.097	0.922	47.223	17.104	0.623	0.222	0.336	0.140	0.347	0.121	5.542	2.628
5	Female	3.813	2.059	3.428	1.070	59.605	30.664	1.455	0.721	0.869	0.438	0.840	0.423	5.776	1.782
	Male	2.196	0.654	3.320	0.960	52.469	23.217	0.752	0.356	0.425	0.226	0.419	0.203	6.007	3.186
6	Female	3.360	2.018	3.178	0.988	44.259	27.678	0.988	0.587	0.585	0.359	0.590	0.384	6.439	2.139
	Male	2.340	0.668	3.135	1.052	44.700	19.647	0.609	0.228	0.334	0.142	0.342	0.143	6.429	2.872
7	Female	2.813	1.104	3.481	1.245	39.753	20.191	0.828	0.416	0.488	0.257	0.471	0.236	7.175	2.638
	Male	2.522	1.005	3.781	1.121	56.554	26.736	0.711	0.337	0.373	0.210	0.384	0.182	6.559	4.217
8	Female	3.048	1.229	3.278	1.211	47.776	28.272	0.935	0.520	0.515	0.282	0.514	0.303	8.734	3.589
	Male	3.022	1.164	3.845	1.211	56.961	31.464	0.817	0.407	0.441	0.258	0.440	0.220	6.961	3.410

Age Group	Gender	ShdB		Shim		NHR		VTI		SPI		SEG		PER	
		Mean	STD	Mean	STD	Mean	STD	Mean	STD	Mean	STD	Mean	STD	Mean	STD
1	Female	0.531	0.162	5.951	1.771	0.141	0.032	0.065	0.019	6.005	3.861	17.745	3.836	162.115	42.432
	Male	0.534	0.243	5.786	2.485	0.138	0.036	0.061	0.021	5.646	3.618	17.191	5.110	155.604	52.080
2	Female	0.536	0.188	6.017	2.321	0.149	0.032	0.074	0.029	6.387	4.398	15.283	3.763	124.477	24.369
	Male	0.484	0.193	5.417	2.282	0.144	0.035	0.063	0.030	7.971	3.740	12.271	2.238	96.640	24.703
3	Female	0.457	0.164	5.051	1.783	0.135	0.029	0.055	0.020	10.296	4.956	11.542	2.509	90.938	21.484
	Male	0.454	0.171	4.987	1.979	0.134	0.026	0.051	0.017	13.525	7.358	12.000	2.318	82.294	15.770
4	Female	0.345	0.080	3.852	0.921	0.120	0.017	0.045	0.013	18.048	7.329	17.902	3.177	127.240	24.380
	Male	0.337	0.080	3.745	0.979	0.133	0.019	0.043	0.012	23.770	8.061	18.200	4.437	72.129	14.610
5	Female	0.422	0.137	4.750	1.554	0.130	0.028	0.042	0.013	16.752	8.340	23.250	4.974	172.040	42.852
	Male	0.336	0.089	3.776	0.992	0.136	0.013	0.046	0.013	20.982	9.977	19.224	6.420	82.776	29.001
6	Female	0.370	0.130	4.218	1.492	0.133	0.028	0.041	0.015	17.104	8.374	21.204	6.318	140.958	44.111
	Male	0.332	0.096	3.696	1.085	0.134	0.016	0.040	0.013	19.671	8.270	19.830	4.188	83.340	22.238
7	Female	0.392	0.161	4.483	1.829	0.129	0.016	0.040	0.014	18.121	10.052	25.913	9.101	170.188	62.501
	Male	0.398	0.128	4.491	1.496	0.140	0.023	0.036	0.009	30.552	14.220	19.244	6.216	73.022	24.722
8	Female	0.352	0.127	3.899	1.397	0.128	0.019	0.042	0.013	18.435	8.072	26.136	9.957	164.622	71.439
	Male	0.378	0.131	4.180	1.347	0.131	0.021	0.034	0.011	27.601	11.059	21.711	6.055	105.447	39.883

Gender	vF0		sPPQ		vAm	
	Mean	STD	Mean	STD	Mean	STD
Female	2.120	1.090	0.966	0.453	19.885	6.663
Male	2.000	1.023	0.851	0.470	19.074	6.964

汉语方言声调古今对照与共时分布的研究方法
——基于字音系统实验研究工具

刘新中　曾　玲

摘　要　本文主要基于熊子瑜博士研发的汉语方言字音系统实验研究工具，探讨运用实验语音学手段系统研究汉语方言声调的方法。不同方言点的研究实践说明，熊子瑜博士开发的汉语方言字音系统实验研究工具能够系统地观察、提取、分析相关声学数据，对于全面观察、梳理汉语方言语音特征的演变和共时研究具有重要意义，也为方言字音库的建设奠定了良好的基础，是运用实验方法研究汉语方言字音系统的有效手段。
关键词　汉语方言，声调，声学实验，系统工具

A Method for the Diachronic and Synchronic Study of Tones in Chinese Dialects: Upon the Research Tool of the Phonetic System of Words

LIU Xinzhong　ZENG Ling

Abstract This paper explores the methods of experimental phonetics to systematically study tones in Chinese dialects based on the research tool developed by Dr. Ziyu Xiong. According to the empirical research of various Chinese dialects, the Research Tool of the Phonetic System of words in Chinese Dialects is capable of systematically observing, extracting, and analyzing acoustic data. Not only does it contribute to the evolutionary and synchronic study on the phonetic features of Chinese dialects, but it also lays a solid foundation for constructing the speech corpora of Chinese dialects. Therefore, the Research Tool of the Phonetic System of words in Chinese Dialects has proven to be an effective means to study the phonetic system of words in Chinese dialects in an experimental approach.
Key words Chinese dialects, Tone, Acoustic experiment, Systematic tools

1. 引言

运用实验的方法研究汉语方言的声调，从刘复［2］、赵元任［8］等以来，已经有了长足的进步。这些年来，随着计算机技术的普及，借助计算机程序对汉语方言声调进行系统化、大规模研究的条件已日趋成熟，出现了很多新型的研究工具，其中具有代表性的是中国社会科学院语言研究所熊子瑜的汉语方言字音系统实验研究工具。熊子瑜基于 Praat 软件研发了一套系统观察、提取、分析语音声学数据的脚本工具，这对于全面观察、梳理汉语方言语音特征的演变和共时研究具有重要意义，也为方言字音库的建设奠定了良好的基础。

熊子瑜开发的汉语方言字音系统实验研究工具主要包括语料设计、语音采集、语音标注、参数提取、数据分析等诸多方面。本文我们根据熊子瑜最新优化的版本，结合汉语方言声调系统的研究成果介绍这套脚本工具的主要功能及其对于汉语方言字音系统研究的重要意义。

2. 实验准备

2.1　设计字表

设计字表是方言字音系统研究的基础，例字的选择主要视使用者的研究目的而定。若要研究共时音系，那字表就应尽可能包括该方言所有可能出现的音节，这样，运

行脚本后所提取的声学数据才有可能呈现包括各个音节在内的各类声母、韵母和声调等声学特性。

为了方便使用者设计一个符合自己要求的字表，熊子瑜把《方言调查字表》的3700多个汉字信息整合成一个调查字表，使用者可根据自己的调查需求从中筛选例字，具体做法是：用记事本程序打开脚本文件夹下的“练习数据：方言调查字表（XZY）. txt”文件，然后复制字表的内容并粘贴到Excel表格之中，再细致筛选出要研究的例字，并将其保存为UTF－8编码格式的文本文件。文本文件设置为UTF－8编码格式，是为了防止系统转换时出现乱码。

使用者也可自行设计字表，但为了能够执行后续操作，字表中必须包含如表1所示的10类信息，否则无法成功运行脚本程序。

表1　调查字表所需要的基本信息

编号	X0001	X0002	X0003	X0004
汉字	哀	挨	矮	爱
备注	哀悼悲哀	挨打 挨饿	矮子 个子矮	爱情 喜爱
古声	影	疑	影	影
古韵	咍	佳	蟹	代
古调	平	平	上	去
摄	蟹	蟹	蟹	蟹
呼	開	開	開	開
等	一	二	二	一
普通话拼音	ai1	ai2	ai3	ai4

2.2　脚本工具的安装

用户在关注微信公众号“语音学堂”（曾用名“九州语言网”）之后，向其后台发送关键词“工具脚本”即可获得共享链接和提取密码，当前提供的百度网盘地址和提取密码如下：https：//pan. baidu. com/s/1lmiRJlAaHt5L1bYxE5sggg（提取密码为：8v5c）。

在下载好这套脚本工具之后，应在C盘或D盘的根目录下新建一个文件夹，将其命名为“xPraat”或其他，注意该文件夹名称中不能包含任何特殊符号并尽量不要包含空格字符，以免导致脚本程序运行错误。建好文件夹后，把自己准备好的字表文件和下载的全部脚本文件均放入该文件夹之中。

为便于使用这套脚本，用户应首先运行脚本文件夹中的“00. 生成全部脚本的Praat运行菜单. scp”脚本，在Praat程序中安装相应的操作菜单，该脚本可将字表处理、语音录制、字音标注、数据提取以及字表数据分析和字音数据分析等操作命令按照一定的顺序内置到Praat系统菜单之中，以便于后期操作。这一操作的执行步骤如下：

打开Praat程序，在Praat程序的主窗口中点击Praat菜单，并选择其下拉菜单“Open Praat script”，在弹出的文件对话框中选择打开“00. 生成全部脚本的Praat运行菜单. scp”脚本文件，然后点击脚本编辑器中的“Run→Run”菜单运行该脚本，会弹出如下参数对话窗口：

图1　运行参数设定窗口

用户应在该对话框中输入脚本程序所在的文件夹路径，并以“\”结尾，然后点击对话框上的“确定”按钮，即可完成这套脚本程序的安装。该脚本运行结束后，用户在Praat主窗口的Praat菜单下会看见一个名为“汉语方言字音系统实验研究”的新菜单。此时可以关闭Praat程序，下次再打开运行Praat程序时，该菜单可直接使用，无须再次安装。

提示：如果多次安装，会导致Praat菜单上出现重复条目，使用者可在C盘的用户目录下搜索“Buttons5. ini”文件，该文件属于Praat程序的用户菜单配置文件，找到后删除该文件，即可清除用户自己安装的菜单，不会影响Praat程序的原有功能。这一操作应在Praat未运行的情况下执行。

3. 实验过程

3.1 字音录制

下面本文以声调分析的过程为例，介绍相关操作步骤，所有步骤都依据熊子瑜在其公众号“语音学堂”中发布的相关推文内容为参考进行操作和叙述。

（1）设定全局变量

这一步主要是输入字表文件的储存路径和新建音库的基本信息，让系统识别要处理的数据并生成储存数据的文件夹。菜单操作步骤如下：点击 Praat 主窗口中的 Praat 菜单，并选择其下拉菜单“汉语方言字音系统实验研究”，然后选择“输入全局变量”菜单，会弹出如下参数对话窗口：

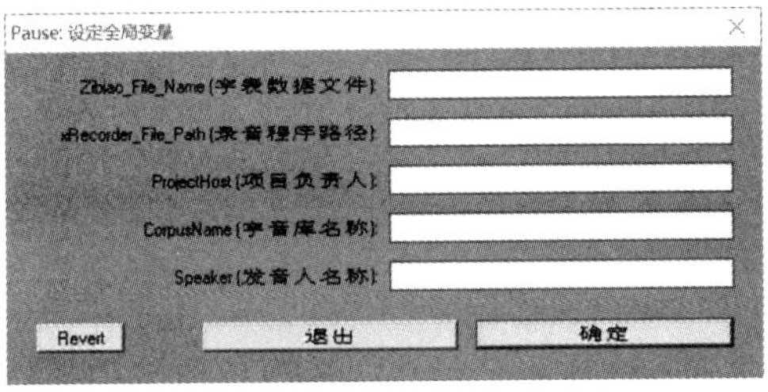

图2 运行参数设定窗口

这里从上到下依次要填写的信息包括：①字表数据文件的路径和文件名，包含该文件的扩展名；②录音程序 xRecorder 的存放路径，后期所有录音文件和数据文件均会保存至该路径之下；③项目承担单位名称；④方言点名称信息；⑤发音人名称信息，这些参数内容都尽量不要包含特殊字符和空格，并要求准确无误，特别是其中的第一项内容，以便于程序能够正确读取字表文件数据。

设定好上述运行参数之后，点击参数对话框上的“确定”按钮即可完成全局变量的设定工作，后期运行的脚本程序将根据这一环节设定的路径参数去保存和读取相应的数据文件。

设定好全局变量之后，接下来在“字音数据处理”菜单下依次运行以下步骤，运行这儿步操作时，无须输入任何参数，但在程序运行过程中不要中断操作。

（2）原始字表数据核查与整理

（3）制作生成录音字表文本文件

（4）调用 xRecorder 程序进行录音

在运行第（4）步调用 xRecorder 程序进行录音时，系统会弹出一个提示框，如下所示：

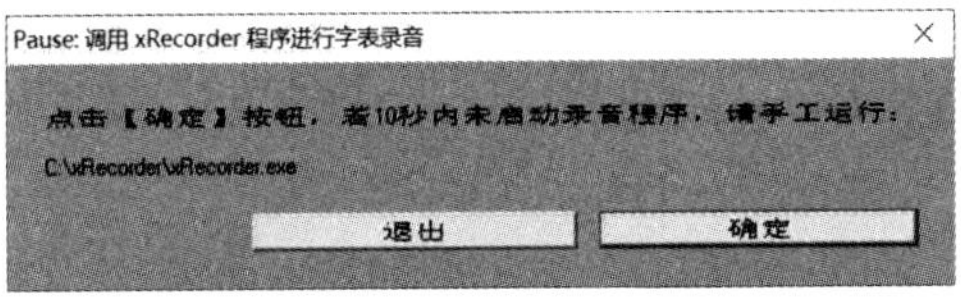

图3 调用 xRecorder 程序时的提示对话框

此时，用户需要点击提示对话框中的“确定”按钮，以便程序去调用 xRecorder 程序，正常情况下会自动打开 xRecorder 程序，其录音界面大致如图4所示：

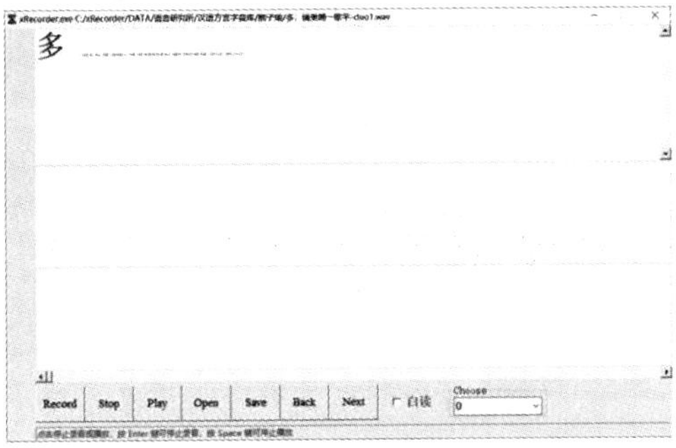

图4 xRecorder 程序的录音界面

如果使用者已经有了与调查字表相一致的录音，可以将已有的声音文件复制粘贴到“DATA”文件夹下“发音人”的文件夹中。如果音频文件名与脚本默认的文件名（如“阿：影果開一歌平 – e1. wav”）不一致，就需在“X 字表数据 . ini”文件中将“文件名”一列的内容修改为与音频文件名一致，并等录音程序打开后将录音文件复制到“发音人”文件夹下，确认录音程序中已显示该录音文件，再将程序关闭。如此，便可让 xRecorder 识别到外部的音频数据文件。因此，可以说 xRecorder 程序及这套脚本工具能够友好地支持和有效利用已有的声音文件。

完成上述 4 步操作过程之后，字音数据就录制结束了。之后用户还可以借助 xRecorder 程序对录音材料进行检查和整理，以提高字音库的数据质量。在录音时，该程序可逐条显示例字及其相关信息，并可将每个例字录制好的声音文件自动保存起来，而且在保存声音文件时可以自动检测其声波振幅大小，当振幅超过用户设定的阈值时会自动报错并提醒用户重新录制，保存好当前例字的声音文件之后，会自动跳转并显示下一个未录音的条目，因此能够在一定程度上提高录音质量和效率，并能够有效防止漏录的情况出现。采用 xRecorder 程序，逐条录制一个方言点 3000 多个字的字音数据，大约需要两天的时间。

3.2 字音数据标注

完成字音文件的采集之后，就需要对录音文件进行细致而规范的音段标注，切分并标注其声韵调信息，具体步骤如下：

（5）自动生成 TextGrid 标注文件

（6）原始标注数据提取

（7）基于原始标注数据还原 Z 字表数据

（8）顺序编校 TextGrid 和 PitchTier 文件。

前面（5）（6）（7）三步都无须设定参数，直接运行即可得到相应结果。第 8 步运行时会弹出如下参数输入窗口：

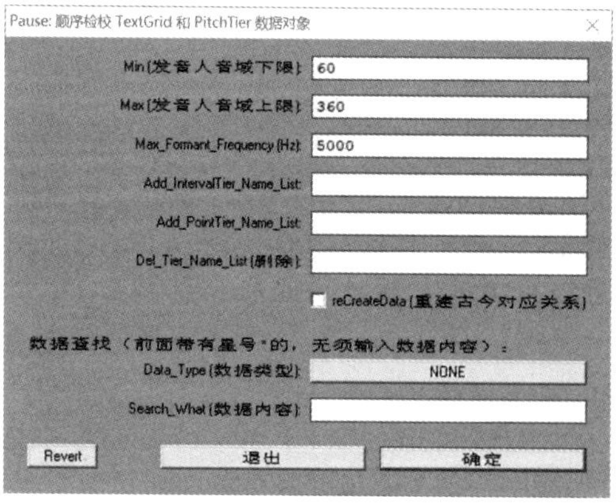

图 5　运行参数设定窗口

对于成年男性发音人的数据而言，一般无须修改图 5 所显示的默认参数，如果是成年女性发音人的数据，可将图 5 中的第三个参数 5000 修改为 5500，然后根据发音人的实际音域范围，适当调整图 5 中的第一个参数和第二个参数，即发音人的音域下限频率和音域上限频率，使音高编辑器窗口能够完整显示该发音人的相应数据。其他运行参数可根据实际需要加以设置。

音段标注和音高数据校准是整个操作过程中耗时最多，也最重要的步骤，它相当于田野调查中的方言记音，标记的准确性对于整个数据的获取、分析至关重要，因此需要耐心、小心、细心。熊子瑜为了方便使用者，还编写了“winPosition”程序固定标注窗口，以方便使用者进行数据标注。另外，每次运行此脚本程序时，所设定的参数应该保持一致。完成参数设置后，点击“确定”按钮即可开始标注例字的声韵调信息，同时也要细致检查音节边界和声韵母边界，并根据发音实际情况对音段边界位置进行适当调整，对声韵调标注信息进行检查和必要的修改。在进行音段标注时要有统一的技术规格，要按同样的标准去处理所有的音节，不要随意处理音段的边界，同样的语音特征要按同样的处理方式。音段标注工作窗口大致如图 6 所示：

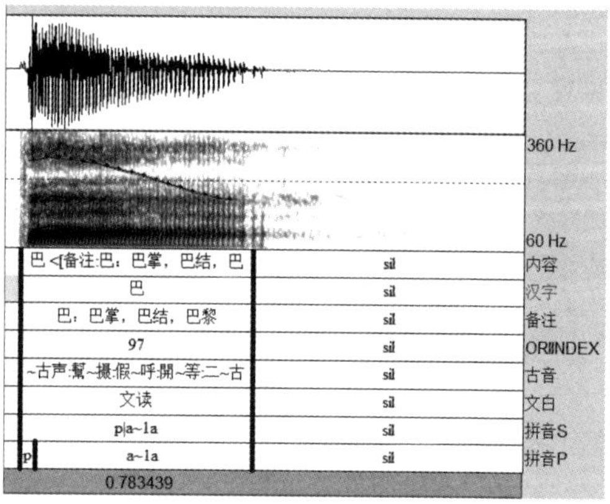

图 6　音段标注工作窗口（未调整边界位置）

从图 6 可以看出，标注对象从上到下包含了“内容、汉字、备注、ORIINDEX、古音、文白、拼音S、拼音P”8层信息内容，前6层都是字表文件中原有的数据，最后2层用于标注例字在方言中的声韵调内容，用户只需要修改第八层“拼音P”层中声母和韵母、调类数据，注意韵母和调类之间采用“~”隔开，另外不要输入空格字符。脚本程序会根据用户在第八层输入或修改的声韵调数据去自动修改第七层的数据，因此用户无须去手动修改第七层的数据。

该脚本程序还会基于用户录入的字音数据，动态更新古今音之间的对应关系，并在此基础上去预测未做记音的汉字的声韵调信息，标注者可以根据实际的读音对预测结果进行调整。自动预测功能可以减少大量的数据录入工作，并能够在一定程度上提高字音数据标注的准确性。当然，基于古今音对应关系不可能完全准确地预测或判断所有汉字的声韵调信息，预测出现错误也是难免的。根据我们目前的数据来看，预测结果的正确率大概能够达到90%，对于某些古今音对应关系较强的方言而言，预测正确率甚至会更高。因此当预测结果与实际读音不一致时，使用者应审慎修改，并思考是不是发音人读错了或者例字的古音分类信息有问题。

对于字音的声韵调标注这一任务来说，一方面要细致确认输入或预测的声韵调信息是否正确，另一方面是要通过拖动标注层的蓝色竖线以精确调整音节边界和声韵母边界的位置，在确定音节边界和声韵母边界时，一开始主要依赖听觉判断，等有一定经验之后可通过查看宽带语图上的声学特征来加以判断。如果研究的重点为声调，也可将默认的宽带语图改变成窄带语图，以帮助查看音高走势并可用于检查音高数据是否出错。具体步骤为：在声音编辑器窗口点击Spectrum菜单，然后选择其下拉菜单Spectrogram settings，并在弹出的对话框中将数值设置如图7所示。

另外需要注意的是，在标注声调的“承载段”时，应该将那些不属于该声调的弯头和翘尾等音高数据给剔除掉，对于音高数据曲线中出现的跳点、断点等错误数据更应加以修改或删除，以提高声调音

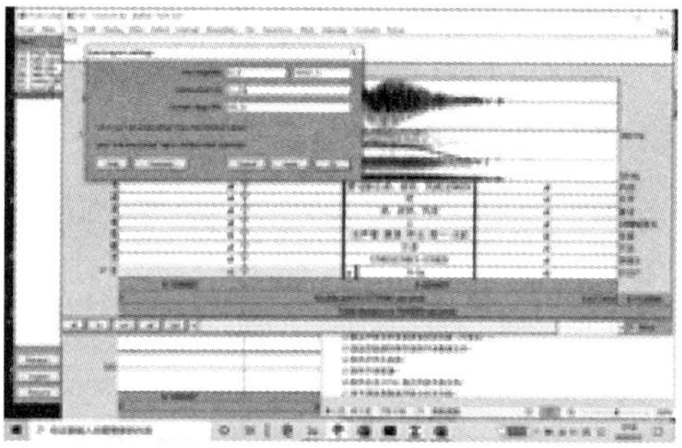

图7 分析窄带语图的参数设定窗口

高数据的准确性。该脚本能够自动读取并保存相关的数据文件，因此能够在一定程度上提高标注工作的效率。尽管如此，音段标注和音高数据校准仍是一件费时费力的工作，但对于字音声学数据分析来说却又是必不可少的。根据我们的经验，完成一个方言点3000多字的音段数据标注和音高数据校准工作大约需要一周甚至更长的时间。

3.3 声学数据分析和提取

在细致完成全部例字的音段标注工作之后，可以进一步开展以下工作：

（9）自动生成各类声学参数文件

运行这一脚本，可以自动批量生成全部录音材料的音高数据文件（*.PitchTier）、音强数据文件（*.IntensityTier）和共振峰数据文件（*.FormantGrid）。一般情况下，无须修改默认的运行参数，只有在分析共振峰数据时需要调整共振峰上限频率这一参数，成年男发音人的共振峰上限频率可设置为5000，成年女发音人的共振峰上限频率可设置为5500，单位均为Hz。脚本程序自动提取并生成的声学参数文件会自动保存至声音文件所在的文件夹之中。

（10）标注数据和声学参数提取

运行这一脚本，可提取各个例字的声、韵、调以及各种古音分类信息等标注数据，还可以进一步提取出韵母段的音高、音强和共振峰等声学数据。通常情况下，用户直接使用默认的运行参数即可。提取生成的标注数据和声学参数数据文件会以文本文件格式保存在声音文件所在的

目录之中，系统默认的纯标注数据文件名为“allData_TextGrid. ini”，标注和音高数据的文件名为“allData_PitchTier. ini”。为便于观察数据结果，用户可以使用记事本打开这些数据结果文件，并全选后复制粘贴至 Excel 表格之中。

（11）基于标注和声学参数文件还原生成 T 字表数据

T 字表数据文件是后续其他脚本运行的基础，里面包含各个例字条目对应的标注文件（＊. TextGrid）所包含的全部标注信息，既有例字的各种古音分类信息，也有用户标注的声韵调信息。之所以要基于标注文件去提取生成新的字表数据文件，一是要把用户标注的声韵调信息纳入字表数据中来，以便于分析古今音对应关系等数据，另外是考虑到用户有可能会对例字的一些古音分类信息加以修改，因此有必要提取出用户检查和修改后的这些基础分类数据，以保证后续研究数据的准确性。

（12）截去声音文件首尾多余的空白段

运行这一脚本，可以将声音文件的首尾空白段时长加以规整，用户可以设定要保留的首尾空白段时长，程序在运行时会自动截去多余的空白段。这项操作除了会影响声音文件之外，还会同步处理标注数据文件（＊. TextGrid）和音高数据文件（＊. PitchTier），以确保它们跟声音文件（＊. wav）能够在时间上一致并对齐。

（13）添加声韵调关联信息到字表数据文件

这一脚本将辅助用户将声韵调所关联的 IPA 或名称、序号、发音特征、调值等数据添加至字表数据文件之中，并与各个例字数据进行关联，特别是其中的声韵调序号信息非常有用，有了给定的排序信息之后，脚本程序在后期输出各类数据表时会以相应的顺序对声母、韵母和声调进行编排，如果没有给定的声韵调序号信息，则只能按照其音序进行编排。这一个脚本至少需要运行两次：第一次运行时会生成一个名为“x 声韵调关联数据 . ini”的数据文件，用户将该文件中的内容拷贝至 Excel 表格中进行编辑，然后将编辑好的内容再从 Excel 表格中拷贝至该数据文件中并保存起来。修改完“x 声韵调关联数据 . ini”数据文件之后应再次运行该脚本，脚本程序会将该数据文件中的内容自动导入至字表数据文件之中并与各个例字条目关联起来。用户可以随时删除或重新编辑“x 声韵调关联数据 . ini”数据文件，然后重新运行该脚本，直到“x 声韵调关联数据 . ini”无须再次修改，每次修改后均应再次运行该脚本程序，以便导入修改后的声韵调关联数据。

3.4 字音数据分析

在完成上述工作之后，用户可根据需要来分析字表数据和字音数据，并自动输出相应的数据结果，下面加以简要介绍。

（14）制作声学元音图

执行这一操作需要用户事先提取并生成“allData_FormantGrid_F. ini”数据结果文件，即所有字音的共振峰数据，若系统提示缺少这一文件，可先返回执行脚本“自动生成各类参数文件”这一步骤，在数据类型（Data_Type）中选择“Formant-Grid”，点击确定，即可生成每个例字的共振峰参数文件，之后再返回执行“标注数据和声学参数提取”这一脚本，在参数类型（Data_Type）中选择“提取标注和共振峰频率数据”，即可提取并生成相应的共振峰数据结果文件“allData_FormantGrid_F. ini”。有了共振峰数据结果文件之后，才能运行“制作声学元音图”脚本。

熊子瑜［6］曾提出，要做出一个精确的元音图，应在标注时专门标出各个单元音共振峰的特征点，以确保提取出来的共振峰数据能够相对准确。

（15）制作字音图谱

运行这一脚本，可批量生成全部例字的字音图谱文件，包含声波图、声韵调标注信息、宽带语图、音高数据图以及例字的古音分类信息等内容。结果大致如图 9 所示。

（16）制作生成 HTML 格式同音字表文件

这一脚本可将字表数据按照一定的编排方式和顺序输出成一个 HTML 格式的表格内容文件，并将声音文件和字音图谱文

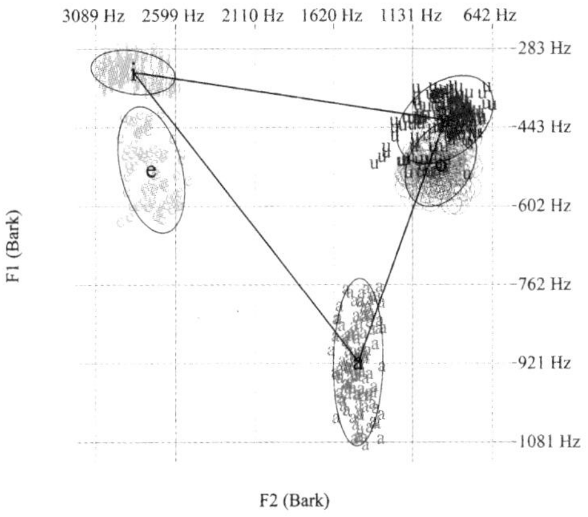

图8　声学元音图示例

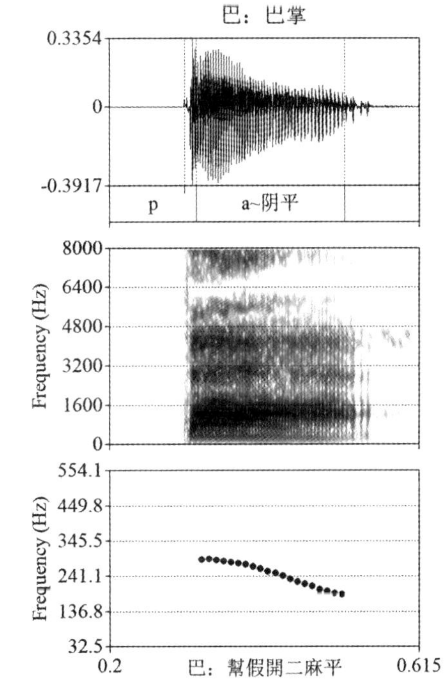

图9　字音图谱示例

件与各个例字进行关联，以便于用户播放语音和查看相应的字音图谱。

（17）单字调音高数据均值分析并作图

执行这一操作需要用户事先提取并生成“allData_PitchTier.ini”音高数据结果文件，即所有字音的音高数据，若系统提示缺少这一文件，可先返回执行脚本“自动生成各类参数文件”这一步骤，在数据类型（Data_Type）中选择“PitchTier”，点击确定，即可生成每个例字的音高参数文件，之后再返回执行“标注数据和声学参数提取”这一脚本，在参数类型（Data_Type）中选择“提取标注和音高数据”，即可提取并生成相应的音高数据结果文件“allData_PitchTier.ini”。有了音高数据结果文件之后，才能运行“单字调音高数据均值分析并作图”脚本。该脚本的运行参数对话框如图10所示：

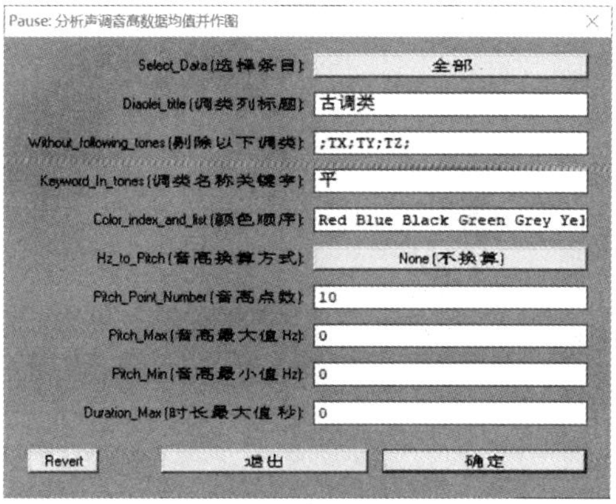

图10　运行参数设定窗口

通过设定图10中第2、3、4这几个控制参数，用户可以筛选出要分析的例字，脚本程序会根据筛选条件分析这些例字的音高数据并制作声调曲线图。因为字表数据文件中既包含古调分类信息，也包含今音调类信息，因此既可以按照例字的古调类来分析作图，也可以按照例字的今音调类来分析作图。此外，对于同一发音人的录音材料，用户还可以通过设定相同的音域范围以及最大调型段时长等参数，以提高不同音高数据图之间的可比性。在作图之前，用户可根据需要在Praat Picture窗口中选定大小合适的作图区域，所选中的粉红色内框，将作为声调曲线图的呈现区域。

本文将在第四部分通过不同方言点的声调音高数据图来说明这一脚本的运行结果及其研究价值，特别是以古调类为控制因素来筛选例字并制作出声调音高图，可以帮助分析古调类在该方言中出现的分化与合并现象。

(18) 自动测算单字调的调值

(19) 自动测算单字调的调类

有研究表明[7],通过合理配置运行参数,利用“自动测算单字调的调值”和“自动测算单字调的调类”这两个脚本程序,可自动测算方言的调值和调类数据,为记录方言字调提供有益参考。

3.5 字表数据分析

在提取生成“T字表数据.ini”文件之后,即可基于该文件中的古音分类信息以及今音声韵调信息,来分析古今音之间的对应关系数据和声韵调组合关系数据,还能按照用户设定的方式输出方言同音字表数据。所用到的脚本程序如下所示。

(20) 分析古今字音对应关系数据

(21) 分析声韵调组合关系数据

(22) 分析输出同音字表数据

这些数据是研究汉语方言语音较为关心的内容,能较好地展示共时的语音面貌和古今对照的情况。此外,对于古今演变规律的研究、跨方言的比较研究等,熊子瑜设计了如下一些能对方言语音的整体性特征、规律进行观察的脚本。

(23) 测算古音分化系数

(24) 测算古音合并系数

(25) 测算古音两两合并系数

(26) 跨点字音对应关系分析

(27) 输出用于weka分析的字表数据

(28) weka决策树结果数据处理

这些系统性、全局性的观察为认识方言演化及方言之间的关系提供了较好的参照角度,能够基本满足汉语方言语音的共时特点概括、古今对应关系的观察等需求。

4. 声调音高数据分析

如前所述,通过运行字音数据分析的脚本所得的声学数据或图表可以呈现方言语音研究所需要的主要结果,在大量声学数据的支撑下完成对声调系统的分析[1,5]。下面我们以古今声调的对比为重点,根据我们已经完成的一些方言实例来进一步说明。

结果呈现首先是运用实验的声学数据表现声调的声学模型,比如江西赣语遂川话以及熊子瑜博士制作的北京话单字调声学模型如图11所示:

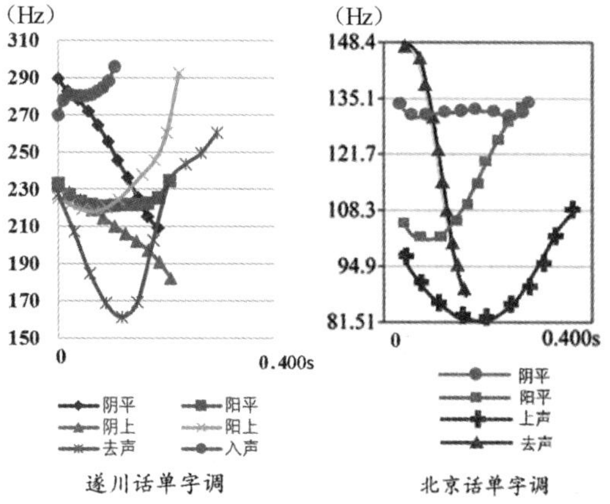

图11 遂川话和北京话的单字调声学模型

图11展示了江西遂川话和北京话的基于调查字表全表例字的单字调,较好地反映了这两个方言点单字调的总体调型特征和声调格局,有利于研究者对该方言点的声调系统有一个整体的认识。

图12是根据3700多个汉字的今读与中古调类的对照制作而成的,从整体上较好地反映了北京话今读与中古四声八调的对应关系,也可看出北京话四声从中古到现代演变的主要规律:平分阴阳(图12平)、浊上变去(图12上)、入派三声(图12入)。

另外,通过实验数据还能清晰表明古调类在现在方言中的共时读音,从而较好地总结该方言点的古今演变规律,对于研究方言的古今演变具有重要意义。

如图13所示,兰银官话声调数量只有三个,但是它的命名、连读调有很多问题。我们使用熊子瑜的字音研究系统,选取兰银官话的一个点,对3500多个汉字的今读进行了系统分析[3]。从图13中我们可以看到兰银官话新疆木垒话声调的古今对应情况,同时也反映出新疆木垒话共时的声调系统。这些数据清楚地显示出兰银官话三个声调的古今演变,也为声调

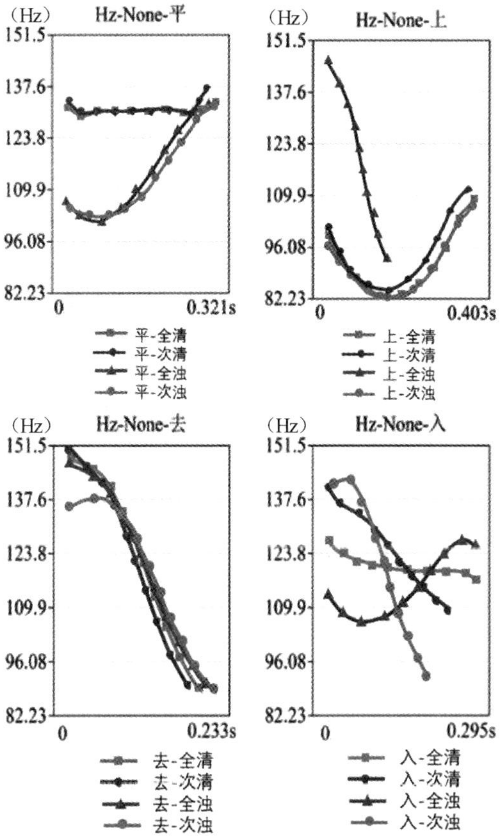

图 12　北京话古今声调对应

（以古调类和古声清浊类型筛选例字并作图）

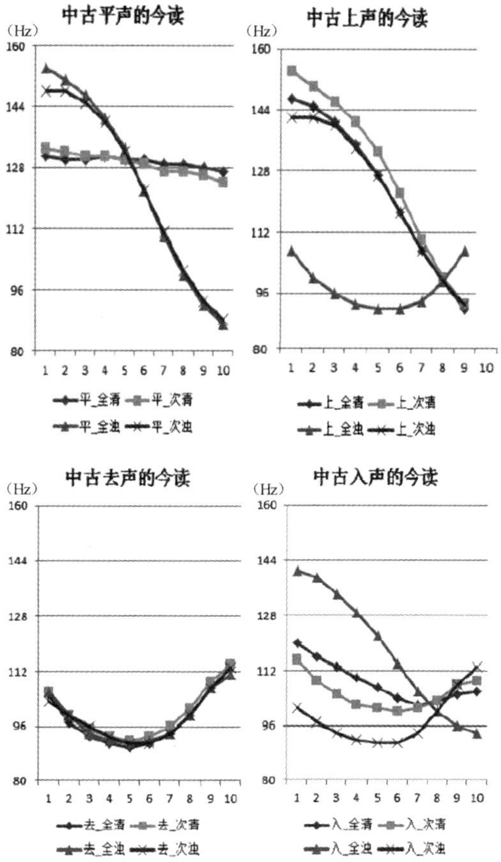

图 13　兰银官话新疆木垒话的古今声调对应

（以古调类和古声清浊类型筛选例字并作图，横坐标时长规整为 10 个点）

的命名提供了实验统计的依据，即兰银官话 3 个声调的合理命名是“平、上、去”，而不是“阴平、阳平、去”或“阴平、阳平上、去”等说法。

5. 结语

本文通过对熊子瑜研发的汉语方言字音系统研究工具的操作步骤及应用实例的阐述，说明该研究工具在汉语方言声调古今对照与共时分布方面起到了重要作用，对于全面观察、梳理汉语方言语音特征的演变和共时研究具有重要意义，是研究汉语方言声调乃至语音特征的一套较为理想的工具。同时也反映出运用实验的方法对汉语方言声调进行研究的优点，不但能优化时间成本、提高效率，还能凭借计算机在大量声学数据分析基础上生成相应的图表，帮助研究者全面且迅速地了解一个方言的字音面貌，这是对传统方言研究方法的重要完善。希望有更多的学界同仁能够了解并充分利用好这套工具，在使用过程中对这套工具提出进一步改进和优化的好建议，共同推动这套工具更好地服务于汉语方言字音实验研究工作。

6. 致谢

本文研究得到了国家社科基金重大项目“汉语方言学大型辞书编纂理论研究与数字化建设”（编号：13&ZD135）、“广东粤、闽、客方言韵律特征研究”（编号：18BYY187）、暨南大学《语言学概论》本科教学团队项目（编号：TD2020030）的支持。在研究和写作过程中也得到了熊子瑜的指导，谨致谢忱。

参考文献

[1] 梁嘉莹、刘新中：《基于大数据的粤方言阳江话（市区）声调实验研究》，《南方语言学》2016 年第 11 辑。
[2] 刘复：《四声实验录》，上海群益书社 1924 年版。
[3] 刘新中、梁嘉莹：《新疆木垒方言的单字调——基于声学数据的研究》，《方言》2017 年第 3 期。
[4] 刘新中、吴艳芬、梁嘉莹：《海南付马话的文白两套声调的实验研究》，《中国语音学报》2017 年第 8 辑。
[5] 谭洁莹、熊子瑜、刘新中：《基于大数据的粤方言新会话声调系统分析》，《实验语言学》2017 年第 5 卷。
[6] 熊子瑜：《语音库建设与分析教程》，西安交通大学出版社 2017 年版。
[7] 梁嘉莹、熊子瑜、刘新中：《粤方言肇庆端州话的声调系统实验研究》，《中国语音学报》2015 年第 5 辑。
[8] 赵元任：《中国言语字调底实验研究法》，《科学》1922 年第 9 期。

刘新中 暨南大学文学院，博士，教授，主要研究汉语方言学、语音学、语言理论与语言应用。
E - mail：liuxinzhongjn@ 163. com

曾 玲 暨南大学文学院，在读硕士，主要研究汉语方言学、赣语。
E - mail：zengling20@ 163. com

人工耳蜗植入儿童普通话卷舌元音的习得研究

于 珏 林裕鑫 金倩雯

摘 要 本文从普通话卷舌元音/ɚ/的声学特征入手，对比人工耳蜗植入（CI）儿童与健听（NH）儿童产出的普通话卷舌元音在发音清晰度及声学特征上的差异，探讨人工耳蜗植入儿童在习得卷舌元音时存在的发音困难，为该群体的语言康复教学，尤其是卷舌元音的教学，以及言语清晰度的提升提供一定的参考。发现：（1）总体而言，8.2 岁左右的 CI 儿童能基本正确掌握卷舌元音的发音特征，但发音得分仍显著低于同龄 NH 儿童；（2）在不同的构词位置，CI 儿童产出的卷舌元音时长均显著长于 NH 儿童；（3）CI 儿童与 NH 儿童的共振峰模式存在明显差异，相比较而言，CI 儿童的卷舌元音发音部位相对靠前、舌位相对较高、开口度相对较大；（4）CI 儿童产出的卷舌元音卷舌色彩不浓，与 NH 儿童存在显著差异；（5）对于 CI 儿童而言，植入人工耳蜗装置的年龄与其产出卷舌元音的发音清晰度存在显著的负相关。

关键词 卷舌元音，汉语普通话，构词位置，语前聋人工耳蜗植入儿童，儿童语言习得

Acquisition of Mandarin Retroflex Vowel in Children with Cochlear Implants

YU Jue LIN Yuxin JIN Qianwen

Abstract The present paper examined the speech intelligibility and acoustic profiles of the Mandarin retroflex vowel /ɚ/ articulated by prelingually deaf children with cochlear implants, and by normal - hearing children. The main purpose is to obtain a comprehensive understanding about the difficulties CI children facing when acquiring this target vowel. The research findings may shed some light on the speech rehabilitation training, especially on the retroflex vowel training, and the improvement of speech intelligibility for children with cochlear implants. The results show that, (1) CI children, averagely aged 8.2, could produce the retroflex vowel with moderate intelligibility, but made significantly more articulatory errors than their NH counterparts; (2) CI children tended to produce the vowel with significantly longer duration in various phonetic contexts; (3) CI children showed significant difference in the formant pattern of the retroflex vowel from that of the NH group, which displayed a more front and higher articulatory position with a larger jaw opening; (4) significant differences were found in the rhoticity between the two distinct groups; (5) a negative correlation was found between the age of implantation and the intelligibility performance of the retroflex vowel.

Key words Retroflex vowel, Mandarin, Lexical position, Prelingually deaf children with cochlear implants, Language acquisition

1. 引言

人工耳蜗通过内置电极将外界声波转化成神经电脉冲信号，直接刺激植入者耳蜗内残余的听神经，从而使其获得听觉[10]。在我国，越来越多的听障儿童（尤其是重度及极重度）通过人工耳蜗植入手术重获听觉，这一听觉路径补偿为其语音感知及语言习得提供了先决条件。然而，囿于电极数量及频谱分辨率（spectral resolution）等诸多技术限制，目前的人工耳蜗设备尚无法有效地传递完整的基频及频谱信号［9］，因而植入者无法获得完整的声学信号，这在一定程度上对植入者的语音感知、言语产出乃至言语交际都造成了

困难。

大量的前人研究表明，人工耳蜗确实能够在一定程度上促进植入者言语感知及产出的发展，但是相对于健听（normal hearing）儿童（下文简称NH儿童），语前聋人工耳蜗植入（cochlear implants）儿童（下文简称CI儿童）在元音［32］、辅音［7］、声调［16，21］、韵律层面［5，8］的感知与产出均存在不足。从发音清晰度（speech intelligibility）上看，CI儿童与NH儿童相比仍有一定差距［1］。发音清晰度是指说话人意图传递的信息内容所能被听者获取的程度范围［29］，是用以评估口语交际能力的一项重要指标［21］。此外，人工耳蜗植入儿童的语言习得表现存在较大的个体差异性［23］。影响其语言习得成效的因素相当多，Tseng等人［25］指出，研究听障儿童的言语产出可以从非语言因素及语言因素两个方面入手。非语言因素包括人工耳蜗植入前的听力水平、失聪年龄、失聪时长、残余听神经情况、人工耳蜗使用时长、人工耳蜗植入年龄，心理、教育与社会因素，甚至双亲教育背景，等等；语言因素包括时长、基频、音强及共振峰模式等［2，3，11，16，25，27］。

关于CI儿童言语习得的前人研究大都以印欧语言为母语的儿童为主，涉及元音、辅音及韵律等多个层面［4，14，26，28］，但探讨以汉语普通话为母语的CI儿童的语言习得及言语特征的文献则相对较少。其中Yang等［31］和Yang & Xu［32］的研究基本涵盖了语前聋CI儿童汉语普通话单元音及双元音的习得情况，但是唯独没有谈到普通话（北京话）中极具特色的卷舌元音。卷舌元音反映到汉字上，最典型的承载字便是“儿”。从语图上看，卷舌元音最明显的特征是，从韵腹的开头部分开始，共振峰F1缓慢地下降，F2上升，F3下降，大幅下降的F3与F2贴得越紧，听感上的卷舌色彩就越重［34］，听感上接近于美式英语单词“berth”的元音部分［12］。卷舌元音的习得对于NH儿童而言，从习得顺序来看也相对较后，如Selby & Robb［20］的案例研究考察了各位母语为美式英语的儿童元音习得轨迹，发现被试在36月龄时才能产出卷舌元音。Pollock［18］的大样本研究中也发现，在16位母语为美式英语的NH儿童中，36—41月龄组产出的卷舌元音正确率仅为79.59%，只有48—53月龄组（即4周岁以上）的正确率才达到90%以上。事实上，即便对于某些汉语方言区的成人来说，在学习汉语普通话时，习得卷舌元音的卷舌色彩也一直是个难点［37］。

总之，习得卷舌元音对于大多数NH儿童来说均不是易事。考虑到CI儿童在元音、辅音、声调等方面表现均不如NH儿童，可以推测其卷舌元音的发音清晰度及习得水平也很有可能亚于NH儿童。其次，梳理目前国内现有的研究，我们发现还鲜有从声学分析入手研究儿童的普通话卷舌元音的习得情况。以普通话为母语的语前聋CI儿童，有关其卷舌元音习得表现的研究则少之又少。基于此，本研究将通过对比人工耳蜗植入儿童与健听儿童在产出卷舌元音时，其发音清晰度及声学特征方面存在的差异，深入探讨语前聋人工耳蜗植入儿童普通话卷舌元音的习得情况。拟解决的具体问题如下：

（1）人工耳蜗植入儿童产出的普通话卷舌元音发音清晰度如何？

（2）与健听儿童相比，人工耳蜗植入儿童所产出的普通话卷舌元音在声学特征方面有何差异？

（3）人工耳蜗装置的使用经历对极重度语前聋儿童的普通话卷舌元音习得有何影响？

2. 材料与方法

2.1 实验被试

本研究共招募两组被试：一组为CI儿童，共24例（10男，14女），年龄范围为5.2—11.0岁，平均年龄为8.2（标准差SD=1.8）岁，均佩戴人工耳蜗三年以上且进行过一年以上的听觉言语康复训练。所有CI儿童在术前的听力阈值均大于95dB；除听力障碍外，无智力发育问题或认知障碍。另一组被试为相同听龄的健听儿童，共24名（11男，13女），年龄范围为5.7—11.5岁，平均年龄为8.0（标准差SD=1.8）岁，无智力发育问题及任何构音问题。两组被试在日常生活中使用的语言均为普通话。参加本研究的所有儿童，其父母已阅读知情同意书并同意孩子参与本研究。

2.2 实验材料

有研究指出，不同的构词位置会影响语流中音节的时长等相关声学参数［17］。由于本研究在研究卷舌元音时，均以“儿”为承载字，因此在设计实验材料时，也将构词位置考虑在内，以便更深入地考察在不同的构词位置上，CI儿童普通话卷舌元音的产出情况。录制的材料包括五个位于词首位置的“儿”双字词及五个位于词中位置的三字词及四字词组。所有词汇均为儿童熟悉的名词或成语，且均标注汉语拼音及汉字。每个词读两遍，每位被试按要求则需产出20个目标词，共计960个目标词（48×20=960）。

2.3 实验步骤

录音前，对所有被试儿童进行了相关的录音培训及词表熟悉。录制过程中，被试儿童佩戴专业的挂耳式耳麦（Shure PGA31），在隔音环境下，按正常语速及音量产出目标词，每个目标词朗读两遍。录音软件为Adobe Audition CS6，采样频率为44100Hz。录制后，每个语音资料实时独立保存为“.wav”格式。

录音完成后，由三位语音学专业的评测员独立地对每位被试儿童的每一目标字的发音正确程度进行主观评分，评分时参照同一评分标准，采用Likert五度值法进行（共5个等级），发音正确得5分，发音错误得1分。评分者间均进行信度（inter-rater reliability）检验。然后，将发音清晰的语料用于Praat声学分析软件［15］，进行人工手动切分和标注。最后，借助FormantPro脚本［30］自动提取每一目标字“儿”的时长参数及前三条共振峰参数。其中，每一目标字按等距提取F1、F2及F3三条共振峰上各11个点值（如图1所示），绘制相应的共振峰制图。

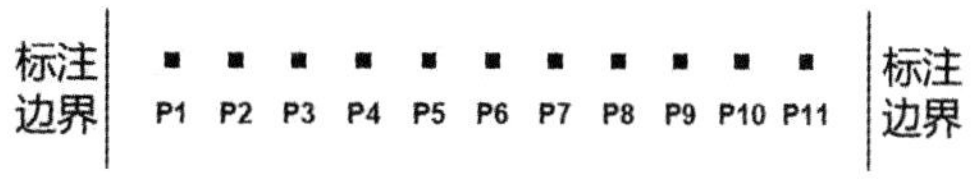

图1 共振峰取点示意图

在时长参数层面，分别计算出每位被试产出的“儿”平均时长，并进一步分类计算不同构词位置的平均时长。此外，考虑到被试儿童个体间存在语速差异，因此进一步对测量所得时长作Z-score归一化处理（见公式1），得出每一被试在不同词位下产出的卷舌元音归一化时长。

$$Z\text{-score}(x) = (x - \text{mean}) / SD \quad (1)$$

其中，x为某被试产出的某一卷舌元音的原始时长，mean为该被试产出的所有卷舌元音的平均时长，SD为该被试产出的所有卷舌元音的时长标准差。

在提取共振峰参数时，考虑到人的听感并不以频率线性变化，脚本自动将Hz值转化为Bark值，每一目标字则共计有33（3×11）个值。同样，分别计算出每位被试所产出目标词的前三条共振峰Bark值，组内每位被试数据叠加后，绘制出相应的组间普通话卷舌元音共振峰模式对比图。另外，本研究计算每一发音人的平均F3斜率，以便量化其产出的普通话卷舌元音的卷舌程度。本研究所有数据均借助R语言软件［19］进行相关的数据分析，并通过Origin（Pro）软件［13］绘图。

3. 结果

3.1 CI儿童与NH儿童卷舌元音发音清晰度对比

所收集的语料共计951个目标字。首先，在R语言软件中，使用肯德尔相关系数（Kendall's W）对三位语音学专业评测员的评测结果进行一致性检验，结果显示三位评测员的相关度较高（r=0.91）。对同一个目标字的三个评分求出平均值，从而计算出每一位被试的平均发音得分。如

表1所示，总体上看，CI儿童组和NH儿童组的卷舌元音清晰度得分分别为4.314和4.983。当目标字位于词首时，两组平均得分分别为4.323和5.000；位于词中时，两组平均得分分别为4.311和5.967。

双因素方差分析结果显示，两组间的发音清晰度得分存在极显著的组别差异（F（1，92）=105.67，$p<0.001$），但是不受构词位置的影响（F（1，92）=0.005，$p=0.942$），亦不存在组别乘以词位的交互效应（F（1，92）=0.004，$p=0.950$）。由此可见，在普通话卷舌元音产出的清晰度层面，人工耳蜗植入儿童的表现虽然达到基本掌握水平，但仍显著亚于健听儿童。

表1　组间总体及在不同构词位置下卷舌元音发音得分情况

组别	发音得分		
	总体	词首	词中
CI	4.314	4.323	4.311
NH	4.983	5.000	5.967

3.2　CI儿童与NH儿童卷舌元音声学特征的量化对比

剔除所有平均得分仅为1分（即三位评测员一致认为该音发音错误）的目标字，最后可进行声学分析的合格目标字共计947个。本节将从普通话卷舌元音的声学特征入手进行详细的量化分析。

3.2.1　两组被试普通话卷舌元音时长对比

首先探讨两组被试儿童产出的普通话卷舌元音的时长差异。从图2看，相较于NH儿童组，CI儿童组无论是在词首还是在词中位置产出的卷舌元音时长均更长、语速更慢，其中在词中位置时这一情况更加显著。

具体而言，NH儿童组的总体平均时长为0.24s，而CI儿童组的平均时长为0.28s，比前者长出16.7%。从不同的构词位置上看，两组在不同构词位置的卷舌元音时长分配上存在差异。在词首位置

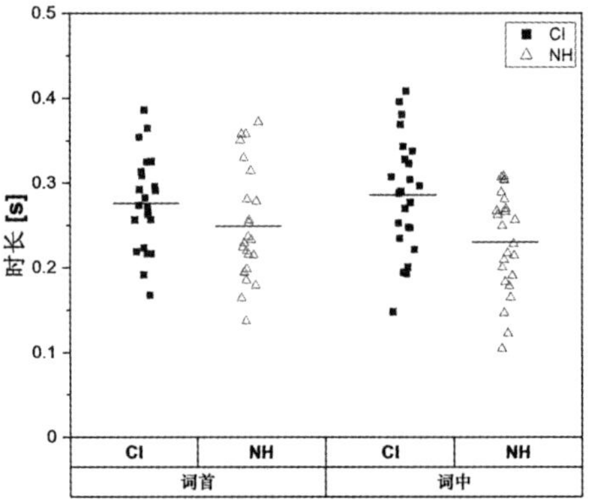

图2　不同构词位置CI儿童与NH儿童组间平均时长对比
（注：图中横杠为均值；下同）

时，NH儿童组产出卷舌元音的平均时长为0.25s，CI儿童组则需0.28s，比前者长出12%；在词中位置时，CI儿童组的平均时长为0.29s，而NH儿童组仅需0.23s，前者比后者长出26%。Lindblom & Rapp［6］研究表明，位于词组中间的音节在时长上会受到挤压，从而短于同一词组中的其他音节。NH儿童在词首和词中的时长差异符合这一研究结果。当卷舌元音“儿”位于词中位置时，NH儿童产出的平均时长短于其位于词首位置。但是值得注意的是，在CI儿童组当“儿”位于词中位置时，平均时长反而要长于其位于词首的位置。这一结果表明，人工耳蜗植入儿童在语流中时长分配的策略不同于健听儿童，本应弱化的词中音节，在产出时反而更加用力。

双因素方差分析结果显示，时长在组别变量条件下存在显著性差异（F（1，92）=10.398，$p<0.05$）。也就是说，总体而言CI儿童的平均时长显著大于NH儿童。另外，时长在词位变量条件下并无显著性差异（F（1，92）=0.120，$p=0.729$），亦不存在组别×词位交互效应（F（1，92）=1.294，$p=0.258$）。

考虑到被试儿童的发音语速可能存在不同，因此对上述时长数据作了归一化处理。从图3看，时长归一化后，多数CI儿童在词首位置的时长较短，而在词中位置的时长则较长。也就是说，对多数CI儿

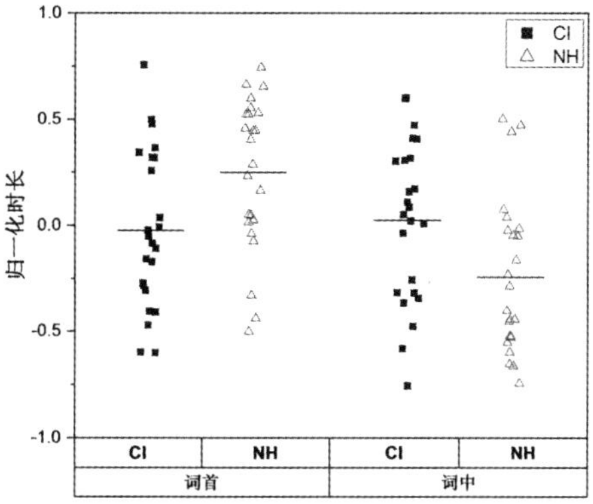

图3　不同构词位置CI儿童与NH儿童组间归一化时长对比

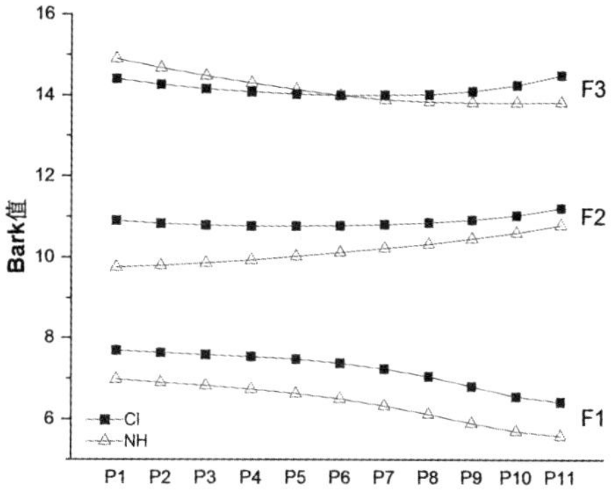

图4　CI儿童与NH儿童组间共振峰模式对比

童而言，当卷舌元音位于词中时，发音时长比位于词首时还要长。这一情况与NH儿童组则恰恰相反。其次，时长归一化后的组间对比结果与绝对时长的对比结果相一致，即CI儿童在语流中时长分配时，本应弱化的词中音节并没有得到弱化，反而会更加用力。双因素方差分析结果显示，归一化时长在组别变量条件下（F（1，92）=0.002，$p=0.964$）不存在显著性差异，但在词位变量条件下（F（1，92）=8.724，$p<0.01$）存在显著性差异，并存在极显著的组别×词位交互效应（F（1，92）=12.893，$p<0.001$）。

3.2.2　*两组被试普通话卷舌元音的共振峰模式对比*

图4是CI儿童组与NH儿童组组间共振峰模式对比图。从图上可以清楚地看到，CI儿童与NH儿童的共振峰模式在空间分布及F3走势上均存在较为明显的差异。虽然就F1、F2走势而言，两组基本相同，但是在空间分布上，CI儿童组的F1及F2均高于NH儿童组，也就是说，相对于NH儿童而言，CI儿童的卷舌元音整体发音部位相对靠前、舌位相对较高、开口度相对较大。

考虑到CI儿童组内或存在较大的个体差异性，我们将24位CI儿童共振峰模式以及24位NH儿童的共振峰模式进行详细的对比（见图5、图6）。结合图5及图6，我们发现：总体而言，NH儿童组内的

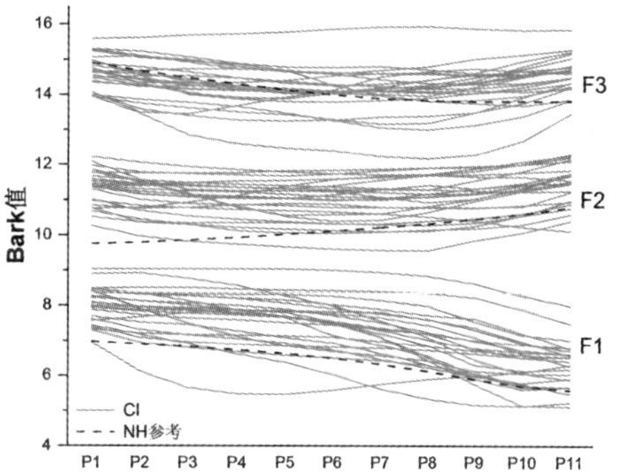

图5　24位CI儿童共振峰模式与NH儿童组间共振峰模式对比

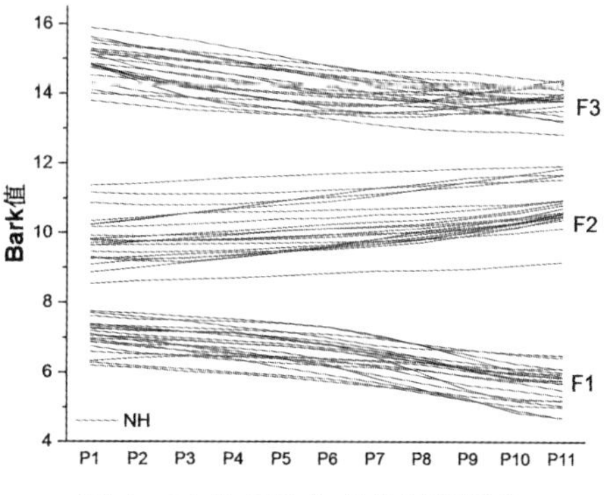

图6　24位NH儿童共振峰模式

共振峰模式个体差异较小，三条共振峰的走势基本相同。相比较而言，F2的组内差

异稍大。反观CI儿童，组内的共振峰模式呈现出较大的个体差异，其中有些CI被试的共振峰走势呈现特异性。不仅如此，CI儿童组F1及F2的起点范围、终点范围跨度较大；从F1及F2的分布来看，几乎所有CI儿童均高于NH儿童组平均；此外，CI儿童的F2的走势相对一致，均呈现出上升的走势，但F1所呈现出的共振峰走势则更加多样。我们知道，F1及F2分别反映了发音部位的前后及舌位的高低，也就是说，CI儿童在产出卷舌元音时发音部位与舌位存在较大的个体间差异。就F3走势而言，多数CI儿童的F3后段带有不同程度的上升走势。

众所周知，普通话卷舌元音的卷舌色彩主要表现在F3上，F3从起点持续下降至终点，其下降幅度越大，意味着卷舌色彩越浓。NH儿童组的F3在图4中表现为平缓下降，反映到其卷舌元音的言语表现上则是具备一定的卷舌色彩。但是反观CI儿童，其F3从起始段到中间段均表现为平稳的、小幅度的下降，在其后半段则表现出上升趋势，这也解释了为何CI儿童在产出卷舌元音时卷舌色彩不浓，甚至不带卷舌色彩。实际上，几乎所有CI儿童能够发出央元音（schwa），也就是“儿”的前半部分元音。至于后半部分的卷舌动作，在发音时舌部需要有一个动程，显然这一过程对于CI儿童而言，在习得过程中较难捕捉，而且在产出时亦是存在一定的困难。

3.2.3 普通话卷舌元音的F3斜率对比

图7显示，CI儿童与NH儿童在F3斜率上存在明显差异。几乎所有NH儿童的F3斜率为负值，但对于多数CI儿童而言，无论是在词首还是词中位置，F3斜率为正值，只有少数CI儿童呈现为负值。此外，CI儿童在词中位置时的F3斜率均值大于其位于词首位置之时，也就是说当卷舌元音位于词中位置时，CI儿童的卷舌色彩反而会更弱一些。在探讨卷舌元音发音时长时，我们已经发现CI儿童在词中位置产出时会更加用力一些，分配了更长的发音时长到位于词中位置的卷舌元音上，在本节我们也可以发现，在卷舌色彩上，当卷舌元音位于词中位置时，对于CI儿童而言同样也是更为用力的。总之，无论是在词首还是词中位置，NH儿童组的平均F3斜率值均远小于CI儿童组。双因素方差分析结果表明，F3斜率在组别变量条件下存在极显著差异（$F(1, 92) = 101.301$，$p<0.001$），在词位变量条件下不存在显著性差异（$F(1, 92) = 1.865$，$p=0.175$）；不存在组间×词位交互效应（$F(1, 92) = 0.531$，$p=0.468$）。由此可以看出，在卷舌色彩方面，CI儿童是显著亚于NH儿童的。

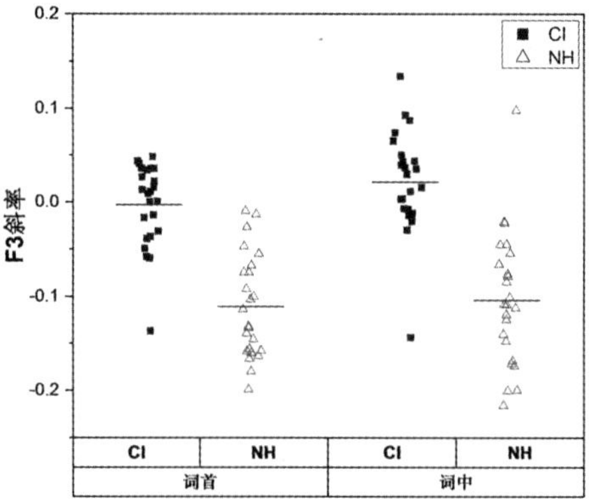

图7　不同构词位置CI儿童与NH儿童组间F3斜率的对比

3.3 人工耳蜗装置对普通话卷舌元音习得的影响

考虑到人工耳蜗装置本身的使用过程会影响到耳蜗儿童的言语习得，本研究对本实验中的CI被试儿童植入人工耳蜗的年龄及佩戴时长与普通话卷舌元音的产出情况作相关性分析。结果如图8的相关性矩阵（correlation matrix）所示，发现：CI组儿童唯有植入年龄与普通话卷舌元音清晰度（发音得分）之间存在统计学意义，两者之间存在显著的负相关关系（$r = -0.403$，$p<0.05$）。这表明，人工耳蜗植入年龄越早，植入者的发音清晰度越好。因此，较早地植入人工耳蜗设备可以在一定程度上更好地提升植入者卷舌元音的习得表现。这一结果与前人有关语前聋CI儿童普通话习得

的研究结果一致［31，32］。

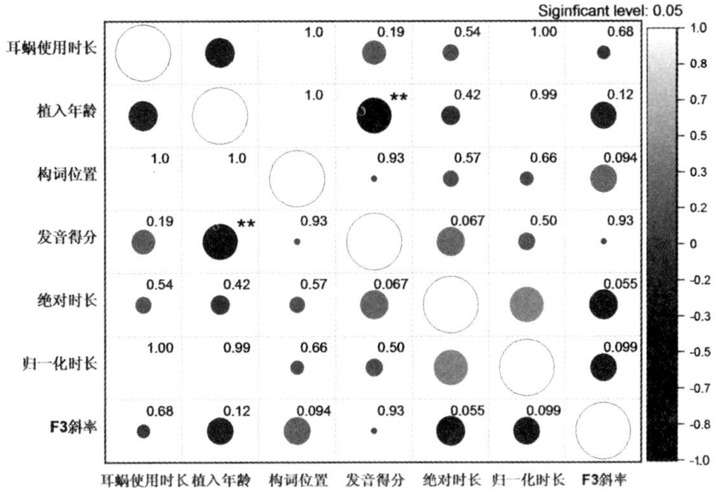

图8 人工耳蜗装置因素与声学特征参数之间的相关性矩阵

4. 讨论与总结

1. 语言的学习与理解是一个复杂的过程，言语信息能否输入取决于听觉传导路径是否正常。听力正常是语言习得的重要前提，但是有感音性听力障碍的儿童，如语前聋患儿，其语言尚处于发育学习的萌芽阶段，在此阶段丧失听力会导致一定程度的语言障碍［33］，进而影响到认知能力的发展。李胜利［35］指出，感音性耳聋是指人耳听觉系统对声音的频率、声压及时间性等变化的情报进行分析时存在功能障碍，其结果是人耳在感知声音时，在“量”方面衰减，在“质”方面歪曲。所幸的是，随着科学技术的发展，植入人工耳蜗为听障儿童提供了听觉径路补偿，为其提供语言发展非常必要的听觉信息。

2. 本研究通过对比人工耳蜗植入儿童与健听儿童产出的卷舌元音在发音清晰度及声学特征方面的差异，发现：（1）语前聋儿童植入人工耳蜗并且接受听觉言语康复训练后，可以基本掌握普通话的卷舌元音，虽然正确率与NH儿童相比仍有一段差距。（2）就共振峰模式而言，CI儿童在产出卷舌元音时，发音部位相对靠前、舌位相对较高、开口度相对较大，共振峰F3在后半段并非如预期一样下降，而是有向上趋势。（3）进一步的统计分析表明，CI儿童组与NH儿童组在F3斜率上存在显著的组别差异，这解释了为何CI儿童所发卷舌元音的卷舌色彩在主观听感上并不浓厚，甚至不携带卷舌色彩。（4）人工耳蜗儿童的植入年龄与发音清晰度呈现显著的负相关关系，这一结果在我们的预期之内。正如Tomblin等［24］所指出的，在语言习得的“敏感期”（sensitive period）内，儿童越早植入人工耳蜗，则越早融入语言环境（linguistic environment）中，其言语表现自然也就更佳。

3. 综合本研究各项结果可以说明，产出卷舌元音对于人工耳蜗植入儿童而言具有一定的挑战。言语康复师在培训CI儿童时需要强化该音的训练，并强调该音在产出时需涉及舌部的动程，从而帮助CI儿童更好地产出卷舌元音，使普通话在听感上更加地道。

4. 另外，需要说明的是，普通话中“儿”位于词尾时发音规则较为多样、复杂。有些可与前字音节合音形成音变现象［36］，这种情况下必须要读成儿化韵，如“尖儿”，而有些词尾“儿”可以是有实义的语素，故不能与前字连读，如“婴儿”，还有词尾“儿”可连读也可以不连读，如“鸟儿”。因此，本文没有讨论“儿”位于词尾处的言语产出情况，在以后的研究中可以做进一步的考察。本研究只考虑人工耳蜗植入年龄及使用时长这两个因素，往后的研究可以将听损程度、家庭因素及康复训练时间等因素考虑进去。此外，本研究只考虑了不同构词位置影响下，CI儿童普通话卷舌元音的产出情况，事实上，影响CI儿童言语产出的因素较多，进入连续语流后情况较为复杂，因此在泛化本研究结果时还需谨慎。

参考文献

[1] Chin, S. B., Bergeson, T. R., Phan, J. Speech intelligibility and prosody production in children with cochlear implants. *Journal of Communication Disorders* 45, 355 – 366.

[2] Connor, C. M., Hieber, S., Arts, H. A., Zwolan, T. A. 2000. Speech, vocabulary, and the education of children using cochlear implants: Oral or total communication? *Journal of Speech, Language, and Hearing Research* 43(5), 1185 – 1204.

[3] Connor, C. M., Craig, H. K., Raudenbush, S. W., Heavner, K., Zwolan, T. A. 2006. The Age at Which Young Deaf Children Receive Cochlear Implants and Their Vocabulary and Speech – Production Growth: Is There an Added Value for Early Implantation? *Ear & Hearing* 27(6), 628 – 643.

[4] Faes, J., Gillis, S. 2017. Consonant cluster production in children with cochlear implants: A comparison with normally hearing peers. *First Language* 37(4), 319 – 349.

[5] Geers, A., Nicholas, J., Tobey, E., Davidson, L. 2016. Persistent language delay versus late language emergence in children with early cochlear implantation. *Journal of Speech, Language, and Hearing Research* 59(1), 155 – 70.

[6] Lindblom, B., Rapp, K. 1973. Some temporal regularities of spoken Swedish. *Papers from the Institute of Linguistics,* University of Stockholm.

[7] Liu, Q. Y., Zhou, N., Berger, R., Huang, D., Xu, L. 2013. Mandarin consonant contrast recognition among children with cochlear implants or hearing aids and normal – Hearing children. *Otology & Neurotology* 34(3), 471 – 476.

[8] Luo, X., Fu, Q. J., Galvin, J. J. 2007. Vocal emotion recognition by normal – hearing listeners and cochlear implant users. *Trends in Amplification* 11 (4), 301 – 315.

[9] Moore, B. C. J. 2003. Coding of sounds in the auditory system and its relevance to signal processing and coding in cochlear implants. *Otol Neurotol* 24(2), 243 – 254.

[10] Niparko, J. K., et al. 2009. *Cochlear Implants: Principles & Practices*. Philadelphia, PA: Lippincott Williams & Wilkins.

[11] Niparko, J. K., Tobey, E. A., Thal, D. J., Eisenberg, L. S., Wang, N. Y., Quittner, A. L., Fink, N. E. 2010. Spoken language development in children following cochlear implantation. *Journal of the American Medical Association* 303 (15), 1498 – 1506.

[12] Norman, J. 1988. *Chinese*. Cambridge: Cambridge University Press.

[13] Origin(Pro), Version 2021. Origin Lab Corporation, Northampton, MA, USA.

[14] Parkinson, A. J., El – Kholy, W., Tyler, R. S. 1998. Vowel perception in prelingually deafened children with multichannel cochlear implants. *Journal of the American Academy of Audiology* 9, 179 – 190.

[15] Boersma, P., Weenink, D. 2019. Praat: doing phonetics by computer [Computer program]. Version 6. 1. 03, http://www.praat.org/ visited 28 – Dec – 20.

[16] Peng, S. C., Tomblin, B., Cheung, H., Lin, Y. S., Wang, L. S. 2004. Perception and production of Mandarin tones in prelingually deaf children with cochlear implants. *Ear & Hearing* 25 (3), 251 – 264.

[17] Peng, S. H. 1994. Effects of prosodic position and tonal context on Taiwanese tones. *OSU Working Papers in Linguistics* 44, 166 – 190.

[18] Pollock, P. K. 2013. The Memphis vowel project: vowel errors in children with and without phonological disorders. In Ball, M. J., Gibbon, F. E. (eds.), *Handbook of Vowels and Vowel Disorders*. Hove: Psychology Press, 260 – 287.

[19] R Core Team 2020. R: A language and environment for statistical computing. Version 4. 0. 3, https://www.R – project.org/ visited 24 – Dec – 2020.

[20] Selby, J., Robb, M. P. 2000. Normal vowel articulations between 15 and 36 months of age. *Clinical Linguistics & Phonetics* 14(4), 255 – 265.

[21] Subtelney, J. D. 1977. Assessment of speech with implications for training. In: Bess, F. H.

(eds.), *Childhood Deafness: Causation, Assessment, and Management*. New York: Grune & Stratton, 183 – 194.

[22] Sucher, C. M., McDermott, H. J. 2007. Pitch ranking of complex tones by normally hearing subjects and cochlear implant users. *Hearing Research* 230(1 – 2), 80 – 87.

[23] Szagun, G., Stumper, B. 2012. Age or experience? The influence of age at implantation and social and linguistic environment on language development in children with cochlear implants. *Journal of Speech, Language, and Hearing Research* 55, 1640 – 1654.

[24] Tomblin, J. B., Barker, B. A., Hubbs, S. 2007. Developmental constraints on language development in children with cochlear implants. *International Journal of Audiology* 46(9), 512 – 523.

[25] Tseng, S. C., Kuei, K., Chou, P. C. 2011. Acoustic characteristics of vowels and plosives/affricates of Mandarin – speaking hearing – impaired children. *Clinical Linguistics & Phonetics* 25 (9), 784 – 803.

[26] Turgeon, C., Trudeau – Fisette, P., Fitzpatrick, E., Ménard, L. 2017. Vowel intelligibility in children with cochlear implants: an acoustic and articulatory study. *International Journal of Pediatric Otorhinolaryngology* 101, 87 – 96.

[27] Tyler, R. S., Summerfield, A. Q. 1996. Cochlear implantation: relationships with research on auditory deprivation and acclimatization. *Ear & Hearing* 17, 38 – 50.

[28] Van de Velde, D. J., et al. 2018. Prosody perception and production by children with cochlear implants. *Journal of Child Language* 46 (1), 1 – 31.

[29] Whitehill, T. L., Ciocca, V. 2000. Perceptual – phonetic predictors of single – word intelligibility: a study of Cantonese dysarthria, *Journal of Speech, Language and Hearing Research* 43(6), 1451 – 1465.

[30] Xu, Y., Gao, H. 2018. FormantPro as a tool for speech analysis and segmentation. *Revista de Estudos da Linguagem*. 26(4), 1435 – 1454.

[31] Yang, J., Brown, E., Fox, R. A., Xu, L. 2015. Acoustic properties of vowel production in prelingually deafened Mandarin – speaking children with cochlear implants. *J. Acoust. Soc. Am.* 138 (5), 2791 – 2799.

[32] Yang, J., Xu, L. 2017. Mandarin compound vowels produced by prelingually deafened children with cochlear implants. *International Journal of Pediatric Otorhinolaryngology* 97, 143 – 149.

[33] 鲍怀翘、林茂灿等:《实验语音学概要（增订版)》, 北京大学出版社 2014 年版。

[34] 孔江平:《实验语音学基础教程》, 北京大学出版社 2015 年版。

[35] 李胜利:《言语治疗学》, 华夏出版社 2004 年版。

[36] 林焘、王理嘉:《语音学教程（增订版)》, 北京大学出版社 2013 年版。

[37] 于珏、李爱军、王霞:《上海普通话与标准普通话卷舌元音声学特征对比研究》,《当代语言学》2008 年第 3 期。

于 珏 同济大学外国语学院，博士，主要研究领域为病理语言学及语音学。
E – mail: erinyu@ 126. com

林裕鑫 同济大学外国语学院，硕士在读，研究方向为实验语音学。
E – mail: 1930865@ tongji. edu. cn

金倩雯 同济大学外国语学院，硕士在读，研究方向为实验语音学。
E – mail: wonderlandjin@ 163. com

DURATION AND AMPLITUDE OF TONE PRODUCTION IN CHILDREN WITH COCHLEAR IMPLANTS

YANG Jing, XU Li

AbstractThe purpose of the present study was two-fold: (1) to examine whether Mandarin-speaking children with cochlear implants (CIs) show distinctive durational and amplitude features for the four lexical tones in their tone production; (2) to compare the durational and amplitude patterns of Mandarin lexical tones in monosyllables produced in citation form by children with CIs with those by age-matched normal-hearing (NH) children. The participants included 14 prelingually deafened Mandarin-speaking children with CIs and 14 NH children, all aged between 2.9 and 8.3 years old. Each participant produced five CV syllables (fa /fa/, fu /fu/, pi /pʰi/, xu /ɕy/, ke /kʰɤ/) in four tones through a tone drill activity. The vowel duration and root-mean-squared amplitude values at nine equidistant time locations over the vowel duration were obtained. The results revealed that the children with CIs produced distinctive durational and amplitude features for the four lexical tones. Their durational pattern and amplitude contours were highly similar to the NH children on tones 1, 2 and 4 but differed from the NH children on tone 3. These findings suggested that the children with CIs may utilize the secondary features of tone duration and amplitude to realize tonal differences.
Key Words Cochlear implants, Mandarin-speaking children, Tone duration, Tone amplitude

1. INTRODUCTION

Tonal languages adopt pitch change to differentiate lexical or grammatical meanings. Mandarin is the most widely used monosyllabic tonal language. Each stressed syllable in the citation has one of the four lexical tones, namely tone 1, tone 2, tone 3, and tone 4. So far, a large number of studies have examined the acoustic correlates of Mandarin tones [1, 2, 3, 4, 5]. It has been widely acknowledged that the primary acoustic feature for tonal identity lies in the fundamental frequency (F0). The pitch patterns corresponding to tone 1, tone 2, tone 3, and tone 4 are high-level, mid-rising, low-dipping, and high-falling.

In addition to the F0 pattern, previous studies revealed that Mandarin tones also differ in their intrinsic duration and overall amplitude contour of the syllable rhymes that carry the tones [3, 6, 7, 8]. Many studies reported that in isolated Mandarin words, tone 3 has the longest duration and tone 4 has the shortest duration. Tone 1 and tone 2 just fall in between [3, 8]. Ho [3] reported that the order of tone duration in Mandarin isolated monosyllables was tone 3 > tone2 > tone1 > tone 4. Chang [9], Lee and Hung [10] confirmed this durational pattern in isolated Mandarin lexical tones. The amplitude contour varies in these four Mandarin tones. Ho [3] described the amplitude contours of Mandarin tones as level/level-falling, rising/level, double-peak, and falling/level-falling, corresponding to tones 1, 2, 3, and 4, respectively. Lin [7] divided Mandarin tone amplitude into five categories: level, higher at the onset, higher at the offset, higher in the middle, and double-peak. He summarized that tones 1, 2, and 4 normally show an amplitude contour with a higher onset or a higher offset, while tone 3 normally presents a double-peak amplitude contour. Although previous studies might show inconsistent categorization or description of the amplitude shapes, most of them consistently demonstrated a positive correlation between the pitch contours and amplitude contours in Mandarin lexical tones of isolated monosyllables [8, 11, 12].

For normal-hearing listeners, the primary perceptual cue for tone identification lies in pitch-related properties [6, 13, 14]. Other types of co-varying features such as duration or amplitude play a very limited role in tone perception [7, 12, 15]. In comparison to normal-hearing listeners who receive a full range of auditory information, hearing-impaired listeners with cochlear implants only obtain partial auditory information. The acoustic signals conveyed through the prosthesis are vocoder processed, in which pitch information is poorly coded. In this scenario, CI users, in general, demonstrated poorer recognition of pitch-related information (e.g., tones) than normal-hearing (NH) listeners [16, 17, 18, 19, 20]. In addition to the overall poor tone recognition performance, the cue-weighting pattern in tone recognition between the CI users and NH listeners was different [21, 22].

The deficits of pitch coding in CIs are reflected not only in speech perception, but also in speech production. Researchers found that children with CIs, in general, demonstrated monotonous pitch contours and produced all four tones with substantially lower accuracy than children with NH. Children with CIs produced less definable F0 contours and less separable F0 categories than the children with NH [23, 24, 25, 26, 27, 28]. While these studies focused on the F0 pattern of tone production, very little research has been conducted to examine the duration or amplitude of Mandarin lexical tones produced by children with CIs. Given that temporal and amplitude information is relatively well-maintained in CIs, we wonder whether children with CIs will show a NH-like pattern on the durational and amplitude features in their tone production. Deroche et al. [22] found that children with CIs exaggerated the durational contrast for tone 1 and tone 4 in comparison to the children with NH. Further, the authors reported that the children with CIs who showed greater reliance on duration in tone perception also showed poorer control in voice pitch in tone production. Extending from the Deroche et al. [22] study that only focused on tone 1 and tone 4, the present study was conducted to examine the duration and amplitude of all four lexical tones in citation-form monosyllables produced by Mandarin-speaking CI children with reference to age-matched NH children. Specifically, there are two related research questions: (1) whether the children with CIs show distinctive durational and amplitude features for the four lexical tones in their tone production; (2) whether the children with CIs show duration and amplitude patterns of lexical tones in citation-form monosyllables similar to agematched NH children.

2. METHODS

2.1 Participants

A total of 28 Mandarin-speaking children were included in the present study. All participants were from previous studies [25, 26]. Fourteen of them (8 boys and 6 girls) were prelingually deafened children with CIs, aged between 2.9 and 8.3 years old (Mean = 5.16 yrs, SD = 1.80 yrs). Fourteen age-matched children with NH (6 boys and 8 girls) (Mean = 5.15 yrs, SD = 1.77 yrs) were recruited to serve as the control group. All children were recruited in Beijing, China and raised by Mandarin-speaking parents or caregivers. The 14 children with CIs were nonverbal prior to implantation and received unilateral cochlear implantation between 1.16 and 7.09 years of age (Mean = 3.43 yrs, SD = 1.91 yrs). The length of device use varied between 0.31 and 2.60 years (Mean = 1.73 yrs, SD = 0.76 yrs). They all received post-implantation training focusing on basic language and speech skills at a professional rehabilitation center in Beijing. The 14 children with NH reported having no speech-language or hearing impairments.

2.2 Data collection

Five CV syllables fa /fa/, fu /fu/, pi /pʰi/, xu /ɕy/, ke /kʰɤ/ from each participant were used for the present study. These five syllables all had voiceless obstruents at the syllable onset and contained the five basic monophthongal vowel phonemes /a, i, u, y, ʁ/ in Mandarin. Each participant was recorded separately in a quiet room. A tone drill activity was used to collect speech samples. The experimenter produced each syllable in tone 1 and the participants were asked to follow the experimenter and produce all four tones for the target syllable in consecutive order. Each tone of individual target syllables was produced once. All speech samples were collected through a digital recorder with a 44.1 kHz sampling rate and a 16-bit quantization rate. Due to missing tokens and peak-clipping issue, a total number of 469 tokens (223 from the children with CIs and 246 from the children with NH) were used for further analysis. Note that all measurable tokens were included, regardless of whether the token was produced correctly or not.

2.3 Acoustic measurement

Although the domain of tones remains controversial, the present study followed Howie's [2] notion that syllable rhyme carries the tone. Because all five tested syllables were in the form of CV structure, the tone duration was defined as the duration of the vowel in each word. Specifically, the onset and offset of the vowels were determined by a visual check of waveform accompanied by a spectrogram display. The vowel onset was set at the start of vowel periodicity, and the vowel offset was set at the end of vowel periodicity with both F1 and F2 present.

The amplitude contour was extracted at nine equidistant time points (10% - 20% - 30% - 40% - 50% - 60% - 70% - 80% - 90% point) over the course of vowel duration. In particular, a root-mean-squared (rms) value was obtained at each time location. The rms value was calculated for a set of 10 ms vowel portions with the midpoints located at these nine time points, using a custom-written MATLAB program. If peak clipping occurred in certain tokens, those tokens were excluded from further analysis. Because the recording environment was not consistently or strictly controlled across all participants to better compare the amplitude contours across different speakers and maintain the relative pattern of the four tones in each speaker, the extracted rms amplitude was normalized for individual participants following the formula:

$$A'_{n[s]} = A_{n[s]} - MEAN_{[s]} \qquad (1)$$

Where $A'_{n[s]}$ is the normalized rms amplitude value for point n of subject S, $A_{n[s]}$ is the original rms amplitude value for the point n of subject S, and $MEAN_{[s]}$ is the grand mean of rms amplitude values for all nine points of four tones from the five tokens of subject S.

Based on the normalized amplitude, the sum of squared differences (SSD) was calculated to evaluate the similarity between the amplitude contours of each tone between the NH and CI children. This value is defined as the sum of the squares of the distance between two corresponding points in the examined groups for a given tone.

$$SSD = \sum_{n=1}^{i} (A_{xn} - A_{yn})^2 \qquad (2)$$

Where A_{xn} is the rms amplitude value of

point n for a given tone in group x and A_{yn} is the rms amplitude value of point *n* for the same tone in group y.

The F0 data from the 28 participants has been analyzed and reported in previous studies [26]. Specifically, the F0 of an articulated vowel was extracted using an autocorrelation algorithm implemented in a custom-written MATLAB program. Errors with automatic extraction were fixed with a manual check. Given that the absolute duration of the articulated vowel in each token of each participant was different, the number of F0 data points in each token varied. Therefore, the interpolation method was used to make F0 data comparable on the same normalized duration scale. F0 values selected from the same nine equidistant points over the course of vowel duration were used to plot F0 contours.

3. RESULTS

Fig. 1 shows the durations of the four tones in the NH and CI children. The children with CIs produced all four tones with significantly longer durations than the NH peers. In addition, the CI group demonstrated a different durational pattern across four lexical tones in comparison to the NH group, which was mainly caused by tone 3. While the NH children produced tone 3 and tone 4 shorter than tone 1 and tone 2, the children with CIs produced tone 4 significantly shorter than the other three tones, and tone 3 slightly longer than tone 1 and tone 2. The longest duration of tone 3, and the shortest duration of tone 4 in the children with CIs matched the durational pattern of four lexical tones in isolation reported in previous studies.

To better compare the tone duration in CI and NH groups, a repeated-measures ANOVA was conducted with the hearing group as the between-subject factor and tone type as the within-subject factor. The results revealed a significant main effect of group ($F(1, 26) = 14.549$, $p = 0.001$), tone ($F(3, 78) = 12.054$, $p < 0.001$) and a significant interaction effect of group by tone ($F(3, 78) = 5.884$, $p = 0.001$). The significant interaction effect suggested that the duration at pattern of the four tones in the children with CIs differed from that in the children with NH. To compare the duration pattern of four tones in each group, a repeated-measures ANOVA was conducted for the CI and NH groups, respectively, with the tone type as the within-subject factor. The post-hoc contrast comparison revealed that for the CI children, tone 1, tone 2, and tone 3 were all significantly longer than tone 4 (all $p \leqslant 0.006$), but none of the tone contrast among tones 1, 2, and 3 were significantly different. For the NH children, tone 1 and tone 2 were significantly longer than tone 3 and tone 4 (both $p \leqslant 0.001$).

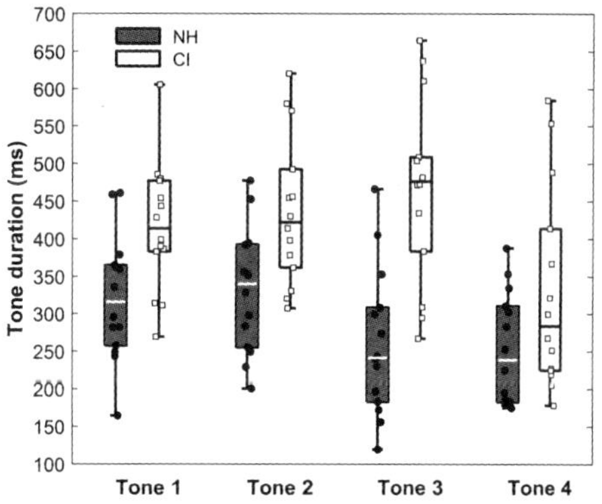

Figure 1 Box plot of tone duration for the four lexical tones in isolated monosyllables produced by the NH and CI children. Each data point represents one subject

Fig. 2 shows the amplitude contours of the four lexical tones in individual CI and NH children and the comparison of group mean amplitude contour and F0 contour between the two groups. The F0 data was adopted from a previous study [26]. The comparison of group mean F0 data revealed that the CI children approximated the NH peers in tone 1, but they deviated from the NH peers in the direction and/or absolute F0 height for the other three tones. Note that the NH children produced tone 3 with a falling F0 contour, not a typical low-dipping contour.

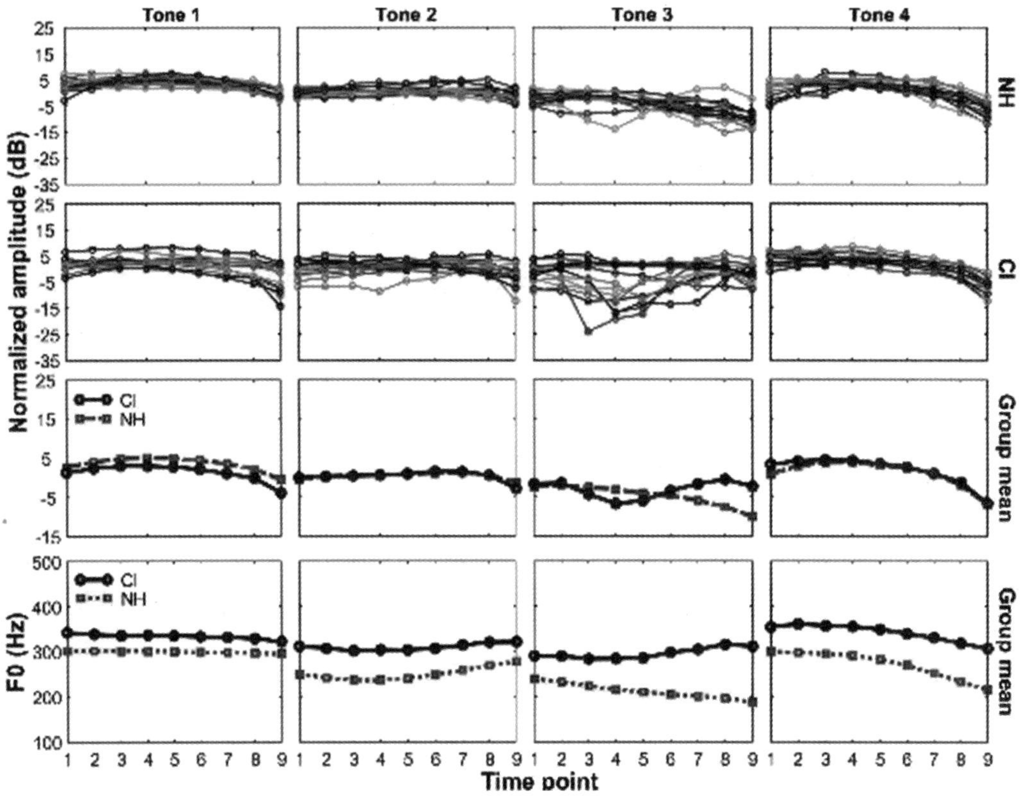

Figure 2 Top three rows: Amplitude contours of the four lexical tones in tested monosyllables by the NH and CI children and the group mean data. Each line in the top two rows represents amplitude contour data from one subject. The rms amplitude was extracted at nine equidistant time points (10% -20% -30% -40% -50% -60% -70% -80% -90%) over the vowel duration and normalized. Bottom row: Group mean F0 contour for each lexical tone. The F0 data were adopted from [26]

As for the amplitude contour, it can be observed that the variability of the amplitude contours is larger for the CI than the NH groups for all tones except tone 4. In the meantime, the two groups of children demonstrated a similar overall pattern of amplitude changes for tones 1, 2, and 4 but not for tone 3. In particular, both groups of children showed a falling amplitude contour for tones 1 and 4, and a slightly rising amplitude contour for tone 2. For tone 3, the majority of NH children presented a falling contour. By contrast, some children with CIs showed a double-peak amplitude contour while the others showed a relatively flat amplitude contour. The SSD value between the CI and NH children was 36.7 for tone 1, 1.8 for tone 2, 149.9 for tone 3, and 9.1 for tone 4. The very small SSD value for tone 2 and tone 4 reflected the highly compatible and overlapped group mean amplitude contours in the NH and CI groups for these two tones. The larger SSD value in tone 1 was caused by the consistently higher amplitude of NH group than the CI group even though the shape of the contours for this tone in these two groups was highly similar. The largest SSD value for tone 3 reflected the substantial difference in the shape of the amplitude contours between the two groups.

A repeated-measures ANOVA was conducted to compare the amplitude data of each tone between the NH and CI groups, with the nine measurement points as the within-subject factor and hearing group as the between-subject factor. The results showed that for all four tones, there was a significant main effect of the measurement point (all $p < 0.05$). As the amplitude changes as time elapses, the significant effect of the measurement point was expected and would not be discussed further. As for the group effect and group by point interaction effect, the results showed a significant group effect only for tone 1 ($F(1, 25) = 8.826$, $p = 0.006$), and a significant group by point interaction effect only for tone 3 ($F(8, 208) = 7.416$, $p = 0.001$). These results suggested that the CI and NH children showed similar magnitudes of amplitude and contour pattern for tone 2 and tone 4. However, the two groups differed in the magnitude of amplitude in tone 1 and the pattern of amplitude contour in tone 3.

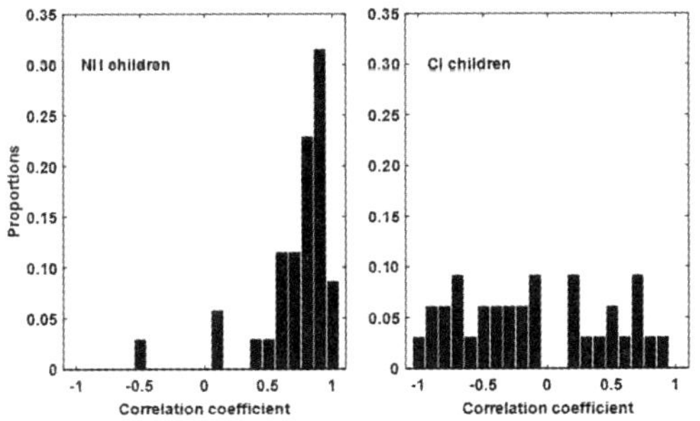

Figure 3 The histogram of correlation coefficients of F0 and amplitude for each token of tone 3 in the NH and CI children

Previous studies suggested that normal adult speakers produced positively matched F0 and amplitude for lexical tones [8, 11, 12]. In the present study, we observed that the NH children produced tones 1, 2, and 4 with similar F0 and amplitude contours as described in previous studies and highly compatible F0 and amplitude contours for tone 3. The CI group showed compatible group mean F0 and amplitude contours as the NH group for tones 1, 2, and 4 but not for tone 3. To further examine the relationship between the F0 and amplitude, the correlation coefficient between F0 contour and amplitude contour was calculated for each token of tone 3 in the CI and NH group, respectively. If the two contours move in the same direction, the coefficient value should be a positive value close to 1. Among the 70 tokens for each group, due to the missing data for F0 and/or amplitude, there were 34 tokens in the CI group and 36 tokens in the NH group with valid F0 and amplitude data. As shown in the distribution of correlation coefficients for each group (Fig. 3), the NH group showed highly matched F0 and amplitude contours, but the CI group produced a large number of tokens with unmatched F0 and amplitude contours.

4. DISCUSSION AND SUMMARY

The purpose of the present study was to investigate whether the children with CIs produce distinctive durational features and amplitude contours among the four lexical tones and whether they follow the NH peers on the patterns of these features in tone production. Our results showed that the CI children produced distinctive durations and amplitude contours for the four tones, which are similar to the canonical pattern reported in Mandarin-speaking adults [6, 7, 8, 9]. For tone durations, the CI children tended to produce tone 3 with the longest duration and tone 4 with the shortest duration. Regarding the amplitude contour, the CI children produced tone 1 and tone 4 with flat or flat-falling amplitude contours, tone 2 with a rising contour, and tone 3 with a double-peak contour. Although the CI children produced tone duration and amplitude with patterns similar to adult norms reported in previous studies, they differed from the age-matched NH children in the present study on both features. At first, the CI children consistently produced all four lexical tones with significantly longer durations than the NH children. Previous literature reported that children with CIs tended to produce longer durations for speech segments than NH peers [29, 30]. Lexical tones are carried by syllable rhymes, which are mainly composed of vowels. The longer tone durations in the CI children than the NH peers provided additional evidence supporting the findings of longer speech segments in children with CIs. Additionally, the CI children demonstrated different durational and amplitude patterns across the four lexical tones in comparison to the NH peers, which was mainly caused by tone 3. The children with CIs produced tone 3 with a double-peak amplitude contour and a relatively longer duration. By contrast, the NH children produced tone 3 with a falling amplitude contour and shorter duration than tone 1 and tone 2.

It is noteworthy that the duration and amplitude patterns of the NH children in the present study did not follow the patterns of adults reported in previous studies. This may be related to the tone drill activity used in the present study in which the participants were required to produce the four tones of a given monosyllable in consecutive order. Most of the NH children did not produce a full version of tone 3 with the rising part because they did not pause enough between every two tokens and the token was not produced in citation form in a truly isolated environment. The CI children were recorded with the same procedure but they produced the duration and amplitude features with similar patterns to normally-speaking Mandarin adults. We speculate that this might be associated with the slower articulatory movements in CI children relative to NH children. Our earlier studies revealed that CI children produced vowels with longer duration than NH children [29]. As the domain of tone is over the syllable rhyme in which the nucleus vowel mainly carries the tone, the longer vowel duration corresponded to the longer tone duration in the CI children relative to the NH children. Accompanying with the slow articulatory movement, the CI children were less likely to make the transition from one token to the next token as fast as the NH children. On the other hand, although pitch information is poorly transmitted through CI devices, the temporal and amplitude information is relatively well-maintained. Therefore, the CI children were likely to perceive the differences in duration and amplitude among the four lexical tones through the language input. Previous studies reported that children with CIs could hardly produce distinctive F0 contours as children with NH did, but they relied more on the secondary cues to perceive tonal identity. Because of this, some CI children might fully produce tone 3 with a complete falling-rising amplitude contour to make distinguishable tones in their speech production.

Many previous studies revealed a positive correlation between F0 contour and amplitude contour in normally-speaking Mandarin adults [8, 11, 12]. In the present study, we observed well-matched F0 contour and amplitude contour in the NH children. However, the CI group presented unmatched F0 and amplitude contours for many tokens. These observations indicate that the amplitude contour may not necessarily be positively correlated to the F0 contour, which is consistent with the finding of Kuo et al. [31] who found that the amplitude contour of a tone and the F0 contour of the same tone were not always most highly correlated.

In general, the present study revealed that the Mandarin-speaking CI children produced distinctive durational and amplitude features for the four lexical tones. Their durational pattern and amplitude contours differed from the NH children mainly in tone 3, but they followed the patterns of these two features in normal adult speakers reported in previous studies. The difference between the CI and NH groups might be associated with the limitation of the elicitation procedure in this study. The NH children did not really produce the monosyllabic words in a true isolation environment, which might cause systematically biased tone production in the two groups. In the future, a more strictly controlled procedure should be used to collect the production data. Some earlier studies suggested that the phonetic features of Mandarin tones in spontaneous, connected speech become less distinctive [9, 32]. Correspondingly, children with CIs may show more difficulty in producing tonal differences in spontaneous speech. For future studies, we shall recruit a larger size of speakers producing isolated monosyllables and spontaneous speech to better examine the tone production in CI users. Additionally, the acoustic analysis of tone production shall be connected with the perceptual data of the four tones or tone contrasts in children with CIs to examine whether and how different acoustic cues (i. e., F0, duration, and amplitude) are perceived in this population.

REFERENCES

[1] Chao, Y. R. 1968. *A Grammar of Spoken Chinese*. Los Angeles: University of California Press.

[2] Howie, J. M. 1974. On the domain of tone in Mandarin. *Phonetica* 30, 129 – 148.

[3] Ho, A. T. 1976. The acoustic variation of Mandarin tones. *Phonetica* 28, 353 – 367.

[4] Gandour, J. T., Harshman, R. A. 1978. Cross language differences in tone perception: a multidimensional scaling investigation. *Language and Speech* 21 (1), 1 – 33.

[5] Jongman, A., Wang, Y., Moore, C. B., Sereno, J. A. 2006. Perception and production of Mandarin Chinese tones. In: Lin, P., Tan, H., Bates, E., Tzeng, O. J. L. (eds.), *The Handbook of East Asian Psycholinguistics*. NY: Cambridge University Press, 209 – 217.

[6] Howie, J. M. 1976. *Acoustical Studies of Mandarin Vowels and Tones*. Cambridge: Cambridge University Press.

[7] Lin, M. C. 1988. Putonghua shendiao de shengxue texing he zhijue zhengzhao (The acoustic characteristics and perceptual cues of tones in Standard Chinese). *Zhongguo Yuwen (Chinese Linguistics)* 204, 182 – 193.

[8] Whalen, D. H., Xu, Y. 1992. Information for Mandarin tones in the amplitude contour and in brief segments. *Phonetica* 49, 25 – 47.

[9] Chang, C. Y. 2010. *Dialect Differences in the Production and Perception of Mandarin Chinese Tones*. (Doctoral Thesis) Retrieved from ProQuest Dissertations and Theses. (UMI No. 3435661).

[10] Lee, C. Y., Hung, T. H. 2008. Identification of Mandarin tones by English-speaking musicians and nonmusicians. *Journal of the Acoustical Society of America* 124 (5), 3235 – 3248.

[11] Gårding, E., Kratochvil, P., Svantesson, J. O., Zhang, J. 1986. Tone 4 and Tone 3 discrimination in modern standard Chinese, *Language and Speech* 29 (3), 281 – 293.

[12] Fu, Q. J., Zeng, F. G. 2000. Identification of temporal envelope cues in Chinese tone recognition. *Asia Pacific Journal of Speech, Language and Hearing* 5, 45 – 57.

[13] Gandour, J. T., Harshman, R. A. 1978. Cross language differences in tone perception: A multidimensional scaling investigation. *Language and Speech* 21 (1), 1 – 33.

[14] Massaro, D. W., Cohen, M. M., Tseng, C. Y. 1985. The evaluation and integration of pitch height and pitch contour in lexical tone perception in Mandarin Chinese. *Journal of Chinese Linguistics* 13, 267 – 289.

[15] Xu, L., Tsai, Y., Pfingst, B. E. 2002. Features of stimulation affecting tonal-speech perception: Implications for cochlear prostheses. *Journal of the Acoustical Society of America* 112 (1), 247 – 258.

[16] Wei, W. I., Wong, R., Hui, Y. Dennis, K. K., Au, B. Y., Wong, W. K., Ho, A. T., Kung, P. and Chung, E. 2000. Chinese tonal language

rehabilitation following cochlear implantation in children. *Acta Oto-Laryngologica* 129 (2), 218 - 221.

[17] Ciocca, V., Francis, A. L., Aisha, R., Wong, L. 2002. The perception of Cantonese lexical tones by early-deafened cochlear implantees. *Journal of the Acoustical Society of America* 111 (5), 2250 - 2256.

[18] Lee, K. Y., Van Hasselt, C. A., Chiu, S. N., Cheung, D. M. 2002. Cantonese tone perception ability of cochlear implant children in comparison with normal-hearing children. *International Journal of Pediatric Otorhinolaryngology* 63 (2), 137 - 147.

[19] Wong, A. O., Wong, L. L. 2004. Tone perception of Cantonese-speaking prelingually hearing-impaired children with cochlear implants. *Otolaryngology-Head and Neck Surgery* 130 (6), 751 - 758.

[20] Zhou, N., Huang, J., Chen, X., Xu, L. 2013. Relationship between tone perception and production in prelingually-deafened children with cochlear implants. *Otology & Neurotology* 34 (3), 499 - 506.

[21] Peng, S. C., Lu, H. P., Lu, N., Lin, Y. S., Deroche, M. L., Chatterjee, M. 2017. Processing of acoustic cues in lexical-tone identification by pediatric cochlear-implant recipients. *Journal of Speech Language and Hearing Research* 60 (5), 1223 - 1235.

[22] Deroche, M. L., Lu, H. P., Lin, Y. S., Chatterjee, M., Peng, S. C. 2019. Processing of acoustic information in lexical tone production and perception by pediatric cochlear implant recipients. *Frontiers in Neuroscience* 13, 639.

[23] Peng, S. C., Tomblin, J. B., Cheung, H., Lin, Y. S., Wang, L. S. 2004. Perception and production of Mandarin tones in prelingually deaf children with cochlear implants. *Ear and Hearing* 25 (3), 251 - 264.

[24] Xu, L., Li, Y., Hao, J., Chen, X., Xue, S. A., Han, D. 2004. Tone production in Mandarin-speaking children with cochlear implants: a preliminary study. *Acta Oto-Laryngologica* 124, 363 - 367.

[25] Han, D., Zhou, N., Li, Y., Chen, X., Zhao, X., Xu, L. 2007. Tone production of Mandarin-Chinese-speaking children with cochlear implants. *Journal of the Acoustical Society of America* 71, 875 - 880.

[26] Zhou, N., Xu, L. 2008. Development and evaluation of methods for assessing tone production skills in Mandarin-speaking children with cochlear implants. *Journal of the Acoustical Society of America* 123, 1653 - 1664.

[27] Lee, K. Y., van Hasselt, C. A., Tong, M. C. 2010. Age sensitivity in the acquisition of lexical tone production: evidence from children with profound congenital hearing impairment after cochlear implantation. Ann. *Annals of Otology Rhinology & Laryngology* 119 (4), 258 - 265.

[28] Mao, Y., Chen H., Xie, S., Xu, L. 2020. Acoustic assessment of tone production of prelingually-deafened Mandarin-speaking children with cochlear implants. *Frontiers in Neuroscience* 14, 592954.

[29] Yang, J., Brown, E., Fox, R. A., Xu, L. 2015. Acoustic properties of vowel production in prelingually deafened Mandarin-speaking children with cochlear implants. *Journal of the Acoustical Society of America* 138 (5), 2791 - 2799.

[30] Yang, J., Xu, L. 2017. Mandarin compound vowels produced by prelingually deafened children with cochlear implants. *International Journal of Pediatric Otorhinolaryngology* 97, 143 - 149.

[31] Kuo, Y. C., Rosen, S., Faulkner, A. 2008. Acoustic cues to tonal contrasts in Mandarin: Implications for cochlear implants. *Journal of the Acoustical Society of America* 123 (5), 2815 - 2824.

[32] Yang, J., Zhang, Y., Li, A., Xu, L. 2017. On the duration of Mandarin tones. *Proceedings of the 18th Annual Conference of the International Speech Communication Association (INTERSPEECH 2017)*, Stockholm, Sweden 1407 - 1411.

YANG Jing PhD She is an associate professor in the Department of Communication Sciences and Disorders at the University of Wisconsin-Milwaukee. Her research focuses on the speech development of bilingual children and children with cochlear implants.
E - mail: jyang888@ uwm. edu

XU Li MD, PhD He is a professor in the Division of Communication Sciences and Disorders at Ohio University. His current research focuses on speech perception in noise, tone perception and production in children with cochlear implants.
E - mail: xul@ ohio. edu

唐氏综合征合并听力障碍儿童听觉言语康复的个案研究

涂顺顺　沈新佳　张蓓华　陈伟民　倪佳伶　赵艳嫔　吴志远

摘　要　唐氏综合征合并听力障碍是一种临床常见的多重障碍类型。相较于其他单一的疾病类型，多重障碍康复难度更大，进展更缓慢。现阶段针对此类患儿的早期系统性听觉言语康复缺乏一种有章可循的干预模式。为尝试提供一种可资借鉴的干预方式，本文以一名低龄的唐氏综合征合并听力障碍儿童为个案对象，经过专业的评估和分析，制订了个性化的早期阶段性听觉言语康复计划，经过传统听觉言语康复和专业技术方法的干预后，个案在听觉功能、认知言语和社交功能、构音能力等方面均有了显著的提高。通过对该个案康复治疗过程的分析，本文认为针对此类患儿进行阶段性特异性的听觉康复和认知言语治疗并辅助以应用行为分析法和社会性游戏法，是一种行之有效且趣味性强的干预方式。

关键词　唐氏综合征，听力障碍，多重障碍，听觉康复，言语治疗

A Case Study of Hearing and Speech Rehabilitation for Children Suffering from Down Syndrome and Hearing Impairment

TU Shunshun　SHEN Xinjia　ZHANG Beihua　CHEN Weimin　NI Jialing　ZHAO Yanpin　WU Zhiyuan

Abstract Down syndrome combined with hearing impairment is a common clinical type of multiple disorder. Children with multiple impairments are more difficult and slower in recovery than children with other single diseases. At present, there is a lack of a systematic intervention model of the early auditory and speech rehabilitation for such children. In order to try to provide an exemplary model as such, this paper focuses on a young child suffering from Down syndrome and hearing impairment. We have developed a personalized early periodical auditory and speech rehabilitation program through professional evaluations and analyses. After the intervention of traditional auditory speech rehabilitation and professional technical methods, the child has significantly improved in auditory function, cognitive function, speech and social function, sound articulation and other aspects. Through the analysis of the rehabilitation process for the case, this paper holds that it is an effective and interesting intervention method for these children through carrying out the stage-specific auditory rehabilitation and cognitive speech therapy, with the adjuvant therapy of applied behavior analysis and social games.

Key words Down syndrome, Hearing impairment, Multiple impairments, Auditory rehabilitation, Speech therapy

1. 引言

唐氏综合征又称先天愚型，是一种常见的染色体疾病。国内发病率为0.56‰—0.64‰，男女比例为3∶2［10］。听力障碍，指听分析器因病变或损伤，致使听力减退或丧失的状态［4］。第二次全国残疾人抽样调查显示，我国听力残疾人数为2780万人，低龄儿童发生的听力残疾，如果不能得到及时、科学的康复，将引起严重的言语障碍［5］。多重障碍是指具有两种或两种以上残疾而导致在生活功能体验方面存在障碍［9］。相较于其他单一的疾病类型，多重障碍康复难度更大，进展更缓慢。而现阶段国内外对于多重障碍儿童的言语康复研究缺乏一种有迹可循、适用性较广的模式。

本文以一例低龄唐氏综合征合并听力障碍的儿童为研究对象，对其进行了专业的言语康复评估和分析，制订了一套针对性的阶段性早期听觉言语康复计划，探究

干预前后效果对比，尝试提出一种针对此类患儿早期阶段性听觉言语康复的可资借鉴的方法，为今后对此类患儿进行更深入的研究奠定基础。

2. 研究方法

2.1 研究对象

王某，女，2016年9月出生，同年12月，经复旦大学附属儿科医院诊断患有唐氏综合征、耳聋、弱视及先天性心脏病。双耳中重度听力下降，听力损失均在90dBHL以上，听反应延迟；确诊后即右耳佩戴助听器，但由于佩戴不良，助听效果不理想。于2017年6月开始进行听觉言语康复。

2.2 研究过程

2.2.1 评估流程和初评结果

（1）听力评估：专业听力师分别对个案治疗前后进行听力评估。初次听力评估显示：畸变产物耳声反射双耳均未通过；声导抗左右耳均为B型（平坦性）；听性脑干反应（Auditory Brainstem Response，ABR）左耳、右耳反应阈分别为80dBnHL、70dBnHL；听觉多频稳态反应（Multiple Auditory Steady-State Responses，MASSR）气导测试结果如表1所示。

表1 听觉多频稳态反应（MASSR）初测

MASSRHz/dBHL	250	500	1000	2000	4000
左耳	/	105	90	80	100
右耳	105	60	75	90	95

综合结果提示：先天性双耳重度混合性语前聋。

（2）听觉功能评估：儿童言语治疗师分别对个案治疗前和每30次治疗进行一次听觉功能评估。测试环境选择在噪声≤45分贝的评估室，根据孙喜斌、刘巧云和黄昭鸣编制的《听觉功能评估标准及方法》［14］和林氏六音法，分别对个案听觉察知、分辨、识别和理解功能进行评估。初次听觉功能评估显示个案处于听觉察知阶段，且对高频音和低频音存在察知障碍。

（3）基本康复评估：康复治疗师分别对个案治疗前和每30次治疗进行一次基本评估，包括大运动、精细运动、感觉统合及言语评估（个案为多重障碍儿童，全面发展落后，需要全面康复介入）。因本文重点研究个案的言语康复，所以笔者重点进行言语评估资料的收集、归纳和整理。

认知言语评估采用黄昭鸣等编制的《构音语音能力评估》记录表［8］、王丽燕等修订的《听障儿童语言功能评估》［16］和本院自制的认知与语言理解量表、语言表达量表。

认知与语言理解量表主要包含三大项目：基础认知（30分）、概念类（70分）和高级认知（28分）。基础认知包括反应能力（5小项）、观察力（2小项）、模仿能力（2小项）、听者反应（2小项）、记忆力（2小项）；概念类包括物品概念（11小项）、颜色概念（3小项）、形状概念（3小项）、比较概念（2小项）、时间概念（4小项）、空间概念（8小项）、数概念（4小项）；高级认知包括因果关系（6小项）、判断对错（2小项）、推理和想象（6小项）。共64个小项目，每个项目满分2分。计分标准：独立、部分、无法完成评估项目分别计2分、1分、0分。初评结果：4分。

语言表达量表主要分为语言与沟通前能力（16分）和言语表达能力（76分）两大项目。语言与沟通前能力包括非言语沟通（7小项）和分辨声音（2小项）；言语表达能力包括单音（1小项）、词汇运用（5小项）、句子复述运用（6小项）、提要求（4小项）、回答问题（8小项）、主动提问（9小项）、描述和叙事（5小项）。共46个小项目，每个项目满分2分。计分标准：独立、部分、无法完成评估项目分别计2分、1分、0分。初评结果：2分。

结果显示：个案全面发展落后，低于

6 个月正常婴儿水平，无言语，反应差，均不能追听追视，口面部感知觉低敏。

2.2.2　评估分析

对各项初评结果进行整理，应用临床常用分析框架——ICF-CY 框架（简版）进行听觉言语功能的分析，并对个案优势和劣势进行剖析，进而根据结果进行康复目标和方案的制定。

（1）ICF-CY 框架分析（简版）

根据 ICF-CY 框架对个案言语、认知及听觉等方面进行全面分析，见图 1。

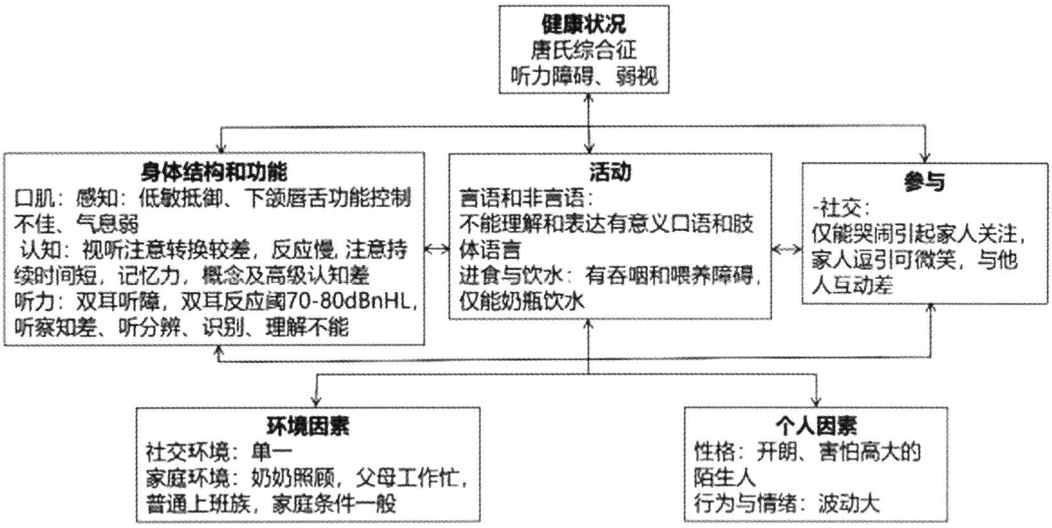

图 1　ICF-CY 分析简图

小结：经 ICF-CY 框架分析，根据发育里程碑规律，个案听力障碍、认知发展落后及口部肌肉感知和控制的障碍较大程度上限制了个案活动和参与功能的发展。其中，听力及轻微视力障碍又影响其认知的发展。个案尚处于听察知阶段，即不能明确觉察到声音的有无。针对小龄患儿，应在其佩戴助听器初期即重点进行听力康复训练，辅以基础认知言语治疗，从而提高其残余听力和发展认知。后期考虑唐氏综合征全面发展落后的特点，需进行认知和社交沟通等全面干预。

（2）优势和劣势分析

对个案进行优势和劣势分析，能帮助治疗师把握个案的整体情况，避免过多地关注个案功能不足之处，进而在干预过程中取长补短，更好地推进康复进程。

优势：模仿能力较好，有助于认知、言语等功能的发展；②干预年龄小，发展空间大；③性格开朗，有利于社交能力的发展。

劣势：①先天条件较差，有听力视力缺损（仅轻微斜视，其他视力缺陷不明显）；②注意力持续性差，影响治疗效果；③反应较慢，对言语声反应延迟 1—2 分钟；④家庭条件有限，仅支持一只助听器适配。

2.2.3　阶段性目标和言语语言康复方案

考虑到个案言语康复治疗频率为 3 次/周，20—40 分钟/次，康复时间和强度有限，结合康复评估结果，所以每半年作为一个康复阶段，拟定阶段性康复目标和方案，具体见表 2。

表2　　阶段性目标和言语语言康复方案

阶段	时间	阶段性目标	治疗方案
Ⅰ阶段：个训	2017.7—2018.1	改善听觉察知能力和进食障碍：1. 每节课能在安静状态下对声音有反应能追听，完成率3/5；2. 每次辅助下进食50ml糊状食物，呕吐或噎食呛咳少于3次	1. 听力康复：呼名反应训练、追听追视训练；2. 进食训练：口面部肌肉感知结合力量训练
Ⅱ阶段：个训	2018.1—2018.7	改善听觉综合分辨能力和进食障碍：1. 每节课能在安静状态下，进行三种动物声和交通工具声分辨，准确率2/3；2. 吸管独立饮水每30ml，呛咳少于2次	1. 听觉训练：动物声分辨，交通工具声音分辨等，儿歌及拟声词分辨；2. 进食训练：口面部肌肉感知结合力量控制训练
Ⅲ阶段：个训情境教学	2018.1—2019.1	改善听觉精细分辨能力、基础认知和促进发音：1. 每节课能在安静状态下，进行音长、音节、语调等分辨，准确率3/5；2. 每节课能在少量辅助下模仿大动作5个，完成率3/5；3. 每节课能在诱导下发元音3种，发音频率达20次/课	1. 听觉训练：单元音时长分辨、词语分辨（音节）、声强分辨、语调分辨、听声复述；2. 认知训练：模仿操作玩具和大动作；3. 言语训练：诱导发音
Ⅳ阶段：个训情境教学	2019.1—2019.7	改善听觉识别能力和基础认知，促进仿说言语：1. 每节课能识别词语、图文等，准确率7/10；2. 每节课能独立模仿简单口型圆唇、抿唇、咧唇等，完成率3/5；3. 每节课能仿说简单元音和唇辅音20个，完成率3/4	1. 听觉训练：自然声识别训练，词语、音位识别训练，识别图文训练法，视触辅助法；2. 认知训练：大动作模仿、口型模仿和功特类模仿；3. 言语训练：口型提示仿说元音和简单唇辅音
Ⅴ阶段：个训结合小组教学	2019.7—2020.1	改善听觉理解和概念类认知，促进言语和社交：1. 每节课能进行三选一听指认10组，完成率7/10；2. 每节课听一步指令8个，准确率8/10；两步指令3个，完成率1/3；3. 每节课能在少量言语提示下与人打招呼3次，能命名日常等卡片10张，准确率2/5	1. 听觉训练：听指认训练、听者反应训练、回答简单问题训练；2. 认知训练：听一步指令、指认日常物品。3. 言语沟通训练：简单命名、招呼语、称呼

2.2.4　辅助治疗技术

本研究主要采用两种治疗技术辅助推进临床治疗和家庭康复进程——应用行为分析法和社会性游戏训练。

（1）应用行为分析法（Applied Behavior Analysis，ABA），是一种利用分解步骤、重复强化和反馈、辅助提示的手段来改变特定行为的治疗方法［2］。举例：模仿发音a：①分解步骤练习：要求模仿张嘴嘴型—要求张嘴发出声音—要求发出近似“a”的声音——要求发音“a”；②反复依次训练每个步骤并强化，如初始步骤中每当孩子完成模仿张嘴即给予强化或表扬；③适当给予提示和辅助：如孩子不能完成模仿张嘴时，给予镜子辅助或训练者用手帮助孩子进行口型模仿；④给予强化物及强化手段：每完成一个小目标即给予孩子喜欢玩的玩具或吃的食物进行强化并表扬。

（2）社会性游戏训练：指以“游戏是孩子的天性”为前提，通过游戏的方式，提高特殊儿童参加社会交往的意愿和动机，让其感受快乐的同时，也能进行针对性的功能训练。在社会性游戏中训练患儿，不仅能使教育变得欢乐，也能提高患儿认知社交的发展；如缺乏该技能，患儿可能会陷入孤独、抑郁状态，影响学习主动性，甚至影响孩子全面发育［13］。Ingersoll 和 Dvortcsak［1］通过直接和交互式教导技术，整合并进一步阐述了将游戏作为自然强化物、在情境中进行教学并及时反馈的训练方法。湖南省残疾人康复研究中心对听障儿童听觉语言游戏训练也进行了深入研究及分析，提供了一系列的康复小游戏集［23］。本文参考和借鉴了上述游戏方法，让个案在游戏中不知不觉地接受训练，提高自身技能。

2.2.5　方案执行

按原计划执行阶段性康复治疗，并配合家庭干预，康复进程调整见表3。

表3　康复进程

<table>
<tr><th>阶段/模式</th><th>计划时间</th><th>实际干预时间</th><th>干预情况和重点调整</th><th>治疗调整及原因分析</th></tr>
<tr><td>Ⅰ阶段：个训</td><td>2017.7—2018.1</td><td>2017.7—2017.11</td><td>听觉察知和进食改善快，提前完成Ⅰ阶段目标，进入Ⅱ阶段训练</td><td rowspan="3">提前完成第Ⅰ、Ⅱ、Ⅲ阶段目标：
1. 家长重视，发现早，听力重建及时，早期重点进行听觉康复，听力改善快；
2. 患儿模仿能力好，性格开朗，学习主动性高，配合度好；
3. 进行家庭宣教和指导，家长在生活中即进行训练；
4. 其他科室如OT、PT同步进行康复，相互促进</td></tr>
<tr><td>Ⅱ阶段：个训</td><td>2018.1—2018.7</td><td>2017.11—2018.4</td><td>能分辨动物声和交通工具声，咀嚼力量增加，尝试咿呀学语，尝试模仿，提前进入Ⅲ阶段</td></tr>
<tr><td>Ⅲ阶段：个训教学</td><td>2018.7—2019.1</td><td>2018.4—2018.9</td><td>能分辨简单元音和辅音，模仿简单动作和发元音；分辨复杂音节和语音特性差，考虑为不理解。调整训练重点为超音段语音分辨训练</td></tr>
<tr><td>Ⅳ阶段：个训情境教学</td><td>2019.1—2019.7</td><td>2018.9—2019.6</td><td>能口型模仿并发简单音节，能模仿进行简单的假扮游戏，能听指认音节差别大的图片，不能指认相似音节的图片。考虑分辨高频音节差，进行助听器复查和助听器调整。后期训练重点置于听觉识别训练</td><td>延后完成第Ⅳ阶段目标：
1. 逢春节，回老家，暂停治疗月余，专业综合康复减少；
2. 家长工作调动，忙碌，家庭干预和康复治疗强度均降低；且交由老人照看，孩子助听器佩戴不良；
3. 认知增加，顽皮，倔强，情绪波动大，学习效率降低</td></tr>
<tr><td>Ⅴ阶段：个训结合小组融合教学</td><td>2019.7—2020.1</td><td>2019.6—2020.1；2020.8—2020.11</td><td>听力训练后，认知和言语词汇量增加明显，治疗师指令多次重复下可独立完成一步指令，可辨别两条件词（颜色+果蔬）；能简单命名人物、动物、果蔬图片。但沟通较少。中期调整重点为小组社交游戏中与人互动沟通训练</td><td>完成第Ⅴ阶段：
1. 2020年1月至7月，患儿回老家过年，又逢疫情，治疗暂停，前期治疗结果未能巩固和维持；
2. 开展小组情境融合教学，并于2020年9月进入幼儿园学习，促进认知及社交技能提升</td></tr>
</table>

3. 结果

3.1　末期评估

（1）末期听力检查：听性脑干反应ABR：左右耳反应阈均为55dBnHL，听觉多频稳态反应（MASSR）结果如表4所示。

表4　听觉多频稳态反应（MASSR）末评

MASSRHz/dBHL		250	500	1000	2000	4000
骨导	左	/	25	30	60	30
	右	/	20	25	45	30
气导	左	30	45	60	75	60
	右	30	40	60	60	85

结果提示双耳中度混合性听力损失。

（2）听觉功能评估：个案处于听觉理解阶段，可理解两条件词。

（3）基本康复评估：认知及言语评估提示个案能力处于两岁水平，社交能力处于三岁水平，可基本回归幼儿园生活。构音清晰度：72.2%，轻中度构音障碍。

3.2 各阶段评估统计

对各阶段进行认知、言语和构音等功能评估，整理数据，制图如下。初评及各阶段干预后统计结果如下。

（1）初评及末评听力结果统计见图2，数据来源于复旦大学附属儿科医院。ABR：左右耳反应阈分别为70dBnHL、80dBnHL改善至双耳反应阈55dBnHL。分别取初评、末评MASSR（气导）各频段评估结果的平均值计算，可知MASSR平均听阈（气导）左耳93.75dBHL，右耳85dBHL，改善至左耳54dBHL，右耳55dBHL。

（2）采用本院认知与语言理解量表评估个案认知与语言理解能力，统计初评和各阶段治疗后评估结果中的基础认知、概念类、高级认知和总认知得分情况见图3。

（3）采用本院语言表达量表评估个案各阶段语言表达能力，统计初评和各阶段治疗后评估结果中的语前能力、言语表达和总言语表达能力得分情况见图4。

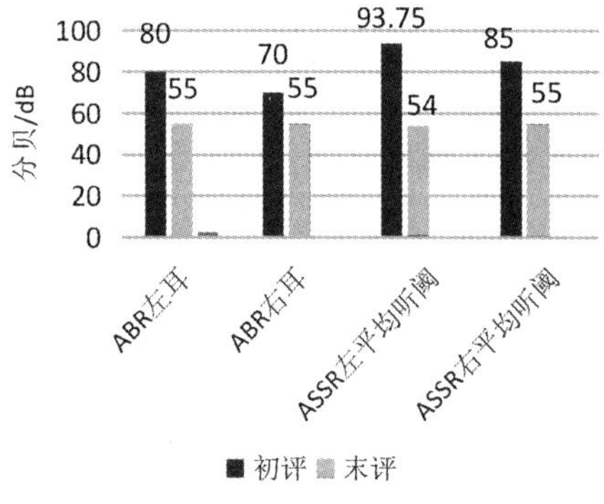

图2 听力评估统计

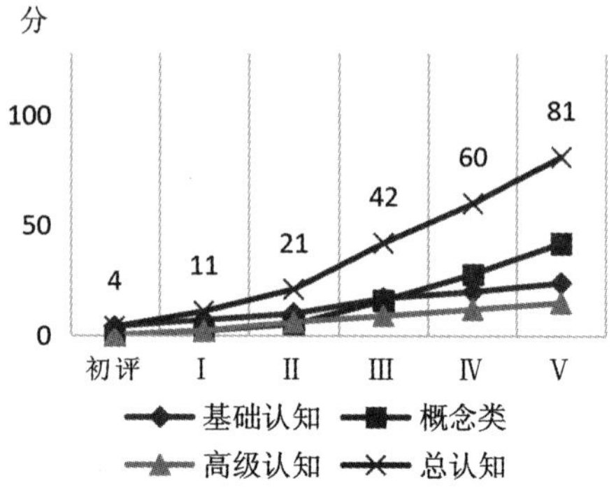

图3 认知与语言理解功能评估统计图

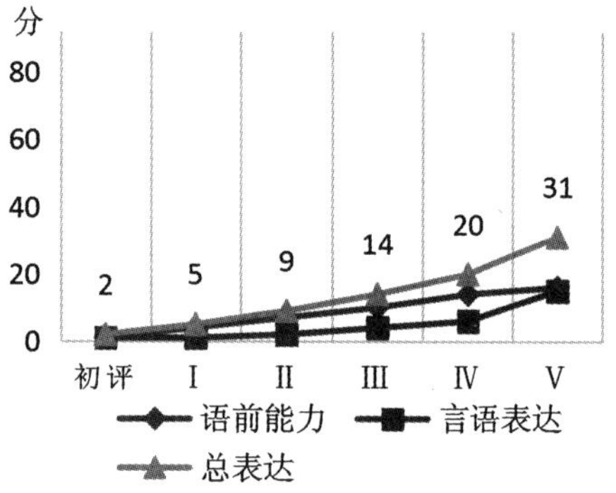

图4 语言表达功能统计

（4）采用黄昭鸣等编制的《构音语音能力评估》记录表［8］，统计初评和各阶段治疗后评估结果中的声母、韵母、声调和总构音清晰度得分结果见图5。

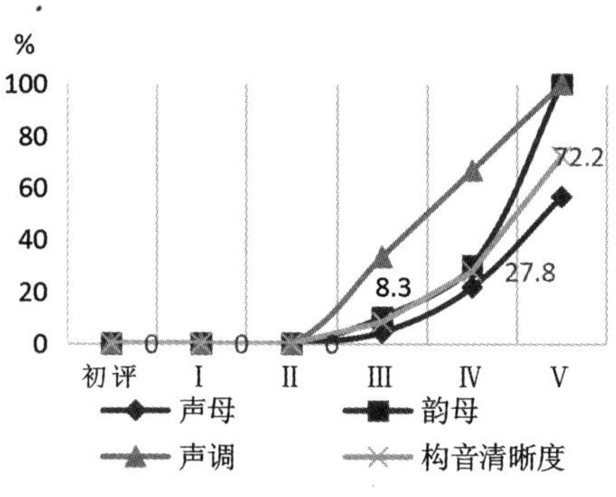

图5 构音清晰度统计

3.3 治疗前后评估小结

个案在听力、听觉功能、口部肌肉、认知、言语构音和社交功能方面均较未干预前有了显著提高。①双耳残余听力恢复多，听力损失由重度改善为中度；②听觉功能由不能察知高频和低频音提高至听觉理解两条件词阶段；③口部肌肉功能由口面部感知觉低敏，下颌唇舌控制差，不能吹笛改善至口部肌肉功能接近正常儿童；④认知能力显著增加（得分由4分增加至81分）；⑤言语能力由无言语（<6个月水平）提高至短语短句阶段（2岁水平），构音清晰度提高72.2%；⑥社交功能由呼名无反应，不能追听追视（<1岁水平）改善至能主动与人用言语打招呼和提简单需求，回归幼儿园进行基本社交（3岁水平）。

4. 思考和讨论

通过对个案的阶段性评估可知，个案整体达到了阶段性康复目标，康复取得了初步成功，故本文提出的早期阶段性的听觉言语康复方式对本个案来说，是一种行之有效的干预方式，也是值得后期深入研究借鉴的。

4.1 唐氏综合征合并听力障碍的多重障碍儿童听觉言语康复的方法

患儿干预前后评估结果显示听力、听觉功能、认知及言语功能有显著的提高，说明为其制定的康复方法是全面而有效的。

（1）早期根据听觉功能发育规律进行阶段性的听觉康复对个案听力重建后残余听力的发展有着至关重要的作用。在个案进行听力重建前，个案因为重度听力损失，接收的听觉刺激较少，且信息多不完整，影响了个案整体的发育。当个案进行分阶段听觉察知、分辨、识别和理解训练后，图2显示个案残余听力恢复多，听力损失程度降低，听觉功能提高。王娜娜［18］、崔方方［3］也提出听觉训练能最大限度地开发和利用聋儿的残余听力，减少听力损失对聋儿产生的不利影响，有效提高儿童的语言理解和认知能力，帮助其参与社会生活。何怡、庞子健［6］通过研究也指出听觉识别训练可提高构音障碍的治疗效果。所以对低龄的唐氏综合征合并听力障碍的多重障碍儿童进行早期听觉发育四阶段的功能训练有助于发展其残余听力、改善其听觉功能和构音能力。

（2）以模仿为基础的认知训练在帮助个案提高认知发育中起着重要的作用。图3显示，从第Ⅲ阶段开始，认知功能整体增长较之前更快。对比表3康复进程表可知，第Ⅲ阶段较前两阶段增加了较多的认知训练，推测模仿训练促进了个案认知功能的发育。相关研究表明，模仿是学习的重要方式，理解和模仿他人行为是人类社会认知的重要组成部分。王协顺等［19］通过研究提出未来可以通过简单的动作模仿控制训练，为社会认知受损个体（如孤独症和述情障碍者）进行康复训练。

（3）口肌训练结合语言社交训练也在很大程度上提高了个案的言语表达能力和构音清晰度。本个案在第Ⅳ、Ⅴ阶段重点介入了小组语言社交训练，在对图4、图5进行分析可知，第Ⅳ、Ⅴ阶段的言语表达能力和构音清晰度的改善速率最大，表3也提示个案从第Ⅳ阶段只能进行简单的元音仿说提高到第Ⅴ阶段能应用简单词汇进行命名、提要求和打招呼；清晰度也由27.8%提高到72.2%。故个案后期进行口肌训练结合诱导发音的社交言语训练有效地改善了个案社交语言表达。据研究发现［15］口肌训练与认知语言训练相结合，确实可以提升自闭症儿童语言训练的兴趣和速度；将应用行为分析中的分化应用于构音训练中有利于提高构音的精确度。

（4）辅助治疗技术也发挥了不可替代的作用。本研究采用了专业的治疗技术——应用行为分析法和社会性游戏训练——贯穿于康复治疗的全程。唐氏综合征儿童往往脾气倔强，配合度不高，畏难心理严重；应用行为分析疗法把个体的复杂行为都分解为小单元行为，并及时强化和适当提示，给予反馈，个性化明显，功能性强。赵维维［25］对自闭症儿童研究中指出基于ABA法的听觉统合训练可提高ASD患儿的认知行为能力、语言和社交能力。张蕾、黄昭鸣等［22］也对游戏在听障儿童听觉康复和言语矫治的应用研究中提出游戏使康复过程更加有趣丰富，更能吸引儿童的注意力，促进儿童全面发展，康复效果更加显著。利用应用行为分析法中的正强化和负强化，把社会性游戏作为自然强化物，在趣味性的社交游戏中不知不觉地进行干预，能较好地帮助患儿建立正面性的社交行为，增强患儿的自信心，提高患儿的学习效率，帮助患儿尽早回归幼儿园和学校。

4.2 影响唐氏综合征合并听力障碍的多重障碍儿童听觉言语康复的因素

此个案家长发现疾病早，并及时进行了听力重建和康复干预，为其后期功能提高奠定了良好的基础。李玉香［12］、梁巍［11］和王娜等［17］通过研究发现，早期干预对听障儿童听觉言语康复有着重要的影响，干预越早，听觉言语功能恢复越快，回归学校和社会越早。王中柱、李丹华等［20］也提出早期干预对特殊儿童发挥着关键性的作用。所以早期干预是影响特殊儿童言语康复的重要因素之一。笔者在多年临床康复实践中，遇到多例此类唐氏综合征合并听力障碍的多重障碍儿童，多为偏远地区儿童，他们或因疾病发现较晚，或因条件有限，未能及时进行听力重建和康复干预，后期介入治疗时已错过最佳干预时期，康复效果不明显。所以在此呼吁广大家长们加强对儿童疾病的筛查意识，医生们加大对儿童相关疾病的宣传，让更多特殊儿童早日被发现，及时进行干预。

对患儿进行专业系统的阶段性评估和分析，制订个性化的阶段性康复计划亦是十分必要的。本个案根据阶段性的评估，进行了阶段性综合康复计划和方法的调整，及时、专业而有效，大大促进了个案全面听觉言语能力的发展。所以阶段性的评估、分析和调整能确保患儿康复顺利有效进行。

本研究个案是有多重障碍的特殊儿童，针对其制定的康复方案包括了传统的言语康复和听觉康复，还贯穿着专业治疗技术——应用行为分析法和社会性游戏。个案进行言语康复的同时，还进行着大运动、精细运动和感觉统合训练的全面干预。黄昭鸣、杜晓新等［7］也提出多重障碍儿童需要多重干预的理念，并构建了综合康复体系。所以多重干预、综合康复也是影响此类多重障碍儿童康复的关键因素之一。

对患儿康复进程进行长期跟踪可知，家庭人员的配合度和康复治疗的持续性对其听觉言语功能康复有着关键性的影响。当其家庭人员配合度降低，如正确佩戴、使用和维护助听器减少，家庭康复强度减弱和临床康复减少时，患儿出现较明显的功能倒退或迟滞不前的情况。姚晓旭［21］、张燕敏等［24］也提出家长在特殊儿童康复过程中发挥着不可替代的作用。所以为促进患儿更快更好地康复，我们需要一定强度的临床康复和家庭康复，并且需要患儿家庭积极配合和巩固支持。

5. 结束语

本文研究对象是一名低龄的早期进行听力重建和康复干预的儿童，在系统的听觉康复训练基础上，结合口面部肌肉感知和运动功能训练、基础康复认知和言语训练；辅助以专业技术手段——应用行为分析疗法和社会性游戏训练；最终个案在听力、语言、认知和社交各方面均取得了显著进步。随着社会的进步与医学的发展，多重障碍儿童能被及时发现并得到及时的治疗。如果康复机构及时提供较为专业、全面的技术指导与跟踪，患儿家庭积极配合康复，那将会有更多的患儿改善其功能水平以回归学校和社会。本文仅为个案研究，后期可扩大样本量和不断完善康复技术以继续进行研究，为低龄唐氏综合征合并听力障碍的儿童康复提供更多借鉴和帮助。

参考文献

[1] Ingersoll, B. , Dvortcsak, A. 2012. *Teaching Social Communication to Children with Autism*. New York: The Guilford Press.

[2] Leaf, R. , McEachin, J. , Harsh, J. D. 2012. *A Work in Progress: Behavior Management Strategies and a Curriculum for Intensive Behavior Treatment of Autism*. New York: Different Roads to Learning.

[3] 崔方方:《听力障碍合并孤独症倾向儿童听觉言语康复训练个案分析》,《中国听力语言康复科学杂志》2021 年第 19 期。

[4] 顾佳云:《融合教育促进学前听障儿童社会性发展的个案研究》,硕士学位论文,宁波大学,2019 年。

[5] 何娴、李刚、郑芸:《听障儿童听力康复需求家长问卷调查》,《听力学及言语疾病杂志》2012 年第 20 期。

[6] 何怡、庞子健:《听觉辨别训练对儿童构音障碍的疗效》,《中国康复理论与实践》2020 年第 26 期。

[7] 黄昭鸣、杜晓新、孙喜斌等:《"多重障碍、多重干预"综合康复体系的构建》,《中国特殊教育》2007 年第 10 期。

[8] 黄昭鸣、万勤、张蕾:《言语功能评估标准及方法》,华东师范大学出版社 2007 年版。

[9] 雷诺兹、弗莱 - 詹:《简明特殊教育百科全书(第二版)》,赵向东译,求真出版社 2013 年版。

[10] 林青、卢红云、刘巧云、黄昭鸣:《"医教结合"理念下唐氏综合征儿童个别化言语康复课例分析课例(三)》,《唐氏综合征儿童个别化言语康复课》,《中国听力语言康复科学杂志》2016 年第 21 期。

[11] 梁巍:《历史新阶段开展聋儿早期康复教育工作的观念与对策》,《中国听力语言康复科学杂志》2004 年第 1 期。

[12] 李玉香:《聋儿康复早期干预的实践与体会》,《中国听力语言康复科学杂志》2005 年第 2 期。

[13] 毛颖梅:《应用游戏治疗提高孤独症儿童社交能力的个案研究》,《中国康复理论与实践》2007 年第 9 期。

[14] 孙喜斌、刘巧云、黄昭鸣:《听觉功能评估标准及方法》,华东师范大学出版社 2007 年版。

[15] 石雅倩:《口肌训练结合语言认知训练对自闭症儿童构音训练成效的干预研究》,硕士学位论文,辽宁师范大学,2020 年。

[16] 王丽燕、孙喜斌、吕明臣等:《〈听障儿童语言功能评估〉参考标准的修订及应用研究》,《听力学及言语研究疾病杂志》2014 年第 22 期。

[17] 王娜、杜巧新:《听障儿童听觉言语能力影响因素的研究》,《中国康复理论和实践》2011 年第 4 期。

[18] 王娜娜:《浅谈听障儿童的听觉训练》,《新课程(上)》2015 年第 11 期。

[19] 王协顺、苏彦捷:《从动作模仿到社会认知:自我—他人控制的作用》,《心理科学进展》2019 年第 27 期。

[20] 王中柱、李丹华、魏旭东:《早期干预对精神迟滞患儿的作用效果分析》,《中国健康心理学杂志》2017 年第 25 期。

[21] 姚晓旭:《家长如何在聋儿康复过程中发挥应有的作用》,《中国听力语言康复科学杂志》2004 年第 4 期。

[22] 张蕾、黄昭鸣、杜晓新:《游戏在听障儿童听觉康复和言语矫治中的应用》,《中国听力语言康复科学杂志》2007 年第 5 期。

[23] 周献珍:《聋儿听觉语言康复教学指导》,长沙市精美彩色印刷有限公司,2011 年。

[24] 张艳敏、高超、段佳丽等:《机构协同家庭对精神发育迟滞患儿早期干预的前瞻性研究》,《中国继续医学教育》2019 年第 11 期。

[25] 赵维维:《基于 ABA 法的听觉统合训练对自闭症谱系障碍儿童社交能力和语言发育水平的影响》,《临床护理杂志》2020 年第 19 期。

涂顺顺 上海市养志康复医院,本科,主要研究领域和方向为听力障碍儿童听觉康复和言语矫治,唐氏综合征、精神发育迟缓等行为分析和儿童社交游戏训练。
E-mail:1251725797@ qq. com

沈新佳 上海市养志康复医院,主要研究领域和方向为听力障碍儿童听觉康复和言语矫治,唐氏综合征、自闭症儿童言语康复治疗。
E-mail:309195542@ qq. com

张蓓华 上海市养志康复医院,同济大学在读博士,目前研究方向为自闭症社交干预。
E-mail:helley - 007@ 106. com

共振峰增强对噪音下汉语普通话语音感知的影响

管晶晶　刘　畅

摘　要　噪音背景中语音感知是听力损失患者以及老年人在日常生活中经常面对的困难。本研究旨在探求第二共振峰（F2）的增强是否会提高正常听力以及听力损失的老年人在噪音背景中的语音感知。本研究采用中文版本的坐标响应语料库（Coordinate Response Measure，CRM）进行测试，让两组被试在两种不同的语音型噪音背景（二人语音噪音，two-talker babble；六人语音噪音，six-talker babble）中识别原始的语音以及F2增强过的语音。结果表明，在二人语音噪音中，不管正常听力还是听力损失，在共振峰增强后，两组人的语音识别成绩都有显著提高，但在六人语音噪音中，F2增强对语音识别阈值没有任何影响。另外，在大多数条件下，F2增强带来的益处与老年听者的年龄和平均听力阈值没有显著相关。F2增强会改善老年人在二人语音噪音中的汉语语音感知成绩，可能是因为背景噪音在时域凹陷处有更多可听见的语音信息。
关键词　共振峰增强，语音感知，汉语普通话听者，听力损失

Speech Perception in Noise with Formant Enhancement for Mandarin-speaking Listeners

GUAN Jingjing　LIU Chang

Abstract Listeners with hearing loss often have difficulties in perceiving speech with background noise in their daily life. The purpose of the current study is to examine whether F2 enhancement improves speech perception in noise for Mandarin-speaking elderly listeners with hearing impairment and with normal hearing. Based on the paradigm of Coordinate Response Measure corpus(CRM), Mandarin target words (e. g., color and digit) were tested for two groups in two-talker and six-talker babbles with original and F2 – enhanced speech. Results show that thresholds of both groups improved for enhanced speech signals, primarily in two-talker babble, but not in six-talker babble. F2-enhancement benefits did not significantly correlate with listeners' age and average hearing thresholds in most listening conditions. Speech sounds with F2 enhancement may improve Mandarin listeners' speech perception in two-talker babble, possibly due to a greater amount of speech information available in temporal dips of background noise.
Key words Formant enhancement, Speech perception, Mandarin-speaking listeners, Hearing loss

1. 引言

相比较于正常听力的人群，听力损失患者在噪音背景中的语音识别阈值要差5到15dB，具体取决于语音材料的复杂性（单词、句子等），噪音的类型（语音型噪声、调制型噪音等）以及听力损失的程度[1-4]。通常，听力损失患者的听力阈值较高，因此需要较高音量的语音，以确保语音的可听度。但是，仅仅增加音量无法解决听力损失患者的时域、频域加工能力的不足，最终并不一定能提高语音感知的能力[5，6]。相反，高音量还可能会导致听力损失患者响度重振（loudness recruitment）问题的发生[7]。具体来说，听力损失患者会由于其异常快速的响度增长而感觉不适。此外，感音神经性听力损失患者频谱的内部表征比较差，是由于耳蜗中外毛细胞的锐化效果减弱了。例如频谱中的波峰和波谷之间对比显著地降低而表现出波峰抹平（spectral smearing）的现

象，这是造成听力损失患者在语音感知中所面临难度的重要原因之一［5—7］。助听器可以补偿各个频率点上的听力损失，放大到可听见阈值之上（比如90或95dB），但不能很好地解决波峰抹平的问题［5，6］。

元音分类主要依靠第一共振峰（F1）和第二共振峰（F2）［8］。低频F1的能量峰值相对较高，因此可以较好地在噪音中被识别。先前的研究表明，不论是年轻的、年老的听者，还是正常或听力损失患者，其F1识别阈值是相似的［5，6，9］。相比之下，F2对于中高频听力下降的听力损失患者在噪音背景中的语音感知非常重要，原因主要有以下三点。首先，在嘈杂的环境下，听力损失患者依靠相对准确的F1信息以及部分F2来识别元音［10］。听力损失患者区分F2频率差异存在主要困难。其次，掩蔽的向上扩展（upward spread of masking）效应，即低频噪音或是F1可能会干扰高频信号F2的识别，使得老年人语音感知更困难［11］。最后，高频听力损失是老年人非常常见的一种听力损失的类型。通常，随着年龄的增加，听力阈值在包括F2频率在内的高频区域开始逐渐下降。总而言之，可听见的F2信息对于听力损失患者构建清晰的频谱对比度以及提高语音感知至关重要。

本研究采用了针对第二共振峰（F2）的语音增强（speech enhancement）技术，探讨可否增强噪音下的汉语语音感知。一般来说，语音增强技术通过缩小共振峰的带宽（频谱锐化，spectral sharpening）［12］或通过调整频谱过滤器的权重来提高频谱对比度（频谱扩展，spectral expansion）［13—19］，但各种语音增强技术的效果不一。具体而言，Simpson等人［25］通过自适应滤波器组，发现中度至重度听力损失患者在长时程语谱噪音（long-Term Speech-Shaped Noise，LTSSN）中的句子识别得到小幅度的显著改善。Lyzenga等人［17］发现单独的频谱扩展技术并没有带来影响。但是结合频谱锐化，通过放大高频以阻止掩蔽的向上扩展效应，对于LTSSN中的句子识别阈值，正常听力群体提高了约1.0dB。语音增强技术对语音感知影响的差异比较大，一些研究表明语音增强技术没有带来任何改善［14，15］，有些研究结果显示语音增强技术可以带来3%—5%的提升［12，13，16］。语音增强的效果取决于诸多因素，如听者的听力阈值、阈上声音加工能力、背景噪音的类型以及语音增强算法的差异［13—19］。

最近，在我们的实验室中已经采用一种简单的声学方法来增强F2，以探究这种F2增强是否可以改善语音感知［6，20］。选择F2增强是因为它是一种相对简单的信号处理方法，可以直接增强F2区域而不影响其他频率范围。F2增强过程包括以下几个主要步骤：进行三维语谱图（振幅×时间×频率）的快速傅里叶变换（Fast Fourier Transform，FFT）、F2估算、F2增强、FFT逆过程来重建语音信号。Woodall和Liu［6］用上述步骤将目标元音刺激的F2峰值分别提高了3dB、6dB和9dB，测量对正常听力和听力损失患者的元音共振峰辨别阈值（即可以检测到的最小共振峰偏移）的影响。结果表明，即使把音量从70dB SPL调高到90dB SPL或是单独增强F2，正常听力的大学生元音共振峰辨别阈值没有发生变化。同样地只是简单地提高音量，对听力损失患者来说，也不能提高其成绩。但是提高音量的同时，增强F2，听力损失患者的元音共振峰辨别的阈值显著地提高了42%。Guan和Liu［20］将同样的F2增强技术应用于英语句子识别任务中，年老的正常听力以及听力损失患者在语音型噪音中聆听未被共振峰增强，以及F2增强过的目标语音，结果发现F2增强显著地提高了英语为母语的两组人在二人语音噪音中的语音感知成绩。

目前大多数语音增强研究关注的是英语语音［13—19，6，20］。在此项研究中，我们选择了汉语普通话，因为汉语普通话与英语在声学、语音、音系和语言等方面有很大不同。此外，普通话是一种声调语言，听者除了使用音段音位信息，还需要利用声调信息来辨别单词的词汇信息，而英语是一种非声调语言，只需要音段音位信息即可获得单词的词汇信息。不管是声调语言还是非声调语言，如果F2增强能被证实在不同语言的语音感知上都是有益的，那么这种增强算法的开发和实现就有可能对全球数百万不同语言背景的听力损失患者产生积极影响。为了评估F2增强是否对汉语普通话语音感知产生影响，利用不同的语音型噪音，即二人语音噪音和六人语音噪音，测试听力正常以及听力损失的两组汉语普通话说话者，对未被增强以及F2增强过的句子进行识别。此外，此项研究还会探讨F2增强的效果是否与听者的听力阈值有关。

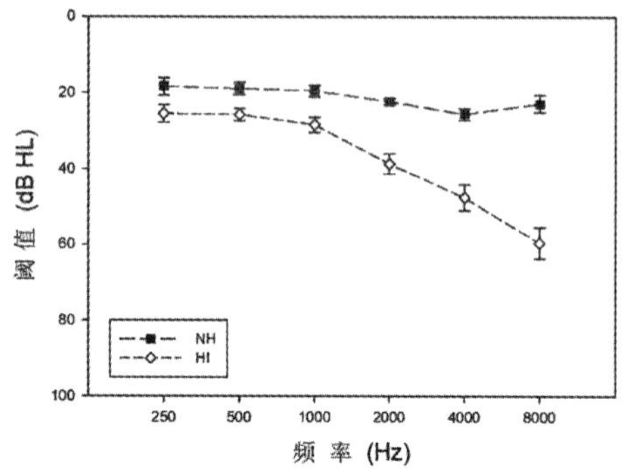

图1 听力正常组（NH）和听力损失组（HI）的平均听力图

2. 研究方法

2.1 实验参与者

在上海交通大学招募了30位汉语普通话母语者。听力正常（Normal Hearing，NH）的听者在250—4000Hz之间纯音的听力阈值≤25dB HL，在8000Hz时的纯音阈值≤35dB HL。另一组听力损失（Hearing Impairment，HI）患者有着轻度到中度重度不等的听力损失，但听损在250—4000Hz范围内不会超过65dB HL。具体来说，听力正常有9名听者（1名男性，8名女性），平均年龄为60.9岁（标准差=2.5岁）。另一组听力损失组有21名感音神经性听力损失的听者（8名男性，13名女性），平均年龄为63.3岁（标准差=4.2岁）。此实验为单耳测试，通常选择被试的右耳作为目标耳朵，而仅当被试右耳有传导性听损或是右耳有手术史时才会选择左耳作为目标耳。图1中为两组被试的平均听力图。

所有被试参与了背景问卷调查。结果显示听力损失组的被试其听损主要是由于衰老和/或噪音暴露而导致的。所有参与者都没有助听器佩戴经验。本研究所有程序均由美国得克萨斯大学奥斯汀的机构审查委员会批准通过的。

2.2 实验材料

本研究的目标语音是CRM语料库的句子，其格式为“准备好［呼号］去［颜色］［数字］”。CRM是Moore针对军事环境开发的一种言语清晰度测试［21］。CRM语句有三个关键词：呼号、颜色和数字。在此项研究中，中文版本的CRM测试是由中文母语者的一名男性录制的。具体来说，四个呼号分别是张军、李婷、王莉、赵华。颜色为蓝色、红色、绿色、黄色。为了匹配英语版本的CRM测试，使用的数字为1—8，但同样排除了数字7，是因为英文数字7是双音节结构，而其他的英语数字，都是单音节结构。因此，本实验使用的中文版本CRM测试一共有四个呼号、四个颜色和七个数字，总共112种组合。

CRM语料库的句子用作基础的目标语音刺激，未被共振峰增强。而另一组目标语音刺激则是F2增强过9dB后的句子。图2显示了元音/i/的频谱在F2增强前后的差异。

首先，在MATLAB程序中为每个句子创建三维语谱图（振幅×时间×频率），采样率为44，100Hz，窗口为10毫秒，所有短窗口之间有50%的重叠。其次，在频谱图的每个时间帧，根据F1、F2的范围确定F1、F2和F3的能量峰值（peaks：P1，P2，P3）以及谷值（valleys：V1，V2，V3），一般来说，F2为800—2500Hz。再次，一旦找到F2，F2的峰值会被放大9dB，F2峰值周围区域在每个时间帧也会被成比例地增加。如果没有找到F2峰值（例如句子中的辅音部分），则不会实施F2增强的处理。最后均通过使用

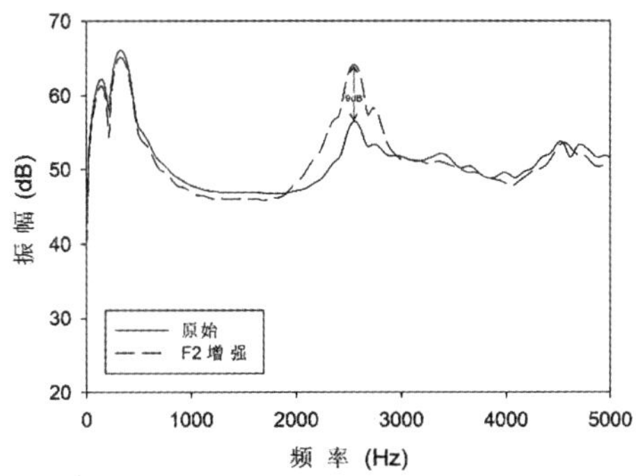

图2 元音/i/未被增强的频谱（实线）以及F2增强了9dB的频谱（虚线）

FFT的逆过程，分别生成无增强的以及/或F2增强过9dB的两组不同的句子，作为目标语音刺激。本实验对背景噪音不做共振峰增强处理，仅对目标句子进行F2增强。两种背景噪音，其中二人语音噪音是一男一女分别录音并混合；六人语音噪音是由三男三女分别录音并混合而成。语音型噪音中每个改成说话人或者发音人，因为谈话人感觉是两个人谈话的录音，录制时是阅读一本中文儿童书中的一段内容，具体内容选自《新儿童百科全书》[22]，每个录音者所录制的录音材料的均方根音量水平一致。

2.3 刺激呈现

CRM目标句子叠加在一个持续4秒的背景噪音的中间播放，该背景噪音是从30秒长的语音型噪音随机截取其中的4秒。噪音音量控制在70dB SPL。

目标句子和背景噪音通过索尼MDR7506耳机呈现给听众的测试耳。所有数据在上海交通大学心理语言实验室的一个安静的测试室中收集。刺激呈现是由TDT移动处理器（RM1）控制的。目标句子以及背景噪音的音量在使用线性权重的Larson-Davis声级计（型号2800）和AEC201－A IEC 60318－1耳模拟器中进行过测量和校准。

2.4 实验程序

被试坐在液晶显示器的前面，液晶显示器以文本框的形式显示28种选项（4种颜色×7个数字），分别对应于每个颜色数字组合。通过4种颜色（行）×7个数字（列）的布局显示28个选项。每次测试要求被试在刺激呈现后尽快单击鼠标，选择认为听到的选项。

本实验是使用自适应上下跟踪程序，基于三种自适应程序获得语音识别的阈值：分别是一下二上（one-down，two-up），一下一上（one-down，one-up），二下一上（two-down，one-up）。三种自适应程序分别对应于在29.3%、50%和70.7%正确率下的阈值[23]，能代表三个不同的难度级别（难度级别Ⅰ：正确率为29.3%时需要的信噪比作为阈值，最高难度级别；难度级别Ⅱ：正确率为50%时需要的信噪比作为阈值，中等难度级别；难度级别Ⅲ：正确率为70.7%时需要的信噪比作为阈值，最低难度级别），基本涵盖了整个动态范围。每个难度级别下的阈值都是单独获得的。噪音水平始终固定在70dB SPL，而目标句子的呈现音量水平则根据被试的反应进行自适应更改。对于每一次测试，目标句子首先从80dB SPL开始播放，经过前三个反向以5dB为步长，然后调整为更小的步长，即1dB进行调整。阈值的计算为最后的偶数反转的平均值，且不包括前三个反转的值。每种条件下的阈值要重复两次测试。如果前两个测试所得的阈值相差超过3dB，则需要额外一次测试。总体而言，针对每个被试，随机分配12种实验条件（3个难度级别×2种背景噪音×2种目标句子）。所有程序均由软件Sykofizx©实施。

3. 结果

3.1 有、无F2增强下的噪音背景中的语音感知

9名平均年龄为60.9岁的正常听力组和22名平均年龄为63.3岁的听力损失组在不同噪音、不同难度级别下的阈值，如图3所示。

对语音识别阈值进行的四因素（被试间因素：不同听力组；被试内因素：难度

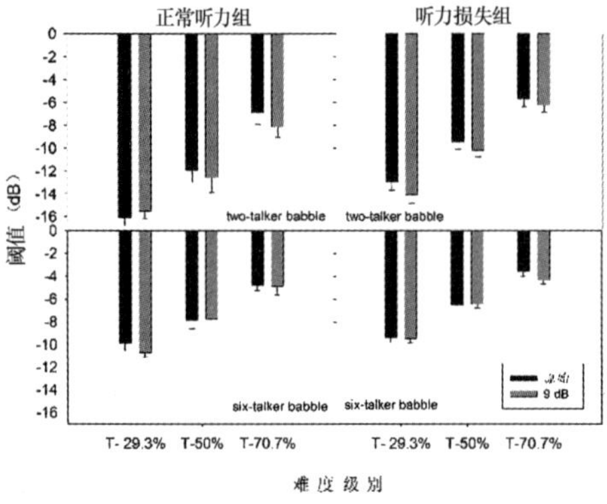

图3　在不同难度级别下，正常听力组和听力损失组在二人和六人语音噪音下有、无F2增强的语音识别阈值

级别×噪音类型×是否F2增强）方差分析（ANOVA）结果表明，阈值会受到难度级别（$F_{2,56}=334.68$，$p<0.05$，$\eta_p^2=0.923$）、噪音类型（$F_{1,28}=140.70$，$p<0.05$，$\eta_p^2=0.834$）以及F2增强（$F_{1,28}=8.558$，$p<0.05$，$\eta_p^2=0.234$）的显著影响。在六个两因素交互作用中，只有一个是显著的：难度级别×噪音类型（$F_{2,56}=12.51$，$p<0.05$，$\eta_p^2=0.309$）。所有四个三因素交互作用都不显著（所有$p>0.05$）。但是，四因素交互作用（难度级别×噪音类型×F2增强×不同听力组）是显著的（$F_{2,56}=5.05$，$p<0.05$，$\eta_p^2=0.153$）。

由于两种类型的噪音在多因素交互作用下效果显著，因此分别对二人语音噪音以及六人语音噪音单独进行分析。在二人语音噪音中，三因素（被试间因素：不同听力组；被试内因素：难度级别×是否F2增强）重复测量方差分析（以阈值作为因变量）结果表明，二人语音噪音的阈值受难度级别（$F_{2,56}=171.763$，$p<0.05$，$\eta_p^2=0.860$）、F2增强（$F_{1,28}=7.702$，$p<0.05$，$\eta_p^2=0.216$）显著影响，并且不同听力组的组间效应边缘显著（$F_{1,28}=4.122$，$p=0.052$，$\eta_p^2=0.128$）。其他的二因素或三因素交互作用均不显著（所有$p>0.05$）。在二人语音噪音中，相比较于原始语音，F2增强后的语音识别阈值显著提高了0.5dB。另外，在二人语音噪音中，听力正常组的阈值比听力损失组低2.3dB，且组间差异是边缘显著的。

在六人语音噪音中，三因素方差分析结果显示难度级别的主效应是所有结果中唯一显著的（$F_{2,56}=195.589$，$p<0.05$，$\eta_p^2=0.875$），其他主效应或是多因素的相互作用均不显著（所有$p>0.05$）。

总之，在不同的聆听条件下，汉语母语者的语音识别阈值与先前英语母语者的研究结果［20］表现出相似的模式。在大多数情况下，二人语音噪音下的语音识别阈值显著低于六人语音噪音下的阈值。值得注意的是，不管听力正常组还是听力损失组，在二人语音噪音下，F2增强后语音识别阈值得到显著改善。但在六人语音噪音下，语音识别阈值在F2增强前后无明显变化。此外，在二人语音噪音下，听力正常组的语音识别阈值比听力损失组的阈值低，且是边缘显著的。

3.2　F2增强带来的益处

F2增强带来的益处，可以通过从F2增强后的语音识别阈值减去F2增强前阈值而计算出来。以F2增强的益处作为因变量，进行三因素方差分析（被试间因素：不同听力组；被试内因素：难度级别×噪音类型）。

结果显示难度级别、噪音类型和不同听力组之间有显著的交互作用（$F_{2,56}=5.046$，$p<0.05$，$\eta_p^2=0.133$），而其他三因素或二因素交互作用中均不显著（所有$p>0.05$）。为了进一步测量不同听力组在不同情况下的简单主效应，首先，在两个难度级别上使用Bonferroni调整后的临界值对两个因素（被试间因素：不同听力组；被试内因素：噪音类型）进行方差分析。进一步的分析表明，在难度级别Ⅰ上，在二人语音噪音中，听力损失组从F2增强获得的收益（D=1.2dB）比正常听力组（D=－0.6dB）多达1.8dB（见图4）。在六人语音噪音中，没有发现不同听力组的组间差异或是任何交互作用是显著的（所有$p>0.05$）。在难度级别Ⅱ上，结果表明，相比较于六人语音噪音，在二人语音噪音下的 F2 增强带来的收益更多。另外，在难度级别Ⅲ上，没有观察到任何显著的交互作用（所有 $p > 0.05$）。

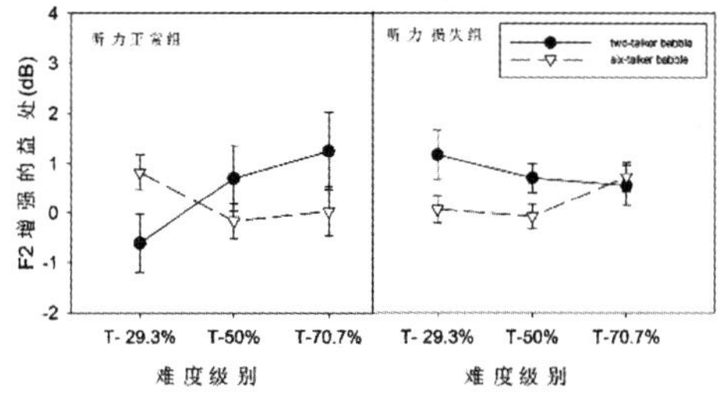

图 4　听力正常组、听力损失组在两种不同的噪音类型以及不同难度级别的条件下 F2 增强带来的益处

总而言之，在某些难度级别上，不论是否听力损失，两组人在二人语音噪音获得 F2 增强带来的益处显著高于在六人语音噪音中的成绩。

3.3　年龄、听阈与 F2 增强前后的语音感知的相关

为了探索听者的背景影响因素，例如年龄和听力损失，如何影响 F2 增强前后的语音识别阈值，以及听者从 F2 增强中获得的益处，对两组人的相关测试结果与背景影响因素分别进行了相关分析。结果表明，在所有聆听条件下，无论是对于正常听力还是听力损失的汉语母语者，均未发现年龄与语音识别阈值或增强效果有显著的相关（所有 $p > 0.05$）。另外，安静环境下的听力阈值与语音识别阈值或增强效果也无任何显著的相关（所有 $p > 0.05$）。这表明年龄或者听力阈值都不是能否获得 F2 增强带来的益处的有效预测指标。

4. 讨论

这项研究调查了有、无 F2 增强下老年听者在噪音中的语音识别，以及探讨了针对汉语母语者的年龄、听力阈值对 F2 增强前后的语音感知的相关关系。

4.1　正常听力以及听力损失的老年听者的语音感知

关于噪声掩蔽对语音识别阈值的影响，本研究结果表明，汉语普通话说话者在二人语音噪音的阈值明显低于六人语音噪音下的阈值。这与之前的研究结果一致。Van Engen 等［24］发现，无论说话者的母语是哪种语言，六人语音噪音下的成绩比二人语音噪音下的句子识别成绩差。Simpson 和 Cooke［25］也发现，六人语音噪音下的辅音得分低于二人语音噪音下的得分。作为语音型噪音，与六人语音噪音相比较，二人语音噪音中包含更多的时间变化和调幅线索。但是二人语音噪音的言语信息比六人语音噪音的言语信息更容易被听到，从而可能导致更高的信息掩蔽（informational masking）。信息掩蔽给语音识别带来更多消极的干扰，但二人语音噪音有更多的调幅，例如在时域上更多、更深的凹陷（temporal tips），从而获得更多的掩蔽释放（masking release），从而获得更低的语音识别的阈值。因此，多人谈话背景语音型噪音下（multi-talker babble）的语音识别成绩的高低取决于信息掩蔽和时域上获得掩蔽释放的混合结果。

听者的听力状态也有可能会影响语音识别阈值。在本研究中，与听力正常的老年听者相比，听力损失的老年人在所有难度级别上，二人语音噪音下的语音识别阈值大约差 2.3dB。但是，在六人语音噪音成绩上，两组没有发现显著的组间差异。此外，相关性结果显示年龄或听力阈值与语音识别阈值无显著相关，这与之前的一些研究发现是一致的。Fogerty 和同事［26］报告说，当将句子用作目标语音时，年龄和听力阈值均与噪声下的语音感知能力无显著相关。也就是说，在安静状态下测量的听力阈值并不是噪声中语音识别能力强有力的预测指标［27］。

4.2　针对老年人的共振峰增强

本研究与之前英语说话者的研究［20］都表明了，不论听者的母语背景是英语还是中文，第二共振峰增强技术让年

纪较大的听者在二人语音噪音下提高了语音识别成绩，更好地克服了噪音带来的消极影响。然而，与正常听力的同龄人相比，听力损失的老龄患者可能更难以利用 temporal tips 来获得更多的噪声掩蔽释放，从而获得较低的语音识别阈值［28］。

另外，噪音掩蔽取决于多个因素，例如目标语音与背景噪音之间的相似性、听者对刺激的熟悉程度（例如，母语或非母语）、刺激的不确定性等。先前的研究表明，老年人和年轻人在噪音中语音感知过程受到信息掩蔽的影响差不多［29—30］，而在一些研究中发现两组明显的差异［31—32］。F2 增强对二人语音噪音下听力正常组以及听力损失组的老年听者的益处，可能与 F2 增强后二人语音噪音有更多可听见的语音信息有关。F2 增强以降低信息掩蔽或是使得时域上获得更多掩蔽释放对于提高语音感知的机制，还需要进一步研究。

4.3 共振峰增强以及其他语音增强技术

在本研究中，F2 增强只针对目标语音，并不是在目标语音和噪音混合之后再进行 F2 增强。与其他语音增强技术研究相比，本研究中的 F2 增强技术有以下优点和局限性。

首先，F2 增强显著地提高了老年人的语音识别阈值特别是在二人语音噪音中（D≈1—1.5dB）。先前一些报告指出语音增强技术可能会让成绩更差并引入意外的信号失真［33］，相比之下，F2 增强被证实还是可靠的。其他一些研究同时在目标语音和背景噪音上同时应用了频谱增强技术，无明显改善或少量成绩提升（3%—5%）也符合预期［13—15］。除了频谱增强外，往往需要结合一些额外的改进，比如适度频率压缩［15］；降噪或高频放大［17］，语音增强效果才能得到些改善。因此，没有依靠额外的技术帮助，本研究仅仅增强了 F2，老年听者的语音识别阈值有了显著改善，似乎是很有可行性的一种技术方法。

其次，本研究中的 F2 增强算法同时检测了频谱的峰值以及频谱的谷值。这样不仅仅针对目标语音的峰值，还加大了峰值和谷值之间的频谱对比，从而为听力损失的患者恢复了更清晰的频谱对比表征。在信噪比较低的聆听环境下，F2 增强让听者获得更多可听见信息。关于目标语音加背景噪音的 F2 增强效果需要进一步的研究。

F2 增强技术有一些局限性。首先，仅目标语音被增强而没有对背景噪音处理。其次，F2 增强的效果有个体差异。能否进行更大的 F2 增强（例如≥ 9dB）而不会导致任何信号的失真，需要进一步研究。为了最大化共振峰增强的效果，在未来的研究中可以考虑针对 F2 和其他高频共振峰（例如 F3）的增强。再次，只对 F2 进行增强，可能不会对句子中的辅音部分（比如摩擦音）进行任何的增强。不确定句子的哪一部分，元音、辅音还是音素之间的共振峰过渡，从 F2 增强中获得更多益处。Franck 等人观察到元音感知分数会随频谱增强而提高，但是辅音感知分数随频谱增强反而下降［16］。在本研究中，F2 增强可能主要作用于元音以及共振峰过渡的部分，而不是辅音部分。因此，需要对诸如元音、辅音和音节等刺激进行更广泛的研究，以评估 F2 增强在不同水平上的有效性。

尽管中文是一种声调语言，而英语是一种非声调语言，本研究和之前的研究［20］均证实 F2 增强能够帮助老年人在二人语音噪音下的语音感知。另外，听力阈值并不是独立预估听者在噪音中的语音识别能力的有效指标。在二人语音噪音中，听者在 F2 增强下的语音感知改善可能是由于动态噪音中有更多的掩蔽释放。共振峰的增强技术仍要进一步的研究，适用于更多听觉场景。

参考文献

[1] Dubno, J. R., Dirks, D. D., Morgan, D. E. 1984. Effects of age and mild hearing loss and age on speech recognition in noise. *The Journal of the Acoustical Society of America* 76, 87－96.

[2] Humes, L. E. 2002. Factors underlying the speech-recognition performance of elderly hearing-aid

wearers. *The Journal of the Acoustical Society of America* 112, 1112 – 1132.

[3] Phatak, S., Allen, J. B. 2007. Consonant and vowel confusions in speech weighted noise. *The Journal of the Acoustical Society of America* 121, 2312 – 2326.

[4] Plomp, R., Mimpen, A. M. 1979. Speech reception threshold for sentences as a function of age and noise level. *The Journal of the Acoustical Society of America* 66, 1333 – 1342.

[5] Liu, C., Kewley-Port, D. 2007. Factors affecting vowel formant discrimination for hearing-impaired listeners. *The Journal of the Acoustical Society of America* 122, 2855 – 2864.

[6] Woodall, A., Liu, C. 2013. Effects of signal level and spectral contrast on vowel formant discrimination for normal-hearing and hearing-impaired listeners. *The American Journal of Audiology* 22, 94 – 104.

[7] Leek, M. R., Dorman, M. F., Summerfield, Q. 1987. Minimum spectral contrast for vowel identification by normal-hearing and hearing-impaired listeners. *The Journal of the Acoustical Society of America* 81(1), 148 – 154.

[8] Peterson, G. E., Barney, H. L., 1952. Control methods used in a study of the vowels. *The Journal of the Acoustical Society of America* 24(2), 175 – 184.

[9] Coughlin, M., Kewley-Port, D., Humes, L. E. 1998. The relation between identification and discrimination of vowels in young and elderly listeners. *The Journal of the Acoustical Society of America* 104, 3597 – 3607.

[10] Parikh, G., Loizou, P. 2005. The influence of noise on vowel and consonant cues. *The Journal of the Acoustical Society of America* 118, 3874 – 3888.

[11] Klein, A., Mills, J., Adkins, W. 1990. Upward spread of masking, hearing loss, and speech recognition in young and elderly listeners. *The Journal of the Acoustical Society of America* 87 (3), 1266 – 1271.

[12] Summerfield, Q., Foster, J., Tyler, R. 1985. Influences of formant bandwidth and auditory frequency selectivity on identification of place of articulation in stop consonants. *Speech Communication* 4, 213 – 229.

[13] Bunnell, H. T. 1990. On enhancement of spectral contrast in speech for hearing-impaired listeners. *The Journal of the Acoustical Society of America* 88(6), 2546 – 2556.

[14] Stone, M. A., Moore, B. C. J. 1992. Spectral feature enhancement for people with sensorineural hearing impairment: effects on speech intelligibility and quality. *Journal of Rehabilitation Research and Development* 29(2), 39 – 56.

[15] Baer, T., Moore, B. C. J., Gatehouse, S. 1993. Spectral contrast enhancement of speech in noise for listeners with sensorineural hearing impairment: effects on intelligibility, quality and response times. *Journal of Rehabilitation Research and Development* 30(1), 49 – 72.

[16] Franck, B. A. M., Van Kreveld-Bos, C. S. G. M., Dreschler, W. A., Verschuure, H. 1999. Evaluation of spectral enhancement in hearing aids, combined with phonemic compression. *The Journal of the Acoustical Society of America* 106 (3), 1452 – 1464.

[17] Lyzenga, J., Festen, J. M., Houtgast, T. 2002. A speech enhancement scheme incorporating spectral expansion evaluated with simulated loss of frequency selectivity. *The Journal of the Acoustical Society of America* 112(3), 1145 – 1157.

[18] Yang, J., Luo, F – L., Nehorai, A. 2002. Spectral contrast enhancement: Algorithms and comparisons. *Speech Communication* 39, 33 – 46.

[19] Chen, J., Baer, T., Moore, B. C. 2012. Effect of enhancement of spectral changes on speech intelligibility and clarity preferences for the hearing impaired. *The Journal of the Acoustical Society of America* 131(4), 2987 – 2998.

[20] Guan, J., & Liu, C. 2019. Speech perception in noise with formant enhancement for older listeners. *Journal of Speech, Language, and Hearing Research* 62(9), 3290 – 3301.

[21] Moore, T. 1981. Voice communication jamming research, in AGARD Conference *Proc.* 331: *Aural Communication in Aviation* Neuilly-Sur-Seine, France, pp. 2: 1 – 2: 6.

[22] Lock, D. 2009. *The New Children's Encyclopedia*. New York: DK Publishing, Inc, 8 – 78.

[23] Levitt, H. 1971. Transformed up-down methods in psychoacoustics. *The Journal of the Acoustical Society of America* 49, 467 – 477.

[24] Van Engen, K. J., Bradlow, A. R. 2007. Sentence recognition in native- and foreign-language multi-talker background noise. *The Journal of the Acoustical Society of America* 121(1), 519 – 526.

[25] Simpson, S. A., Cooke, M. 2005. Consonant identification in N-talker babble is a nonmonotonic function of N(L). *The Journal of the Acoustical*

Society of America 118(5), 2775 – 2778.
[26] Fogerty, D., Kewley-Port, D., Humes, L. E. 2012. The relative importance of consonant and vowel segments to the recognition of words and sentences: Effects of age and hearing loss. *The Journal of the Acoustical Society of America* 132, 1667 – 1678.
[27] Vermiglio, A. J., Soli, S. D., Freed, D. J., Fisher, L. M. 2012. The relationship between high-frequency pure-tone hearing loss, hearing in noise test (HINT) thresholds, and the articulation index. *Journal of the American Academy of Audiology* 23(10), 779 – 788.
[28] Moore, B. C., Peters, R. W., Stone, M. A. 1999. Benefits of linear amplification and multichannel compression for speech comprehension in backgrounds with spectral and temporal dips. *The Journal of the Acoustical Society of America* 105 (1), 400 – 411.
[29] Agus, T. R., Akeroyd, M. A., Gatehouse, S., Warden, D. 2009. Informational masking in young and elderly listeners for speech masked by simultaneous speech and noise. *The Journal of the Acoustical Society of America* 126(4), 1926 – 1940.
[30] Helfer, K. S., Freyman, R. L. 2005. The role of visual speech cues in reducing energetic and informational masking. *The Journal of the Acoustical Society of America* 117(2), 842 – 849.
[31] Marrone, N., Mason, C. R., Kidd, G., Jr. 2008. The effects of hearing loss and age on the benefit of spatial separation between multiple talkers in reverberant rooms. *The Journal of the Acoustical Society of America* 124(5), 3064 – 3075.
[32] Alexander, J. M., Lutfi, R. A. 2004. Informational masking in hearing-impaired and normal-hearing listeners: Sensation level and decision weights. *The Journal of the Acoustical Society of America* 116(4), 2234 – 2247.
[33] Boers, P. M. 1980. Formant enhancement of speech for listeners with sensorineural hearing loss. *IPO Annual Progress Report* 15, 21 – 28.

管晶晶 美国得克萨斯大学言语语言听力系博士毕业，主要研究领域为助听设备的功能、听觉健康。
E-mail：psygjj@ 163. com

刘 畅 美国得克萨斯大学言语语言听力系副教授，博士，研究兴趣包括言语感知和发音、特殊群体的听觉感知。
E-mail：changliu@ utexas. edu

口罩对语音产出及感知的影响

王非凡

摘　要　本文主要回顾了关于口罩影响语音产出与感知的研究文献。从产出角度看，口罩主要充当了低通滤波器的角色，使语音高频段的能量有所衰减，同时也将部分能量转向两边侧面。产出研究目前尚未形成一个标准化的测量及报告程序。从感知角度看，相关研究主要关心口罩如何影响语音可懂度，但结论不尽相同。本文认为这主要是测试方法的不一致所导致的，并从测试材料、背景噪音、被试选择等几方面详细分析了现有研究的方法问题。后续研究应更关注听障群体在口罩环境下的语音感知问题。

关键词　口罩，语音，产出，感知

Communications in the Pandemic Era: A Review on How Face Masks Affect Speech Production and Perception

WANG Feifan

Abstract Face masks have been widely used during the Covid – 19 pandemic. This paper is a review on how face masks affect speech production and perception. From the perspective of speech production, face masks are considered not only as a low-pass filter which might attenuate energy of high frequency (probably above 2000 Hz), but also deflecting sound energy to both sides of the face. So far there has not been a standard procedure of measurement and report on speech production influenced by face masks. From the viewpoint of speech perception, most studies focus on whether (and how) speech intelligibility is affected by face masks, but the results are different. The methods of these studies are critically reviewed and discussed in this paper in terms of speech stimuli, background noise, and selection of subjects, all of which might lead to some biases. It is suggested by this review that further research should focus more on the communication problems of the hearing-impaired group.

Key words Face masks, Speech, Production, Perception

1. 引言

近一年来，新型冠状病毒肺炎（以下简称新冠肺炎）疫情肆虐全球，对全世界人民的生活产生重要影响。作为应对疫情的一项有效防护措施，世界卫生组织在其临时指导意见中强调了佩戴口罩的重要性，但同时也指出了口罩使用的潜在伤害（potential harms）：给清晰交流带来困难，尤其对聋人、听力障碍人士及需要依靠读唇（lipreading）的群体影响甚大［20］。

Chodosh 等［6］用“毁灭性”（devastating）一词来形容口罩对听障人士的影响。他们指出，即便是在没有疫情的时期，一般听障人士的交流就已经非常不便。在戴口罩的情况下，不管是唇部运动还是面部表情都被遮蔽，而这些都是听障人士相对比较重要的感知交流线索。英国的两位聋人医师［9］也指出，他们在世界范围内仅找到一家生产及销售透明防护口罩的厂商。对于像他们这种很大程度上依赖读唇的人士来说，一般不透明防护口罩造成了极大的交流障碍，进而同时影响并损伤了医患双方的权益。对听障人士而言，这种交流上的障碍更容易进一步引发心理层面上的孤独、孤立感，从而导致一些心理问题。

考虑到上述口罩与言语交流之间的密切关系，许多研究开始重视口罩如何影响人们语音的产出与感知，涉及人群不单只是正常听力人士，也涵盖相关听力障碍群体。本文尝试对相关的研究文献进行整理、概括与批评，就现有文献的一些研究结果，讨论"口罩如何影响语音的产出及感知"这个核心问题，并从方法论的角度探讨相关实验设计的优点及问题。

2. 口罩对语音产出的影响

按照语音产出相对经典的"声源—滤波器"模型理论（Source – filter Model），由声带振动产生的声音必须经过整个声门上共振腔体的过滤及修饰。从这个角度出发，基本不难得出这样的预设：口罩作为覆盖在口鼻腔体外面的遮蔽物，实际上参与了"滤波"这一进程。从现有研究来看，Goldlin 等［8］和 Wolfe 等［19］都支持这一预设，并且认为口罩实际上扮演了低通滤波器（low – pass filter）的角色。

Wolfe 等［19］比较了标准的一次性外科口罩（disposable surgical mask）、N95 口罩、布质口罩（cloth mask）及塑料防护面罩（plastic face shield）。他们发现，相较于不戴口罩的情况，标准的一次性外科口罩基本不会造成声音的衰减（attenuation）。N95 口罩及布质口罩能导致 4000—8000 赫兹（Hz）频率范围内的声音能量衰减 2—3 个分贝（dB）。塑料防护面罩则可以使 4000—8000 赫兹频率范围内的声音衰减 3—6 个分贝。

Goldlin 等［8］则是利用人造的头身模拟器（head and torso simulator）发出白噪音（white noise），在距离声源大致 2 米处的位置进行录音。结果表明，在 2000—7000 赫兹的高频段，普通口罩可以导致 3—4 分贝的声音能量衰减，N95 防护口罩则能够造成平均约 12 分贝的声音能量衰减。

为什么要重视不同频带（frequency bands）能量的衰减？主要是因为我们日常交流所产出的语音有着丰富的频率，不同频带上的声音对语音可懂度（speech intelligence）及语音识别（speech recognition）都有着不同的相对贡献（relative contribution），这种相对重要程度的大小可以用频率重要性函数（Frequency Importance Function，FIF）进行量化。比如，图 1 中所展示的是汉语普通话及英语的频率重要性函数（引自［5］，部分翻译为中文）。可以看到，汉语普通话中一个显著的高峰基本落在中心频率 1000—3000 赫兹的频带。在这个范围内的能量衰减，无疑会在很大程度上影响汉语语音产出的清晰可懂度。上述两篇文章中，口罩对语音产出的影响频段最低是 2000 赫兹，Bottalico 等［3］的产出实验结果也支持这一结论。另有 Corey 等［7］的结果表明，口罩对语音产出的影响在 1000 赫兹处就已经开始显现。这无疑会在一定程度上影响语音的清晰可懂度，进而在：（1）听障人群交流；（2）人机对话及智能语音服务等层面产生实际的影响。

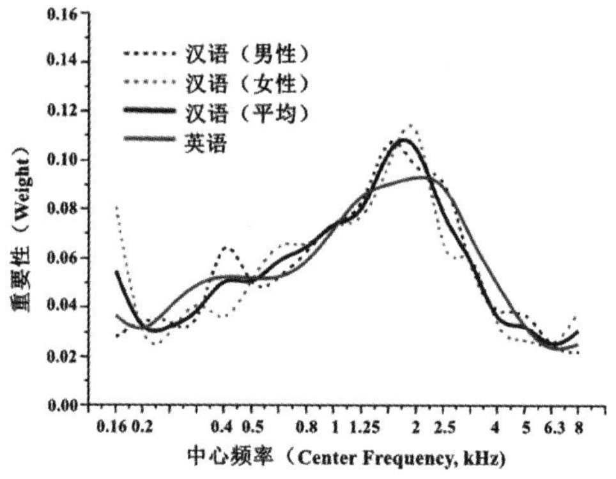

图 1　汉语普通话的频率重要性函数［5］

另一个佐证来自 Palmiero 等［15］关于语音传输指数（Speech Transmission Index，STI）的分析。相较于听者主观感受测试，语音传输指数被认为是一个相对客观的量化指标，能够较好地反映语音可懂度。文章在粉噪音条件下（pink noise，52.5—72.5dBA）比较了两款外科口罩及两款 N95 口罩的语音传输指数。结果发现，相较于不戴口罩的情况，外科口罩大致会影响 3%—4% 的语音传输指数，而 N95 甚至能有 13%—17% 的影响。

Corey 等［7］比较详细地探讨了不同

口罩（医用外科口罩、N95及KN95口罩、不同材质的布口罩、透明口罩及防护面罩）在不同方向上的声衰减（acoustic attenuation）情况。文章有几个比较重要的发现：(1) 研究所选取的两款透明口罩与一款透明防护面罩在高频段的声衰减情况尤其明显。尽管这样的透明口罩与面罩保留了许多必要且有用的视觉辅助信息，但也导致了更多高频段的声衰减。(2) 从方向性上来说，口鼻部前端方向的声衰减是最为显著的，但面部两侧及身后方向的声衰减则相对弱一些（透明防护面罩甚至放大了说话者背后方向的声音能量）。从这个角度上说，单纯把口罩视作低通滤波器可能还不够全面，口罩同时将部分声音能量转向侧面。因此，将麦克风置于侧面位置可能更有利于扩音（sound reinforcement）效果。

从产出的角度来看，目前相关的文献主要集中讨论不同类型的口罩对语音产出的影响，重点探讨口罩影响下语音在不同频段上能量的衰减情况。初步的共识是：不管哪种类型的口罩，都会影响语音的产出，尤其影响高频段的能量。此类研究中，大部分都选取了不止一种类型的口罩，并重点比较了不同类型、材质及款式的口罩对语音产出的影响，提供了相当的基础数据。部分研究（如［7］）也考虑到了麦克风类型、声场方向性等问题，为后续相关应用研究提供了很好的参考。

3. 口罩对语音感知的影响

在讨论口罩对语音感知的影响这一问题时，大部分研究都把重点放在语音可懂度上，主要探讨口罩是否影响，或者说在多大程度上影响人们自然交流过程中对语音的感知与听辨。本文主要选取了八篇相关文献，将其主要信息进行整理总结，见表1。

表1　口罩与语音感知相关研究文献的主要信息整理

文献	测试材料/量表	背景噪音	口罩类型	被试	结果
［1］	◇一位成年男性发音人录制的连贯语音测试（Connected Speech Test，CST）表中部分内容 ◇5种组合：口罩（无/透明）×呈现方式（纯音频/［音频＋视频］）＋纸口罩纯音频	多人人声噪音（＋10dB SNR）	透明口罩（1款） 纸制口罩（1款）	共30位被试，按纯音测试听阈水平分为： 1. 正常对照组（25dB，10人） 2. 中度听障组（41—70dB，10人） 3. 重度听障组（＞71dB，10人）	对正常对照组及中度听障组被试来说，佩戴口罩所产出的语音并未显著影响他们感知语音的清晰可懂度。重度听障组被试则更能明显获益于透明口罩所额外提供的视觉线索
［2］	一名男性发音人分别在有无个人防护设备（Personal Protective Equipment，PPE）情况下录制的： ◇扬扬格词表（spondee words，50个词），用于计算言语接受阈（speech reception threshold）参数 ◇单音节词表，用于计算被试的语音区分度得分（speech discrimination score）	无	个人防护设备：N95口罩＋防护面罩	20名正常听力医务人员（Healthcare Workers，HCWs）	个人防护设备对语音听辨有显著影响，主要体现在：1）显著提高了听者的言语接受阈值；2）显著降低了听者的语音区分度得分

续表

文献	测试材料/量表	背景噪音	口罩类型	被试	结果
[3]	◇头身模拟器所发出的英语单音节词表部分内容（单音节格式为辅音+音节核+辅音：Consonant-Nucleus-Consonant，CNC） ◇口罩（3款口罩+无口罩）×2种室内声学条件［不同的混响时间（reverberation time）及双耳房间脉冲响应（Binaural Room Impulse Responses，BRIRs）］	人声噪音（+3dB SNR）	布口罩（1款） 外科口罩（1款） N95口罩（1款） 其他[a]	40名正常听力大学生	相较于没戴口罩的语音，不同类型口罩皆显著降低语音的清晰可懂度（约12%—16%），布口罩影响最大，外科口罩与N95口罩无显著差异。 房间的混响时间（建筑声学特性）也显著影响了戴口罩的语音清晰可懂度，以及被试的听音费力（listening effort）程度
[12]	◇40个目标词（包含13个音节首音位，12个音节尾音位，4个元音，互相组合） ◇口罩（3款口罩+无口罩）×呈现方式（纯语音/语音+视频）×发音人性别（男/女）=16种组合	无	外科口罩（1款） 其他[b]	13名正常听力人士	佩戴口罩（及其他面罩）情况下的语音基本只造成2%左右的错误听辨率。视觉信息（哪怕遮挡住面部）在言语感知中起到重要作用
[13]	◇5位发音人录制的构音障碍语音清晰度测试（Assessment of Intelligibility of Dysarthria Speech，ASSIDS），包括50个单词和22个句子	无	外科口罩（1款） N95口罩（1款） 布口罩（1款）	5名正常听力人士	不管是单词还是句子，其清晰可懂程度并未显著受到口罩影响，不同类型的口罩之间也并未表现出显著差异
[14]	◇一位成年男性发音人录制的连贯语音测试（Connected Speech Test，CST）表中部分内容 ◇口罩（有/无）×背景噪音（有/无）=4种组合	录制牙科电钻声，将45dB SPL以上的部分复制循环成一小时左右的噪声材料（+5dB SNR）	标准外科口罩	15名正常对照（纯音测试听阈不超过25dB HL）； 15名听障人士 ［距声源1米外］	不管是在安静还是噪声环境中，是否佩戴口罩并不显著影响相关语音的正确听辨，主要还是噪声更易影响语音的听辨
[17]	◇航空机长现场说出20个航空飞行专业术语 ◇口罩（7款口罩+无口罩）×背景噪音（有/无）=14种组合	直升机引擎噪音	外科口罩（1款） N95口罩（1款带有呼吸阀，5款封闭式）	1名机上护士 1名调度员 1名非航空从业人士（对照组） ［戴耳机］	飞机引擎未启动时，无论是否佩戴口罩或佩戴何种口罩，均不影响听辨。飞机引擎启动运行时，部分N95口罩更容易使非专业人士产生一定的听辨困难

续表

文献	测试材料/量表	背景噪音	口罩类型	被试	结果
[18]	◇1男1女两位专业播音人士所录制的噪声中语音感知测试（Speech Perception in Noise Test, SPIN）表中部分内容，被试被要求重复所听句子的最后一个词。 ◇没戴口罩/戴口罩/口罩+面罩	多人人声噪音（+4dB SNR）	外科口罩（1款）外科口罩+防护面罩（组合1款）	6名正常听力人士（纯音测试听阈不超过20dB）	没戴口罩的语音听辨正确率最高，戴口罩的语音听辨正确率次之，口罩叠加面罩的语音听辨正确率最低

注：a. 弹性半遮面式空气净化口罩（Elastomeric Half-mask Air-purifying Respirators，EAPR）；b. 尼卡卜（niqāb，一种伊斯兰式面纱，只露出双眼部分），巴拉克拉瓦头套（balaclava，一种遮蔽面部，仅露出一部分的头套）。

整体来看，这些文献都较注重实际应用，从疫情下的现实需求及问题出发，所考虑到的言语沟通环境包括医院［2，14］、学校［3］、飞机机舱［17］；对象既包括正常听力人士，也包括听力障碍群体，更有专门针对飞机机组服务人员、医务工作者的语音可懂度测试。

从语音可懂度测试的方法来看，所有文章都是在被试主观感知听辨结果的基础上进行分析。听辨材料大多是单词及句子，被试需要重复说出或写下任务要求的目标单词或句子，进而计算相应的正确率及语音可懂度。大多数研究也设置了各种各样的噪音环境，包括人声噪音、真实录制的环境噪音等。在对照比较方面，大部分研究均设置了基本的正常听力被试对照组，以及不戴口罩情况下的语音刺激材料，用以比照不同类型口罩对被试感知语音可懂度的影响。考虑到口罩对视觉信息的影响，部分研究也专门探讨了透明口罩及视觉线索所产生的影响［1，12，18］。

从结果来看，不同研究对口罩是否显著影响语音可懂度这个问题尚未达成一致见解。Bandaru等［2］发现，当说者佩戴个人防护设备（N95口罩加防护面罩）时，被试的言语接受阈值（speech reception threshold）显著提高，同时语音区分度得分（speech discrimination score）显著降低。Bottalico等［3］也发现，相较于没戴口罩的情况，不同类型口罩皆显著降低语音可懂度（12%—16%），尤其以布制口罩影响最大。Wittum等［18］也认为，没戴口罩的语音听辨正确率最高，戴口罩的语音听辨正确率次之，口罩叠加面罩的语音听辨正确率则最低。但是，也有一些研究并没有发现统计学意义上的显著影响［12，13，14］。我们认为，不同文章结论的不一致主要和他们采用的研究方法有关。如表1所示，这些研究在被试、材料、实验设计上相当多样，这些都可能影响最终的实验结果。关于研究方法的描述与批评，将在后文讨论部分进行更为细致的说明。

值得专门介绍的一点是，Llamas等［12］以一个相对“语言学”的手段，设计了包括13个音节首（onset）音位、12个音节尾（coda）音位、4个元音（vowel）组成的40个目标词，给13位正常听力被试进行感知听辨。从总体结果来看，在佩戴口罩的情况下所录制的这些语音材料基本上只导致了大约2%的错误听辨率。但是，文章同时给出了详细的错误类型（pp. 88，103），值得关注：

（1）塞音（stop）与（主要是同部位）擦音（fricative）的混淆，如/t/～/θ/；

（2）塞音不同发音部位（place of articulation）的混淆，如/t/～/p/；

（3）塞音清浊（voicing of stops）的混淆，如/k/～/g/；

（4）擦音不同发音部位的混淆，如/f/～/θ/；

（5）鼻音（nasal）不同发音部位的

混淆，如/n/～/ŋ/。

结合前文所介绍的产出数据，可以发现，这些错误类型并非完全随机。比如：不同部位擦音的一个重要区别是能量集中区域（concentration of energy）的频率范围，一般可用谱重心（Center of Gravity，COG）参数衡量。通常认为，唇齿及齿间部位的擦音本身能量就较弱，/θ/的谱重心常高达8000赫兹左右，而/f/则一般低于4000赫兹［11］。在口罩的高频能量衰减作用下，将/θ/误听为/f/是完全有可能的。又如：塞音在爆破（burst）时能量集中区域的频率也能作为一个重要的感知线索（perceptual cue）。一般认为，/t/爆破时能量集中区域的频率通常在4000赫兹以上，而/p/能量分布相对分散，低频区域能量总体要大于高频区［10］。一旦被口罩影响，高频能量衰减，就很容易把/t/误听为/p/。可见，文章所提及的这些具体的语音听辨错误，实际上和口罩对语音产出的影响息息相关。

4. 讨论

4.1 口罩和语音产出

如前文所述，关于口罩如何影响语音产出这个问题，研究结论较为一致，主要是强调口罩导致语音高频能量的衰减（比较普遍的结论是2000赫兹以上）。至于频率及能量衰减的具体数值，则主要取决于采样的设备及方法。从声源角度来看，不管是用真人还是头身模拟器，都是较为普遍的做法。从论文报告的规范要求角度，我们建议至少考虑并清楚说明如下一些信息：（1）录制环境，实验室相关声学规格参数，如混响时间（reverberation time）；（2）所用设备的规格参数，如话筒需说明指向（全指向、心型指向）、频响范围或特性；（3）声源及录制设备的位置（高度、角度、距离）。同时，建议多人（如果声源为真人）、多次重复测量，以确认信度（reliability）。

关于对口罩的认识方面，在一般的“低通滤波器”的基础上，前文也介绍了另一种更深入的看法，即还有将部分声音能量转向侧面（防护面罩则是放大背面能量）的作用。我们认为，共鸣腔的作用确实不仅仅是低通滤波，而是一组带通滤波，即某些频段的能量会被抑制（产生衰减），而某些频段的能量也有可能被增强（产生共振）。口罩不可能与口腔及面部完全紧贴，中间必然会留有一些空间，防护面罩则更甚。这样一来就会实际在口面部与口罩或面罩间多形成一个小的共鸣腔，这个小共鸣腔可能会对语音产出造成各种各样的影响，这是值得进一步研究的。

在“声源—滤波器”模型中，口罩一时之间或许难以影响声源。相关文献也证实，戴口罩之后并不影响嗓音质量相关分析，如基频与振幅的抖动微扰（jitter，shimmer），谐噪比（Harmonics-to-Noise Ratio，HNR）等［4］。但是也有最新文献表明，因工作需要及日常必要原因而一直佩戴口罩者，更容易在主观上显著感到用声费力（vocal effort），以及嗓音疲劳和不适（vocal fatigue and discomfort）［16］。这也是值得后续深入探究的一个非常实际的问题。

4.2 口罩和语音感知

围绕口罩如何影响语音感知这一问题，研究文献主要考察的是语音可懂度这一参数。具体到这一参数的量化，实际上可以发现，不同文献在实验方法设计上各有不同。以下将结合表1中整理概括的信息，分别就不同方面作详细讨论。

（1）测试材料/量表

不同研究所用的测试材料及量表有很大差异，目前比较常见的有：①连贯语音测试（Connected Speech Test，CST）；②扬扬格词表（Spondee Words）；③构音障碍语音清晰度测试（Assessment of Intelligibility of Dysarthria Speech，ASSIDS）；④噪声环境中语音感知测试（Speech Perception in Noise Test，SPIN）；⑤其他及自制量表。

现成量表的一个好处是，其信度与效度（validity）基本上已获认证，可以很大程度上避免一些因材料而导致的偏差（bias）。但是具体到每一个实验中，有时因实际需要或适配性问题，无法百分之百完成整套测试，又或者进行了修改。这个时候就容易导致一些作者自己未必能察觉到的偏差。

我们认为，其中一个最重要的偏差即是材料本身的语音音位分布。前文所述Llamas等［12］研究中发现某些特定语音音位（如不同部位擦音或塞音，以及部分塞擦音和鼻音）的感知听辨更容易受到口罩的影响。如果在测试词表中没有控制这些语音音位的分布，显而易见将影响最后的实验结果。因此，我们认为测试词表应当做到相对平衡的音位分布（balanced phonemic distribution），这里的平衡大致有两层含义：①控制音位的整体分布，避免在词表中某些音位出现过多或过少；②不追求绝对的“平等分布”，而是按照材料词表本身所属语言的实际情况，使材料中音位的分布大致符合该语言系统中音位的分布［3］。

另一个关于测试材料及量表的问题是熟悉程度及语境（context）问题。在词汇熟悉程度方面，比如Thomas等［17］在探究飞机机舱实际环境中戴口罩的影响时，所用测试材料为20个航空专业术语（aviation term）。被试中既有机组人员，又有非航空专业的对照组。显而易见，非航空专业被试对这些词汇相对陌生，很难排除这个因素对语音感知听辨结果的影响。因此，测试词汇的常用度及词频应该有一定的控制，即便在材料中可能因特定需要而包括不同词频及专业程度的词汇，也应该做到每位被试所接触的词汇分布大致相同。此外，有些量表中可能需要测试句子中的目标词汇，这时需要注意语境的影响。如Wittum等［18］在使用噪声环境中语音感知测试（Speech Perception in Noise Test，SPIN）量表时，就按目标词是否容易被句子语境预测（predictable）而分为“强语境”（high context）和“弱语境”（low context）两个水平。我们认为，这种考虑是严谨且必要的。

具体操作过程中，如果材料内容比较多，影响因素比较丰富，还应注意刺激呈现顺序的随机性，避免较为同质的材料大量连续呈现，从而导致一些可能的学习或疲劳效应（learning and fatigue effects），进而影响实验结果。

关于佩戴口罩情况下刺激材料的制作，Mendel等［14］一针见血地指出，目前最大的一个问题是缺乏一个已知的标准录制程序（no known standardized recordings of speech stimuli）。这实际上和口罩影响语音产出的研究关系重大，只有在产出研究中充分考察各种技术细节，才能为感知研究中刺激材料的制作提供更多的参考。

（2）背景噪音设计

我们考察的文献中，相当一部分研究都加入了背景噪音设计。我们认为，背景噪音设计有两个非常重要的作用：①在日常生活中，很少存在如语音实验室般理想的安静环境。考虑到口罩对语音感知听辨的影响是一个非常实际的问题，有必要加入背景噪音的设计，进而模拟贴近真实环境；②前文产出研究的许多基础数据表明，口罩尽管对语音高频能量有衰减作用，但强度大致也只有10dB左右（一般医用外科口罩可能在5dB左右）。对正常听力的被试而言，如果测试材料信噪比太过理想，很容易产生天花板效应（ceiling effect）。

当然，如果背景噪音做得太大，导致信噪比过低，也会影响实验的结果。从我们考察的文献来看，信噪比基本控制在+5dB到+10dB是一个相对合理的区间，主要的评判标准是正常听力对照组不至于轻易达到100%正确率，但也应基本保证在90%左右。

背景噪音内容方面，按研究实际的需求，可以是实际录制并加工过的真实环境噪音，也可以是经过加工的人声背景噪音。Bottalico等［3］为了贴近学校不同房间的室内声学条件（room acoustic conditions），专门将实际测量的双耳房间脉冲响应（Binaural Room Impulse Responses，BRIRs）做到语音刺激材料中。这些都是很好的尝试。

（3）被试选择

大多数研究在选取正常听力对照组被试方面不存在什么问题，但明显缺乏足量的听障被试群体。考虑到疫情期间口罩的佩戴实际上影响最大的是相关听障群体，以他们为核心对象的研究目前为止尚显不足。这不仅体现在样本量过小（见表 1），而且样本也缺乏广谱代表性，比如至今尚未见到对象为人工耳蜗佩戴者群体的研究文献。这是后续研究可以深入的一个问题。

在样本量的估计上，Bottalico 等［3］做了一个很好的示范：他们根据已有文献数据计算得出的效应量（effect size），按 80% 的统计功效（statistical power）及 $p<0.001$ 的显著性水平（significance level）标准，推估出所需要的样本量（estimated sample size）。这是本文所认可并试图向中文实验语言学界推广的一种方法，这能够在很大程度上避免样本量设计的随意性，也可以有效保障实验结果的信度与效度。

5. 总结

本文主要回顾了关于口罩影响语音产出与感知的研究文献。目前为止，涉及该话题的文献并不特别多，有许多是新近的研究成果。研究取向大体比较实际，属于问题导向。相较于产出研究，感知听辨方面的研究文献更多，涉及的问题更广，结论也不尽相同。

从产出的角度来看，口罩主要充当了低通滤波器的角色，使语音高频段的能量有所衰减，同时也将部分能量转向侧面。产出研究主要关心不同材质及类型的口罩具体在什么频段衰减多少能量。在具体操作层面，目前还未形成一个标准化的测量及报告程序。本文建议，之后的研究应当在实验室环境及设备的相关声学规格参数、声源、录制设备的位置（高度、角度、距离）等方面作详细说明，以形成一套标准化、可重复的范式。同时也建议多人多次重复测量以保证信度。产出研究有其重要性：不管是各类相关语音技术研究中对高频能量的补偿，还是在相关感知测试实验中设计并使用刺激材料，都离不开产出研究中的许多基础数据。

从感知的角度来看，相关研究都聚焦在口罩影响语音可懂度这个问题上，但结论却并不一致。本文认为这可能是测试方法的不同所导致的，并从测试材料、背景噪音、被试选择等几个方面详细分析了现有研究的问题。在后续研究中，本文建议更关注听障群体在口罩环境下的语音感知问题，并在应用层面考虑相应的改善方法，以提升相关人士在疫情期间的沟通质量与生活质量。

6. 致谢

本文研究得到了教育部人文社会科学研究基金青年项目“上海市区方言变异的实验语音学研究”（项目批准号：17YJC740067）的经费支持。

感谢绍兴文理学院人文学院吴生毅老师对本文提出的意见。感谢本刊匿名审稿人及编辑老师的建议。

参考文献

［1］Atcherson, S. R., Mendel, L. L., Baltimore, W. J., Patro, C., Lee, S., Pousson, M., Spann, M. J. 2017. The effect of conventional and transparent surgical masks on speech understanding in individuals with and without hearing loss. *Journal of the American Academy of Audiology* 28, 58 – 67.

［2］Bandaru, S. V., Augustine, A. M., Lepcha, A., Sebastian, S., Gowri, M., Philip, A., Mammen, M. D. 2020. The effects of N95 mask and face shield on speech perception among healthcare workers in the coronavirus disease 2019 pandemic scenario. *Journal of Laryngology and Otology* 134, 895 – 898.

［3］Bottalico, P., Murgia, S., Puglisi, G. E., Astolfi, A., Kirk, K. I. 2020. Effect of masks on speech intelligibility in auralized classrooms. *The Journal of the Acoustical Society of America* 148, 2878 – 2884.

［4］Cavallaro, G., Di Nicola, V., Quaranta, N., Fiorella, M. L. 2020. Acoustic voice analysis in the COVID – 19 era. *Acta Otorhinolaryngologica Italica*. Epub ahead of print.

［5］Chen, J., Huang, Q., Wu, X. 2016. Frequency importance function of the speech intelligibility index for Mandarin Chinese. *Speech Communication* 83, 94 – 103.

[6] Chodosh, J., Weinstein, B. E., Blustein, J. 2020. Face masks can be devastating for people with hearing loss. *BMJ* 370, m2683.

[7] Corey, R. M., Jones, U., Singer, A. C. 2020. Acoustic effects of medical, cloth, and transparent face masks on speech signals. *The Journal of the Acoustical Society of America* 148, 2371 – 2375.

[8] Goldlin, A., Weinstein, B., Shiman, N. 2020. How Do Medical Masks Degrade Speech Reception? *Hearing Review* 27, 8 – 9.

[9] Grote, H., Izagaren, F. 2020. Covid – 19: The communication needs of D/deaf healthcare workers and patients are being forgotten. *BMJ* 369, m2372.

[10] Kent, R. D., Read, C. 1992. *The Acoustic Analysis of Speech*. San Diego: Singular Publishing Group.

[11] Ladefoged, P., Johnson, K. 2010. *A Course in Phonetics* (*sixth edition*). Boston: Cengage Learning.

[12] Llamas, C., Harrison, P., Donnelly, D., Watt, D. 2008. Effects of different types of face covering on speech acoustics and intelligibility. *York Papers in Linguistics* Series 2, 80 – 104.

[13] Magee, M., Lewis, C., Noffs, G., Reece, H., Chan, J. C. S., Zaga, C. J., et al. 2020. Effects of face masks on acoustic analysis and speech perception: Implications for peri-pandemic protocols. *The Journal of the Acoustical Society of America* 148, 3562 – 3568.

[14] Mendel, L. L., Gardino, J. A., Atcherson, S. R. 2008. Speech understanding using surgical masks: A problem in health care? *Journal of the American Academy of Audiology* 19, 686 – 695.

[15] Palmiero, A. J., Symons, D., Morgan, J. W., Shaffer, R. E. 2016. Speech intelligibility assessment of protective facemasks and air-purifying respirators. *Journal of Occupational and Environmental Hygiene* 13, 960 – 968.

[16] Ribeiro, V. V., Dassie-Leite, A. P., Pereira, E. C., Santos, A. D. N., Martins, P., Irineu, R. de A. 2020. Effect of Wearing a Face Mask on Vocal Self-Perception during a Pandemic. *Journal of Voice*. Epub ahead of print.

[17] Thomas, F., Allen, C., Butts, W., Rhoades, C., Brandon, C., Handrahan, D. L. 2011. Does wearing a surgical facemask or N95-respirator impair radio communication? *Air Medical Journal* 30, 97 – 102.

[18] Wittum, K. J., Feth, L., Hoglund, E. 2013. The effects of surgical masks on speech perception in noise. In *Proceedings of Meetings on Acoustics ICA* 2013 Montreal, 060125.

[19] Wolfe, J., Smith, J., Neumann, S., Miller, S., Schafer, E. C., Birath, A. L., et al. 2020. Optimizing Communication in Schools and Other Settings During COVID – 19. *The Hearing Journal* 73, 40, 42 – 45.

[20] World Health Organization. 2020. Mask use in the context of COVID – 19: interim guidance. https://www.who.int/publications/i/item/advice-on-the-use-of-masks-in-the-community-during-home-care-and-in-healthcare-settings-in-the-context-of-the-novel-coronavirus-(2019-ncov)-outbreak.

王非凡 香港大学教育学院人类沟通、发展及资讯科学学部，言语及听觉科学项目博士研究生，研究兴趣包括噪音分析、实验语音学、社会语言及方言学。
E-mail：feifan.wang@hku.hk

汉语人工耳蜗使用者声调感知和产生研究综述

冯 杰 伍新春

摘 要 人工耳蜗的发明给广大听力障碍群体带来了福音，但由于其设计的局限性，不能提供声调语言加工中所需要的精细音高信息，因而使汉语人工耳蜗使用者在声调感知和产生方面都表现出一定困难；并且，汉语人工耳蜗使用者声调感知与产生之间的关系也更加复杂。该领域已有的研究多为行为水平的共时研究，今后有必要从追踪、脑认知神经及干预等研究方向，全面深入地对汉语人工耳蜗使用者声调感知、声调产生及二者关系进行研究，并指导特殊教育实践。
关键词 人工耳蜗移植，声调感知，声调产生

Review of the Perception and Production of Lexical Tones by Chinese Cochlear Implant Users

FENG Jie WU Xinchun

Abstract Artificial cochlea benefit deaf people a lot in hearing and speaking, however, the information processing strategy that is used in the design of artificial cochlea do not include elaborated pitch information, which is very important in lexical tone language. Therefore, Chinese cochlear implant users face certain difficulties in the perception and production of lexical tones, and for them the relationship between perception and production of lexical tones becomes more complex. Most of previous studies in this area are behavioral cross-sectional studies. Longitudinal, neuropsychological and interventional studies are needed in further research in the perception and production of lexical tones in Chinese cochlear implant users to instruct special education practice.
Key words Cochlear implant, Lexical tone perception, Lexical tone production

1. 引言

在我国，具有听力言语障碍的残障人群有 2057 万人，占全国 6000 万残疾人总数的 1/3。现有 117 万聋儿，其中七岁以下聋儿有 80 多万，并且由于药物、遗传、疾病、噪音污染等原因，每年新增聋儿 3 万余名［43］。人工耳蜗植入（Cochlear Implant，CI）是目前帮助重度或极重度听障患者恢复听觉功能的最为有效的方式。针对我国规模巨大的听障人群，由中国残联牵头实施的“国家贫困聋儿人工耳蜗、助听器抢救性康复项目”，在 2009—2011 年为 1500 名极重度聋儿免费植入了人工耳蜗，并提供术后康复训练经费。2011 年又拨款计划五年内为 17000 名听障儿童进行免费人工耳蜗移植［44］。随着我国经济水平的发展和各种慈善资助项目的开展，人工耳蜗的使用量呈快速增长趋势。

人工耳蜗的主要工作原理是将言语信号通过体外的语音处理器转换为一定编码形式的电信号，发送到植入体内的电极系统，通过电极系统直接使听神经兴奋，从而恢复、提高和重建聋人的听觉功能。但是，人工耳蜗的最关键技术——“言语编码策略”在设计时主要是基于西方非声调语言特点研究出来的，对于声调语言中的“调”（tone or pitch）这一声学特征考虑并不周到。目前的人工耳蜗在设计中所使用的语音信息加工策略主要是将语音中的包络信息传递到人工耳蜗植入者的听神经，并不能提供精细的音高信息，这给声调语言文化中的人工耳蜗使用者的语言发

展带来较大挑战。

在声调语言（比如汉语、越南语等）中，声调对词汇意义具有决定性作用。声调是一种音高连续变化的语音信息，相同的音节（声母+韵母）组合搭配不同的声调可以表征不同的语义，比如汉语普通话中的/ma1/妈、/ma2/麻、/ma3/马、/ma4/骂。基频（F0）、音长（duration）和振幅（amplitude）等声学特性都会对个体的声调感知产生影响。基频是健听人群声调感知的最重要的声学参数，当基频起作用时，音长和振幅等声学信息在声调感知中只具有辅助作用，但当基频提取困难时，音长和振幅就可能成为声调感知的重要线索［38］，此外，有研究发现，视觉线索（比如面部线索）对声调感知也有一定作用［2，3］。

以往对普通话健听儿童的研究发现，九个月的幼儿已经能够产出四种不同的声调变化［41］，一岁半以前就基本完成声调习得［40］。健听儿童汉语声调体系获得时间大概是两岁左右，但这时T2（二声）和T3（三声）对幼儿来说仍然是较容易混淆的。在声调习得顺序方面，冯燕［39］对多个代表性研究中声调的习得顺序进行总结，结果发现健听儿童一声和四声的习得普遍早于二声和三声的习得。

当下，在人工耳蜗提供的声调音高信息有限的情况下，人工耳蜗对汉语听障人群的声调感知及产生的帮助和局限成为研究者非常关心的问题。本文主要聚焦于现有汉语人工耳蜗使用者声调感知和产生方面的相关研究，分析并总结汉语人工耳蜗使用者对声调的感知和产生能力及其特点，并对该领域今后的研究趋势进行讨论。

2. 汉语人工耳蜗使用者声调感知的研究

汉语人工耳蜗使用者声调感知的研究主要包括汉语普通话和广东话两种。Chao［5］在五度标调法中使用数字表示声调音高，其中1表示最低音高，5表示最高音高。据此，汉语普通话中的4种声调可分别表示为：一声（55，文中统一用T1表示），二声（35，文中统一用T2表示），三声（214，文中统一用T3表示）和四声（51，文中统一用T4表示）。广东话中除入声外有6种声调，可分别表示为一声（55，文中统一用t1表示），二声（25，文中统一用t2表示），三声（33，文中统一用t3表示），四声（21，文中统一用t4表示），五声（23，文中统一用t5表示）和六声（22，文中统一用t6表示）。括号中的第一个数字表示声调开始时基频F0的水平，最后一个数字表示声调结束时基频F0的水平，中间的数字表示声调拐点处基频F0的水平。广东话中的一声、二声和四声与普通话中的一声、二声和四声较接近。

根据研究者所使用的实验任务类型的不同，可以将汉语人工耳蜗使用者声调感知的研究分成两种：一种是区分任务（discrimination）研究，比如让被试判断所听到声音刺激和所呈现的图片代表的字相同还是不同，这种任务相对容易一些。另一种是确认任务（identification）研究，比如要求被试听到声音刺激后，从所给的图片中挑出目标刺激所对应的图片。确认任务反映被试对该目标声调与其他一个或三个声调的分辨能力。不同的任务形式和实验材料会影响任务难度，因此本文将分别对使用不同任务的研究进行分类论述。

2.1 声调区分任务

Tse等人［30］对母语为广东话的人工耳蜗使用者的声调感知能力进行了测量。研究者将6种声调组成15组声调对比对，要求被试判断所听到的声调对中的两个声调相同还是不同。结果发现，人工耳蜗使用组的表现（74.9%）显著差于控制组（98.1%）；人工耳蜗被试对t3—t4声调对比对区分能力最好，可能是因为三声和四声基频音高和声调轮廓都存在较大差异，他们对t3—t6声调对比对的辨别能力最差（20%），这可能是因为这两个声调轮廓相似，被试仅能依靠较小的音高差别进行区分［30］。同样使用15种声调对比对的声调区分任务，Wong等［34］的研究发现，人工耳蜗植入被试的平均正确率为59.2%，15种声调对比对中只有对t4和t5的区分表现高于机会水平。

2.2 二选一声调确认任务

Li及其同事［19］的研究中使用二选一的声调确认任务研究耳蜗植入儿童在人工耳蜗开启和关闭状态下的普通话声调确认表现，结果发现在人工耳蜗关闭状态下被试的正确率有15%，在人工耳蜗开启状态下被试的正确率有54%（显著高于几率水平），而控制组儿童在该任务上的表现都高于98%。同时，人工耳蜗使用者对六组声调对比的辨别能力也表现出差异，其中对T2和T4声调对比对的判断表现最好，T1和T3的声调对比对表现最差，几组表现依次是T2和T4、T1和T4、T3和T4、T1和T2、T2和T3以及T1和T3。其中，被试对包含四声的声调对区分能力比较好，研究者认为这是由于四声长度最短并且波幅能量最大，因此被试能更好进行识别［19］。但是，该研究中并未对声调长度进行控制。Peng及其同事［25］的研究结果与上述研究类似，同样是使用二选一的声调确认任务，研究者发现30名先天语前聋儿童总体表现显著高于机会水平（72.88%），被试对包含T4的声调对区分度比较高。在一个更大样本量的研究中［31］，研究者对96名人工耳蜗植入的儿童声调感知进行判断，任务形式为二选一声调确认，被试在安静条件下声调感知测验平均得分为77%，其中只有五位被试能达到同龄健听儿童水平。对六种声调对比组的详细分析发现，人工耳蜗使用者对T2和T3对比的表现显著差于对其他组的区分，而其他五组之间无显著差异，被试比较容易混淆T2和T3［31］。研究者认为T2和T3比较容易混淆，可能是因为T2和T3的声调轮廓比较相似，T3声调轮廓是先下降再上升，而T2的声调轮廓在开始部分也有些微下降之后上升，但二声比三声的拐点更靠前［6］。Zhou及其同事［37］的研究中对比了110名语前聋人工耳蜗植入儿童和125名健听控制组声调感知和产生的表现。同样使用二选一的声调确认任务，研究发现人工耳蜗植入被试表现出较大个体差异，正确率从机会水平到接近满分，整体平均得分67.31%，显著差于控制组，但在该研究中并未发现人工耳蜗使用者在六种不同对比对中表现的差异。

Ciocca及其同事［7］有选择地使用了广东话八种对作为实验材料，让人工耳蜗使用被试完成二选一的声调确认任务。其中t1和t3、t1和t6、t3和t6这三组对比对用来研究三种水平音高（高、中、低）差别对被试声调感知的影响；t2和t5、t5和t6、t4和t5、t4和t6这四组对比对用来研究声调结尾部分基频F0的差异对被试声调感知的影响，因为这几组声调对比对在声调开始部分音高基频接近，在这四组中，t5和t6、t4和t5、t4和t6除了结尾部分基频不同外，每一对的声调轮廓也有差异，而t2和t5声调音高轮廓一致，只有结尾部分音高不同；第八个对比对t1和t2声调结尾部分音高相同、开始部分音高不同，因此可以用来研究声调开始部分音高差异对被试声调感知的影响［7］。结果发现，被试对八个声调对的判断的正确率从50%到61%不等，其中对t1和t3、t1和t6以及t1和t5三个对比对的辨别高于机会水平，对t1和t3的辨别显著好于对t3和t6以及t2和t5的辨别。研究者认为人工耳蜗使用者对包含t1的对比对表现较好，这可能是因为t1和其他声调的音高变化差异较大，也可能是因为t1具有较大的总体振幅［7］。Chan的研究中［4］同样使用上述八个声调对比对的二选一任务，他们发现被试对不同声调对的区分的正确率范围为53%—78%，表现最不好的几个对比组分别是t3和t6、t2和t5、t4和t6以及t5和t6，正确率都仅在50%左右，表现高于机会水平的有t1和t3、t1和t6以及t1和t2，其中表现最好的是对t1和t6的辨别。研究者认为人工耳蜗使用者对水平声调中的基频差异比较敏感，并且在声调音长范围内基频所对应的时间变化越大，听者越容易对基频音高进行区分［4］。Lee及其同事［17］比较健听儿童和人工耳蜗使用儿童声调感知能力，其中人工耳蜗植入儿童年龄从 6 岁 1 个月到 11 岁 5 个月不等，人工耳蜗使用时间为 27—53 个月，对照控制组年龄从 2 岁 9 个月到 3 岁 3 个月，与人工耳蜗组被试耳蜗使用时间匹配。研究者选择了较容易习得和区分的三个声调 t1、t2 和 t4，组成三个声调对比对，被试需要完成二选一的声调确认任务。人工耳蜗使用者对声调的确认表现总体差于健听组被试；健听组被试表现最好的是对 t1 和 t4 的辨别，对 t2 和 t4 的辨别表现最差；而人工耳蜗使用被试虽然表现最好的也是对 t1 和 t4 的辨别，但他们对 t1 和 t2 的辨别表现最差。t2 和 t4 具有相似的声调起始音高，t1 和 t2 具有相似的声调结束音高，因此研究者认为健听组被试进行声调区分时可能更多地依赖起始部分音高，而人工耳蜗使用者则更多依赖结束部分音高［17］。Wong 及其同事［34］用/ji/作为实验音节与六种声调组合，使用四选一的声调确认任务，研究发现被试的正确率为 31.2%，显著高于机会水平(25%)，t6 是最难进行确认的声调，很容易与其他声调混淆，尤其是 t2。

2.3 四选一声调确认任务

Wei 等［33］采用四选一的声调确定任务对 7 位语前聋被试和 10 位语后聋被试的普通话声调进行研究，结果发现人工耳蜗使用者在安静状态下声调感知正确率为 70%，显著差于控制组。Wang 及其同事［31］对比了 20 位健听者和 19 位人工耳蜗植入者声调感知能力，同样选用四选一的声调确认任务，并对声调音长进行了标准化。人工耳蜗组被试的正确率为 58.3%，显著差于控制组。人工耳蜗使用者对四种声调的感知能力也有显著差异，对 T4 的感知能力最好，后面依次是 T1、T3 和 T2，被试比较容易混淆 T1 和 T2。研究者认为这可能是由于人工耳蜗所提供的音高信息缺乏变异，使得一些声调听起来比较平［31，32］。最近的一项研究同样发现被试四选一声调感知任务表现显著高于机会水平，达到 80.9%，人工耳蜗使用者表现出对 T2 确认最困难，T1 的表现差于 T4［26］。

2.4 噪音背景下声调感知任务

日常环境并不是完全安静的，存在各种环境噪音，因此研究者也对噪音或有其他语音干扰条件下人工耳蜗植入者的声调感知能力进行了研究。研究者使用白噪音［33］和语音噪音［6］，通过改变信噪比(Signal-to-Noise Ratio，SNR)，研究不同信噪比条件对人工耳蜗使用者声调感知能力的影响。在白噪音的信噪比为 -5dB 和 -10dB时，人工耳蜗使用者的表现只能达到机会水平，而他们在无白噪音条件时正确率可达到 70%［33］。在语音噪音的信噪比为 +10dB、+5dB 及安静条件下，人工耳蜗使用被试声调感知能力表现显著高于机会水平，而当信噪比为 -5dB 和 -10dB 时，分别只有 32% 和 4% 的被试表现高于机会水平［6］。可见，噪音对人工耳蜗使用者声调感知有强烈干扰，并且语音噪音比白噪音对被试的干扰更大，这可能由于语音噪音本身包含了很多声调、声母和韵母，这些对声调感知具有干扰作用。

总体来看，人工耳蜗使用者对汉语声调感知的正确率都显著高于机会水平，并且在人工耳蜗开启状态下的表现显著好于关闭状态下的表现，这些结果一致说明人工耳蜗的使用有助于听障个体的声调感知。但是，人工耳蜗使用者对汉语声调的感知表现一致地差于同龄健听组，说明人工耳蜗对被试声调感知的帮助是存在局限的。此外，各项研究中人工耳蜗被试的表现不尽一致(正确率范围 54%—80.9%)。这一方面可能是因为每个研究中具体使用的实验设计和测试材料不同，从而导致任务难度各异；另一方面，在一些研究中(比如［31］)研究者对音长、振幅等其他声学特征进行了标准化，测试着重在对基频(F0)和音高轮廓(pitch contour)的感知，使得人工耳蜗使用者感知结果与健听组差距较大；而有的研究没有对其他的声调信息进行控制，人工耳蜗使用者在声调感知中可能会使用其他声学线索，进而得到的结果就不是那么差。

2.5 汉语人工耳蜗使用者声调感知的影响因素

以往汉语人工耳蜗使用者声调感知研究中表现出一些不一致甚至相反的研究结果，并且，人工耳蜗使用者声调感知能力具有较大个体差异。这些现象说明人工耳蜗使用者的声调感知可能受很多因素影响，比如人工耳蜗的设计、声调的其他声学特征、语音背景（即音节信息等）、声调的视觉线索、助听器的使用、人口统计学变量及家庭变量等。

人工耳蜗设计中，耳蜗通道越多，其频谱分辨率越高，一项脑电研究［16］证明，人工耳蜗在设计过程中需要至少有8个通道以保证其输入信息的分辨率。不同的语音加工策略传递到人工耳蜗的音高信息也有差异，进而会影响耳蜗使用者的声调感知。在人工耳蜗设计中较常用的加工策略有SPEAK（Spectral Peak）、ACE（Advanced Combination Encoders）和CIS（Continuous Interleaved Sampling）。Fu及其同事［9］比较了这三种加工策略对人工耳蜗使用者声调感知的影响，结果发现使用ACE和CIS加工策略的被试比使用SPEAK策略的被试的声调感知表现更好，并且刺激频率越高被试声调感知的表现越好，因此，在人工耳蜗设计中还需要适当提高刺激频率以帮助耳蜗使用者获得更多的声调信息。

汉语普通话和广东话声调中最重要的声调感知线索是声调基频音高（F0）和轮廓（pitch contour）［12，13，20，29］。此外，声调音长是被试声调感知的另一个重要线索，其中T3最长T4最短［15］；自然声调的振幅也是声调感知的一个线索，T3拥有最低的振幅峰值，而T4拥有最高的振幅峰值［10，11］。研究发现在汉语普通话声调感知中，声母、韵母和声调存在交互作用，其中韵母比声母对被试的声调感知干扰更大［28］。当让人工耳蜗使用者对单个音节进行辨别时，他们对韵母辨别的正确率有90%，声调辨别正确率有63%；当让被试对连续快速呈现的多个音节的声母、声调等进行判断时，正确率均下降40%—60%。该研究说明在多谈话者情况下，声母、韵母和声调对被试语音感知存在相互干扰作用［22］。以广东话为母语的被试在完成声调感知时也受到语音背景干扰，被试对声母韵母都不同的声调辨别最困难，其次是同声母不同韵母的声调，同韵母不同声母的声调对被试来说最难分辨，韵母比声母对被试声调感知的干扰更大［27］。

最近的一些研究（比如［1，23，24］）指出，人工耳蜗使用者虽然F0信息有缺失，但他们能够利用音长（duration）和振幅（amplitude）信息进行声调的辨别。也有很多研究发现，助听器的使用有助于汉语听力障碍被试获得更好的声调感知（比如［21，31］）。此外，生理年龄、失聪时长、人工耳蜗植入年龄、人工耳蜗使用时长、接受特殊训练的时间等人口统计学变量对人工耳蜗使用者的声调感知表演也具有一定预测作用。其中，人工耳蜗植入年龄（比如［19，37］）和人工耳蜗使用时长（比如［6，26，37］）是获得较多研究验证的对人工耳蜗使用者声调感知表现具有稳定的预测作用的两个变量，具体来说，人工耳蜗植入越早、人工耳蜗使用时间越长，耳蜗使用者的声调感知能力越好。也有研究者［26］指出失聪时长与语前聋被试声调感知表现存在显著相关。人工耳蜗使用者的声调感知能力与音乐音高感知能力也存在显著正相关［32］。

3. 汉语人工耳蜗使用者声调产生的研究

感知会影响产生，听与说是相辅相成的。人工耳蜗使用者不仅在声调感知方面表现出一定困难，他们在声调产生方面同样存在很多问题。人工耳蜗使用者汉语声调产生的研究主要集中于以普通话为母语的被试。在人工耳蜗使用者声调产生的相关研究中，根据所使用的评价方法的不同，可分为使用客观的听觉物理分析方法的研究和使用主观人工评价方法的研究，也有一部分研究中同时使用这两类评价方法。不同的评价方法反映人工耳蜗使用者声调产生的不同层面的特点。

Peng及其同事［25］使用人工评价方法，让3位汉语普通话为母语的专家对30名语前聋儿童（平均年龄9岁3个月）声调发音准确性进行5点评分，其中1代表完全错误、5代表完全正确。研究发现，人工耳蜗植入儿童声调发音的平均正确率为53.09%，并且T1和T4发音的准确性显著好于T2和T3。Han等［14］对比了14位人工耳蜗使用儿童和14位年龄匹配的健听儿童声调产生的表现。他们请7名以汉语为母语的成年人对所收集的两组被试的语音材料进行声调判断，评委根据听到的声音刺激四选一确定是哪个声调。人工耳蜗使用儿童声调产生表现显著差于健听被试组，人工耳蜗使用儿童四个声调（T1、T2、T3、T4）发音的正确率依次为71.7%、19.4%、48.1%、55.3%；T1表现最好，T2表现最差，人工耳蜗使用者所发出的二声、三声、四声最易被判断为一声。研究者认为这可能是因为人工耳蜗使用儿童发出的声调基频音高变异不大［14］。张芳等［42］将120名听障儿童分成3岁、4岁、5岁三个年龄段，对其声调产生能力进行测量。他们让儿童进行双字调发音，由经过训练的语训老师进行评分，对的记1分，错的不计分。健听组儿童在3岁时双字调发音已达到100%，听障儿童三个年龄段声调发音均落后于健听儿童；两组儿童T1发音无显著差异，但T2、T3和T4发音上听障儿童比控制组差。

Xu及其同事［35］使用一种模拟神经网络模型对耳蜗使用者发声的语音材料的听觉物理属性进行分析，研究发现被试声调产生的平均准确性为52%，但存在较大个体差异。在另一项研究中，研究者［36］主客观结合的分析方法，既对声调基频进行分析又请4位健听母语评委对被试的声调发音准确性进行11点评分（0代表没有一点调性，10代表完美声调）。结果发现，健听组四种声调发音非常准确，而人工耳蜗使用儿童只有T4发音与健听组相似，T1、T2和T3缺少应有的区分度。耳蜗使用儿童的声调产生具有较大个体差异，其中，S1表现基本与健听儿童类似，S2在T2和T3产生上有较大困难，S3能产生一个迅速下降的音高模式来表征T4但其他三个声调发音较平或稍稍有上升趋势，S4四种声调发音都有困难［36］。Zhou等［37］收集了更大样本的数据，他们比较了110位语前聋和125位健听被试声调产生表现，同时使用主客观两种分析方法。客观的听觉物理分析中，使用三个指标来描述两组声调产生的差异，指标1和指标2用来计算相对于被试产生的音高总变异，四种声调各自的基频F0分布，这两个指标类似心理学研究中的鉴别力指标d’。指标3计算的是每个声调错误探测的可能性，反映一个声调和其他声调的区别性。两组被试在三个指标上都表现出显著差异，人工耳蜗使用者产出的音高和声调基频音高模式不匹配，不同声调的音高分布有较多重叠，说明虽然他们能够产生相当的音高范围，但却不能准确使用有区分度的音高轮廓；同时，主观的人工评价指标也显示两组有显著差异，控制组的正确率有94.8%，而人工耳蜗使用者的正确率为46.8%［37］。

丁馨［38］对汉语人工耳蜗植入儿童声调及重音的感知与产出进行了研究。研究者提取了基频、时长、振幅等多个相关声学参数，系统分析了健听儿童和人工耳蜗植入儿童产出能力的差异。主要结果发现，从基频上来看，健听组儿童的基频最小值显著低于人工耳蜗组，调域也显著宽于人工耳蜗组，说明人工耳蜗组儿童的声调产出存在基频较平的特点；从时长上来看，两组儿童的语音都是上声时长最长，而去声时长最短，但健听组儿童的声调产出时长显著低于人工耳蜗组儿童，这说明健听组儿童的产出语速比人工耳蜗组儿童的声调产出语速更快。

健听儿童汉语声调体系获得时间大概是2岁左右，这时T2和T3对幼儿来说仍然是较容易混淆的［8，18］。通过对汉语人工耳蜗使用者声调产生的研究分析，我们发现人工耳蜗使用者一声和四声发音表现较好，二声和三声发音表现较差，其发展规律与健听儿童是一致的，但人工耳蜗使用者声调产生能力的发展滞后于同龄健听儿童。人工耳蜗使用者声调产生的障碍一方面可能是由于人工耳蜗设计局限导致输入的音高信息不足，使用者对声调的感知和识别不准确，进而影响其声调产生能力的发展；另一方面可能也与人工耳蜗使用者发音器官、构音器官协调运动不足有关，使得人工耳蜗使用者对声调的控制有一定困难，不能准确地提高或降低音高。

以往研究发现，人工耳蜗使用者在声调感知上存在巨大个体差异，这种差异可能来自多方面原因［6，19，26，32，37］；但目前对人工耳蜗使用者声调产生影响因素的相关研究还比较少，或没有发现有效结果。Han及其同事［14］研究中指出人工耳蜗植入年龄和被试声调产生存在显著负相关，越早植入人工耳蜗的被试声调产生表现越好；较长的人工耳蜗使用时间也会促进被试声调产生。但也有研究指出只有人工耳蜗植入年龄对听障被试声调产生具有显著预测作用［37］。

此外，目前人工耳蜗使用者声调产生方面的研究主要集中在儿童受试者的声调产出。人工耳蜗儿童的声调产出让正常成人听辨结果比正常儿童的结果要差，因为正常人群主要依据音高信息来听辨。尚未有让人工耳蜗使用者听辨耳蜗使用者的声调产出的相关研究，他们的感知结果可能会与健听人群的听辨结果有所不同。从这个角度进行的研究对我们认识人工耳蜗使用者的声调感知和产生都非常有意义，这也是该领域今后可以继续探索的方向。

4. 汉语人工耳蜗使用者声调感知与产生关系的研究

感知是产生的基础，科研领域和实践领域都希望通过提高人工耳蜗使用者的语音感知而获得更好的语言产生能力。然而，由于目前人工耳蜗设计方面的局限，它并不能给使用者提供足够的声调音高信息。研究者发现，除了声调音高基频信息外，人工耳蜗使用者的声调的感知和产生还有很多其他线索和影响因素，这些有别于健听人群的声调感知与产生机制。Peng及其同事［25］的研究中发现，语前聋儿童声调感知和产生总体表现出显著相关，但去掉三个极端值后相关便消失了，他们并未找到两者之间稳定的相关关系。但Xu及其同事［35］发现被试的声调感知和声调产生之间存在显著高相关（r = 0.85），说明良好的声调感知能力是声调产生的基础。Zhou等［37］的研究中同样发现，声调感知和产生存在显著正相关，但不同声调上的感知和产生关系不一致，其中T4声调感知和产生存在显著正相关，T1声调感知和产生边缘相关，而T2、T3的声调感知和产生相关不显著。研究者认为，人工耳蜗使用者对T2有较好的感知能力，但未发现感知和产生的显著相关，这可能是因为良好感知并不能保证声调产生，人工耳蜗使用者T2产生困难可能是由于发音困难；对T3的感知能力也不能显著预测其声调产生的表现。

目前，我们对人工耳蜗使用者声调感知与产生之间的关系尚不清楚，研究中所发现的人工耳蜗使用者声调感知和产生之间的复杂关系除了受人工耳蜗本身的因素影响外，还有很多的其他影响因素，人工耳蜗使用者声调加工机制和健听人群也可能存在一定差异。

5. 汉语人工耳蜗使用者声调感知和产生研究展望

以往对汉语人工耳蜗使用者声调感知、产生以及感知与产生之间关系的研究获得了一些规律性的结果：人工耳蜗的使用是严重听力障碍群体声调感知的必要而非充分条件，存在很多其他影响因素；人工耳蜗使用者的声调产生发展相对滞后；声调感知与产生存在一定的相关关系。以往研究都是共时的行为研究，对问题探讨的深入性和延展性仍然有限，对汉语人工耳蜗使用者声调感知、产生及二者关系的机制探讨还不够透彻。鉴于此，有必要对该领域进行更深入和全面的研究。

第一，行为层面的研究有必要控制更多重要的影响因素，比如人工耳蜗植入年龄、人工耳蜗使用时间、语前聋语后聋、是否使用过助听器等；结合使用多种难度水平的测试，研究人工耳蜗使用者对不同类型声调感知和辨认的能力；结合使用主观和客观评价方法，分析人工耳蜗使用者声调产生的行为特点及语音学基础。

第二，已有研究大多是共时研究，对汉语人工耳蜗使用者声调感知和产生的追踪研究有助于刻画人工耳蜗使用者声调感知和产生的发展规律，更好地指导特殊教育实践。

第三，人工耳蜗使用者汉语声调感知、产生及二者关系的研究目前都限于行为水平，研究者还不了解其认知神经机制，借助于 ERP、fNIRS、fMRI 等认知神经研究工具可以使研究者更好地解释人工耳蜗的使用对个体声调感知和产生发生作用的认知神经机制。

第四，目前的关于人工耳蜗使用者的声调感知和产出的研究主要集中在单音节情况下。在连续话语中，汉语声调的表现与单音节情况下有很大不同。后续的研究应从单音节向双音节、连续话语继续推进。

第五，本文关注的主题是声调，但是汉语作为声调语言，同样基于音高信息的声调和语调有着密不可分的关系。因为对音高信息传递和处理的缺陷，人工耳蜗使用者在语调的感知和产出方面的表现，以及人工耳蜗使用者声调和语调的协调机制等都是值得深入探讨的问题。

第六，基于干预的研究对特殊教育实践具有更直接的作用，这也是该领域目前急缺的。需要研究者投入更多的时间和精力，以人工耳蜗使用者声调感知和产生的特点、机制及影响因素研究成果为基础，设计科学有效的干预方案，通过严谨的实验对其进行验证，最终得到有助于特殊教育的实践成果和规律，这也是所有基础研究的最终目的和意义所在。

6. 致谢

本文研究得到了国家社会科学基金重大项目“残疾人语言障碍与学习机制研究”（13&ZD188）和认知神经科学与学习国家重点实验室2013年度开放课题“残疾儿童语言障碍的认知神经机制研究”（CNLYB1311）的经费支持。

参考文献

[1] Barrett, K. C., Chatterjee, M., Caldwell, M. T., Deroche, M. L., Jiradejvong, P., Kulkarni, A. M., Limb, C. J. 2020. Perception of child-directed versus adult-directed emotional speech in pediatric cochlear implant users. *Ear and Hearing* 41(5), 1372 – 1382.

[2] Burnham, D., Ciocca, V., Lauw, C., Lau, S., Stokes, S. 2000. Perception of visual information for Cantonese tones. *Actes de SST(Speech Science and Technology)*.

[3] Burnham, D., Ciocca, V., Stokes, S. 2001. Auditory-visual perception of lexical tone. *Eurospeech Conference* 2001, Aalsborg, Denmark (October), 395 – 398.

[4] Chan, T. K. 2001. *Cantonese Tone Perception by Postlingually Deaf Cochlear Implant Users*. B. Sc. Thesis. Hong Kong: The University of Hong Kong.

[5] Chao, Y. R. 1947. *Cantonese primer*. Published for the Harvard-Yenching Institute, Harvard University Press.

[6] Chen, Y., Wong, L. L. N., Chen, F., Xi, X. 2014. Tone and sentence perception in young Mandarin-speaking children with cochlear implants. *International Journal of Pediatric Otorhinolaryngology* 78(11), 1923 – 1930.

[7] Ciocca, V., Francis, A. L., Aisha, R., Wong, L. 2002. The perception of Cantonese lexical tones by early-deafened cochlear implantees. *Journal of the Acoustical Society of America* 111(5), 2250 – 2256.

[8] Dodd, B. J., So, L. K. 1994. The phonological abilities of Cantonese-speaking children with hearing loss. *Journal of Speech, Language, and Hearing Research* 37(3), 671 – 679.

[9] Fu, Q. J., Hsu, C. J., Horng, M. J. 2004. Effects of speech processing strategy on Chinese tone recognition by nucleus – 24 cochlear implant users.

Ear and Hearing 25(5), 501 – 508.
[10] Fu, Q. J., Zeng, F. G. 2000. Effects of envelope cues on Mandarin Chinese tone recognition. *Asia-Pacific J Speech Lang Hear* 5, 45 – 57.
[11] Fu, Q. J., Zeng, F. G., Shannon, R. V., Soli, S. D. 1998. Importance of tonal envelope cues in Chinese speech recognition. *The Journal of the Acoustical Society of America* 104(1), 505 – 510.
[12] Gandour, J. 1981. Perceptual dimensions of tone: evidence from Cantonese. *Journal of Chinese Linguistics*, 20 – 36.
[13] Gandour, J. 1983. Tone perception in far easternlanguages. *Journal of Phonetics* 11(2), 149 – 175.
[14] Han, D., Zhou, N., Li, Y., Chen, X., Zhao, X., Xu, L. 2007. Tone production of Mandarin Chinese speaking children with cochlear implants. *International Journal of Pediatric Otorhinolaryngology* 71(6), 875 – 880.
[15] Howie, J. M. 1974. On the domain of tone in Mandarin. *Phonetica* 30(3), 129 – 148.
[16] Kuo, Y. C., Lee, C. Y., Chen, M. C., Liu, T. L., Cheng, S. K. 2014. The impact of spectral resolution on the mismatch response to Mandarin Chinese tones: An ERP study of cochlear implant simulations. *Clinical Neurophysiology* 125 (8), 1568 – 1575.
[17] Lee, K. Y. S., van Hasselt, C. A., Chiu, S. N., Cheung, D. M. C. 2002. Cantonese tone perception ability of cochlear implant children in comparison with normal-hearing children. *International Journal of Pediatric Otorhinolaryngology* 63(2), 137 – 147.
[18] Lee, T. H. T. 1993. Theoretical issues in language development and Chinese child language. *In C. T. J. Huang & Y. -H. A. Li (eds.), New Horizons in Chinese Linguistics* (pp. 293 – 356). Boston: Kluwer Academic Publishers.
[19] Li, A., Wang, N., Li, J., Zhang, J., Liu, Z. 2014. Mandarin lexical tones identification among children with cochlear implants or hearing aids. *International Journal of Pediatric Otorhinolaryngology* 78(11), 1945 – 1952.
[20] Lin, M. C. 1988. The acoustic characteristics and perceptual cues of tones in Standard Chinese. *Zhongguo Yuwen* 204, 182 – 193.
[21] Luo, X., Chang, Y. P., Lin, C. – Y., Chang, R. Y. 2014. Contribution of bimodal hearing to lexical tone normalization in Mandarin-speaking cochlear implant users. *Hearing Research* 312, 1 – 8.
[22] Luo, X., Fu, Q. J., Wu, H. P., Hsu, C. J. 2009. Concurrent-vowel and tone recognition by Mandarin-speaking cochlear implant users. *Hearing Research* 256(1 – 2), 75 – 84.
[23] Peng, S. C., Chatterjee, M., Lu, N. 2012. Acoustic cue integration in speech intonation recognition with cochlear implants. *Trends Amplif* 16 (2), 67 – 82.
[24] Peng, S. C., Lu, H. P., Lu, N., Lin, Y. S., Deroche, M. L. D., Chatterjee, M. 2017. Processing of Acoustic Cues in Lexical-Tone Identification by Pediatric Cochlear-Implant Recipients. *J Speech Lang Hear Res* 60(5), 1223 – 1235.
[25] Peng, S. C., Tomblin, J. B., Cheung, H., Lin, Y. S., Wang, L. -S. 2004. Perception and production of mandarin tones in prelingually deaf children with cochlear implants. *Ear and Hearing* 25(3), 251 – 264.
[26] Tao, D., Deng, R., Jiang, Y., Galvin, J. J. 3rd, Fu, Q. J., Chen, B. 2015. Melodic pitch perception and lexical tone perception in mandarin-speaking cochlear implant users. *Ear and Hearing* 36(1), 102 – 110.
[27] Tong, X., McBride, C., Burnham, D. 2014. Cues for lexical tone perception in children: Acoustic correlates and phonetic context effects. *Journal of Speech, Language, and Hearing Research* 57 (5), 1589 – 1605.
[28] Tong, Y., Francis, A. L., Gandour, J. T. 2008. Processing dependencies between segmental and suprasegmental features in Mandarin Chinese. *Language and Cognitive Processes* 23(5), 689 – 708.
[29] Tseng, C. Y., Massaro, D. W., Cohen, M. M. 1986. Lexical tone perception in Mandarin Chinese: Evaluation and integration of acoustic features. *Linguistics, psychology, and the Chinese language* (67), 91.
[30] Tse, W. T., So, L. K. 2012. Phonological awareness of Cantonese-speaking pre-school children with cochlear implants. *International Journal of Speech-Language Pathology* 14(1), 73 – 83.
[31] Wang, S., Liu, B., Dong, R., Zhou, Y., Li, J., Qi, B., Zhang, L. 2012. Music and lexical tone perception in chinese adult cochlear implant users. *Laryngoscope* 122(6), 1353 – 1360.
[32] Wang, W., Zhou, N., Xu, L. 2011. Musical pitch and lexical tone perception with cochlear implants. *International Journal of Audiology* 50 (4), 270 – 278.
[33] Wei, C., Cao, K., Jin, X., Chen, X., Zeng, F. –

G. 2007. Psychophysical performance and Mandarin tone recognition in noise by cochlear implant users. *Ear and Hearing* 28(2 Suppl), 62S - 65S.

[34] Wong, A. O. C., Wong, L. L. N. 2004. Tone perception of Cantonese-speaking prelingually hearing-impaired children with cochlear implants. *Otolaryngology-Head and Neck Surgery: Official Journal of American Academy of Otolaryngology-Head and Neck Surgery* 130(6), 751 - 758.

[35] Xu, L., Chen, X., Lu, H., Zhou, N., Wang, S., Liu, Q., Han, D. 2011. Tone perception and production in pediatric cochlear implants users. *Acta Oto-Laryngologica* 131(4), 395 - 398.

[36] Xu, L., Li, Y., Hao, J., Chen, X., Xue, S., Han, D. 2004. Tone production in Mandarin-speaking children with cochlear implants: a preliminary study. *Acta Oto-Laryngologica* 124(4), 363 - 367.

[37] Zhou, N., Huang, J., Chen, X., Xu, L. 2013. Relationship between tone perception and production inprelingually-deafened children with cochlear implants. *Otology & Neurotology: Official Publication of the American Otological Society, American Neurotology Society [and] European Academy of Otology and Neurotology* 34(3), 499.

[38] 丁馨：《人工耳蜗植入儿童声调及重音的感知与产出研究》，硕士学位论文，南京师范大学，2018年。

[39] 冯燕：《儿童普通话音位范畴感知及其发展》，硕士学位论文，华中师范大学，2018年。

[40] 李嵬、祝华、Barbara Dodd、姜涛、彭聃龄、舒华：《说普通话儿童的语音习得》，《心理学报》2000年第2期。

[41] 吴天敏、许政援：《出生到三岁儿童言语发展记录的初步分析》，中国心理学会发展心理、教育心理专业委员会编《中国心理学会第二届年会——发展心理教育心理论文选集》，1978年。

[42] 张芳、晁欣、史泱、黄露、侯应平、申敏、曲春燕：《3—5岁听障与健听儿童双字调发音的比较研究》，《中国康复理论与实践》2014年第5期。

[43] https://baike.baidu.com/item/%E5%90%AC%E5%8A%9B%E9%9A%9C%E7%A2%8D%E7%96%BE/981911.

[44] http://www.hearingkids.org.cn/sqjz/2012/03/07/c_3622.htm.

冯　杰　北京电子科技学院，博士，讲师，主要研究领域为特殊人群（包括听障、视障及失乐症患者）言语感知和加工。
E-mail: myonly88@126.com

伍新春　北京师范大学，博士，教授，博士生导师，主要研究领域为正常人群和特殊人群语言和阅读能力发展。
E-mail: xcwu@bnu.edu.cn

听力障碍儿童言语语言治疗的研究现状

倪佳伶　陈伟民　张蓓华　沈新佳　涂顺顺　赵艳嫔　吴志远

摘　要　听力障碍指的是各种原因导致的听觉困难，听不到或听不清周围环境及言语声。一般可分为传导性听力障碍、感音神经性听力障碍和混合性听力障碍。儿童正处于听觉、言语和语言发展的关键时期，听力障碍在一定程度上会损害儿童的言语、语言功能，影响儿童的认知、情感、个性形成和社会性发展。本文主要检索了2015—2020年国内外听障儿童言语语言康复的相关文献，分析了听障儿童言语语言的评估和治疗方法，发现根据听障儿童的临床表现，治疗可从构音、嗓音、语畅和代偿方式入手。与此同时，多学科团队合作、早期干预、持续康复和家庭参与的康复模式对听障儿童的预后也非常重要。当然，临床上我们需要结合患儿的具体问题具体分析，创建具有中国特色、汉语特色的听障儿童言语语言介入计划。

关键词　听力障碍，儿童，言语语言治疗

Current Research Situation Review of Speech and Language Therapy for Children with Hearing Loss

NI Jialing　CHEN Weimin　ZHANG Beihua　SHEN Xinjia　TU Shunshun　ZHAO Yanpin　WU Zhiyuan

Abstract Hearing loss refers to hearing difficulties resulted from a variety of factors, with inability to capture or hear environmental sounds or speech sounds clearly. Hearing loss can be subdivided into conductive hearing loss, sensorineural hearing loss and mixed hearing loss. Hearing loss in the critical period of auditory, speech and language development as childhood is detrimental to the speech and language capability of children to a certain extent, further deteriorating their cognition, emotion, personality formation and social development. Domestic and foreign literatures related to speech and language rehabilitation for children with hearing, published between 2015 and 2020, were studied in the present paper, by analyzing the assessment and therapy methods for the speech and language performance of children with hearing loss, this paper found that, (1) articulation, voicing, language fluency and compensatory mode can be selected for treatment according to the individual clinical manifestation. (2) the rehabilitation models composed by multidisciplinary cooperation, early intervention, continuous rehabilitation and family participation are of great significance for their prognosis. Last but not least, in clinical practice, case studies are needed to analyze the specific problem of children with hearing loss, through which the speech and language intervention plan of Chinese characteristics can be expected to devise for the group.

Key words Hearing loss; Children; Speech and language therapy

1. 引言

听觉是人们感知世界，学习言语、语言，阅读，以及发展认知能力最有效的途径之一。儿童正处于听觉、言语及语言发展的关键时期，听力障碍的发生会在一定程度上损害儿童的言语、语言功能，影响儿童认知、情感、个性及社会性发展［1］。

2. 听力障碍相关概念

听力障碍也称听力损失，指各种原因导致的听觉困难，听不到或听不清环境及言语声［20］。

2.1 听力障碍类型

听力障碍可根据其病变部位细分为传导性听力障碍、感音神经性听力障碍和混合性听力障碍。

（1）传导性听力障碍：由于外耳道及中耳的病变，声音在传导过程中出现障碍从而引起听力障碍。儿童受其障碍的常见原因有外耳道耵聍、中耳炎、异物、先天性外耳道闭锁等。

（2）感音神经性听力障碍：指内耳发生病变不能将声波转变成电信号或神经及其中枢途径发生障碍不能将电信号传入。常见于各种急慢性传染病导致的听力障碍，如药物或化学物质中毒、听神经瘤［10］、颞骨骨折及颅脑外伤等。

（3）混合性听力障碍：指传导和感音途径同时存在病变。常见原因多为慢性中耳炎、耳硬化症等［17］。

2.2 引发听力障碍的原因

造成听力障碍的原因及其发生的时间、性质和程度等各不相同。声音从外耳传至大脑形成听觉需要经历一系列复杂的传递及加工过程［24］。在此过程中，相关疾病涉及上述器官、组织病变、功能异常都有可能引起听力障碍［1］，包括：中耳炎、先天性胆脂瘤、颞骨骨折、内耳发育畸形、听神经发育不良［12］、听神经病谱系障碍［6］、小儿耳鸣［11］、小儿脑瘫［2］和镰状细胞性贫血等疾病［8］。

2.3 听力障碍矫正设备类型——助听器/人工耳蜗

（1）助听器

助听器是目前针对轻、中度感音神经性听力障碍、部分混合性及少部分传导性听力障碍的主要干预措施。据统计，目前全球约有4000万听障患者在使用助听器，且每年以5%的速度增长［13］。

（2）人工耳蜗

人工耳蜗是一种直接刺激听神经从而使植入者产生听觉的植入式电子装置。对于在耳蜗处发生病变、不能充分得益于助听器的双耳重度或极重度听力障碍患儿，建议选择人工耳蜗植入。据统计，全球现有19万听力障碍者植入了人工耳蜗，预计植入量今后将以每年15%的速度增长［20］。

3. 听力障碍相关的言语语言功能评估

3.1 听障儿童言语测听介绍

对于重度及以上听力损失儿童来说，人工耳蜗是最具革命性和有效性的植入式听觉解决方案之一，可恢复重度—极重度听力损失儿童和成人的言语交流能力［13］。区别于往常以听损程度作为入选人工耳蜗植入的重要指征，近年来国际上转而专注于优化助听后聋儿听觉言语能力的发育状况，因为听觉—言语能力才能最准确地反映听障儿童的残障程度［25］。临床上主要以言语测听来评估听障患儿言语识别能力，分为闭合式和开放式。对于言语测听材料，一些学者在国外英文版材料基础上，开发出若干与国际接轨，适合我国儿童不同发育阶段的测试材料。如郑芸等［14］仿照英文版PSI（Pediatric Speech Intelligibility）编制原则，结合普通话和中国儿童语言文化特点，开发了闭合式的中文儿童言语理解力（MPSI）测试。张宁生等［34］参照英文版LNT（Lexical Neighborhood Tests）开发了普通话版的词汇相邻性单音节词表和多音节词表，可用于5岁以上听障儿童开放式词汇辨识测试。

3.2 听障儿童言语评估方法介绍

听障儿童在植入助听设备，完成听能创建后，由于言语对大脑的刺激相较于同龄人减少，或多或少存在语言发育迟缓。所以针对听障儿童系统化的言语语言评估十分必要。言语评估方面，由黄昭鸣教授团队设计的《构音语音能力评估》［19］是一套使用较广泛的标准化构音评估工具，该工具由50个单音节词组成，包含21个声母、13个韵母和4个声调。通过18项音位对比、36对最小音位对比和音位习得情况的分析，测评患者声母音位习得的能力、声母音位对比的能力以及构音清晰度，该工具主要适用于3—6岁的儿童。

3.3 听障儿童语言评估方法介绍

在语言评估方面，目前使用较为广泛且信度、效度相对较高的评估工具是由培声听力语言中心研发的《普通话听力理解和表达能力标准化评估》（*Diagnostic Receptive and Expressive Assessment of Mandarin*, DREAM-C），可全面评估儿童的语言理解、语言表达、词义、句法和总体语言情况，该工具主要适用于2岁6个月至7岁11个月儿童。此外，其他常用的语言评估工具包括 PLS-5（Preschool Language Scales-Fifth Edition）、SLDT（Social Language Development Test）、Rossetti（The Rossetti Infant-Toddler Language Scale）等［20］。

由于国内康复起步相对较晚，故在语言沟通方面，全国各医院、机构及特殊学校多使用的是其自行设计的评估工具，具有全国统一性的标准化评估工具较少。

4. 听力障碍儿童言语语言治疗现状分析

4.1 听障儿童言语治疗现状分析

大量研究发现在轻、中度已完成听能创建的听障儿童中，约1/2患儿存在或多或少的言语语言功能障碍。在言语障碍中，根据患儿言语表达功能，又可以将其分为构音障碍、嗓音障碍和语畅障碍等。根据听障儿童言语障碍与语言障碍不同的临床表现可采取不同的治疗策略［32］。

4.1.1 听障儿童的构音障碍治疗

对于听障儿童构音障碍的康复治疗，应遵守由易而难，循序渐进的原则。根据国内一般儿童语音发展，在声母的习得上，双唇音/p/、/m/一般最先习得，儿童2周岁时即有90%出现率。而摩擦音（如/f/、/s/）的出现时间相对较晚。Yang等［5］认为，由于构音时舌位控制，以汉语为母语的人工耳蜗植入儿童相较于正常儿童尚未建立明显的摩擦音分类。在韵母的习得上，也遵循先训练单韵母（如/a/、/o/、/i/）后训练复韵母（如/ai/、/ou/）的顺序。Yang等［6］认为，听障儿童在言语习得早期阶段，没有为复韵母产生建立合适的目标和发音协调。这为进一步研究听障儿童言语康复的训练方法提供参考。构音障碍根据病因分类可分为功能性构音障碍和器质性构音障碍。其中器质性的构音障碍包括结构型、动作计划/神经系统型和感觉/知觉型。听障儿童的构音异常多为感觉/知觉型［3］。

（1）传统治疗法

在国内临床康复实践中对于听障儿童的构音障碍治疗多采用的是传统治疗法（traditional approach），该方法以动作为基础，强调先建立舌头构音行为的概念，给予大量听正确语音的机会，再进入听辨正确与错误音阶段，进而诱发目标语音，从单音、音节到词汇、词组再到长句及对话，逐步从简单到困难的层次，最后运用在日常对话当中。其中五个主要阶段为听知觉的训练（Sensory-perceptual training or ear training）、发音练习（Production training）、语音稳定阶段（Sound stabilization）、泛化阶段（Transfer and carryover training）和维持阶段（Maintenance）。

传统治疗法虽提出较早但沿用至今且使用广泛，因其繁简排列具有逻辑性、动作练习后可逐渐达成目标，使用起来具有高度弹性与应用性。只是，传统治疗法的治疗时间较长，有学者指出若个案存在多重构音错误，源于音系而非构音动作的错误，传统治疗法可能不是最佳治疗策略［15］。

（2）构音PCT法

构音PCT（Phonemic Contrast Therapy, PCT）法［36］是指在构音治疗中结合多种现代化技术，以最小音位对作为训练介质，开展递进式音位对比训练，提高患者连续语音的构音清晰度，为提高连续语音的清晰度、可懂度做准备的一种治疗方法。构音PCT法是一种相对较新的构音治疗技术，其强调对传统构音治疗中“音位对比”训练的延伸与拓展，该方法非常重视连续语音能力的训练，增加方法多样性与有效性。与此同时，该方法在执行时需注意治疗的持续性。有些家长在患儿刚习得目标音后，由于心态上急于求成或经济原因等因素就停止了治疗，而此时患儿尚未将目标音充分泛化，导致治疗不够彻底，甚至出现倒退。所以，康复干预的时间长短也会对最终疗效有重要影响。研究表明［20］，对于重度及以上听障患儿，言语康复干预前的听话识图能力与干预后0—6个月相比无明显差异，但干预后6—24个月，听障儿童的听话识图和模仿能力出现了明显提升。所以，持续康复、长期康复的模式十分重要。

另外，针对听障患儿产生的构音障碍，根据其错误类型及数量，需选择不同的治疗策略。原则上由易而难，循序渐进。一种特定的策略可能并不能适应所有儿童，而且在整个干预过程中，策略可能会随着儿童需求的变化而变化。下面介绍一些构音治疗策略［3］。

（1）纵向策略：对一个或两个目标的错误发音进行集中练习，直到孩子达到一个特定的标准水平（通常是会话水平），然后再进行下一个或多个目标。

（2）横向策略：在同一会话中单独或交互地解决多个目标，在一些目标上减少强度练习，从而接触到更多声音系统的方面。

（3）循环策略：针对多个目标的错误发音进行练习。将错误的发音分为几个阶段练习。然后再次按该顺序练习，至少3个回合。进行到下一个阶段时，不一定要全部掌握上一阶段的发音。

4.1.2 听障儿童的嗓音障碍治疗

与健听儿童相比，听障儿童的嗓音更易出现粗糙的音质及音调异常的问题。在临床中除了需进行常规的呼吸训练（如吸气与呼气发声的协调训练、最大发声时长训练、腹式呼吸训练）之外，还应注重放松声带训练。主要方法有打嘟法、咀嚼哼鸣法、哈欠叹息法、改良喉部按摩法等［37］。针对听障儿童的声调异常，可使用乐调匹配训练［22］，改善听障儿童音调偏高的问题。此外，汪梅梅、刘晋宣等学者［29］的研究显示不同语调的视听提示对于治疗效果良好的学龄前听障儿童的音调和音调变化有一定影响，可为其音调异常矫治提供指导。在国内，对于以上几种嗓音治疗方法在听障儿童方面的研究相对较少，暂缺大样本的群体实验证实其在听障儿童嗓音治疗中的有效性和可靠性。

4.1.3 听障儿童的语畅障碍治疗

听障儿童存在言语不流畅的问题，主要是言语产生系统功能不足所造成的，故从听障儿童的呼吸、发声与呼吸协调性和构音等方面进行干预可改善其言语流畅性。高晓慧、万勤等学者［18］在对3名听障儿童的言语不流畅问题的干预研究实验中首先使用了促进治疗法对其进行基础放松，然后分别且有针对性地采用了重读治疗法、快速用力呼气法、语音切换及轮替法来解决听障儿童在呼吸支持不足、发声与呼吸协调性欠佳、构音运动能力差的问题，综合提高了听障儿童言语产生系统的能力，从而显著改善了听障儿童言语不流畅问题［26］。在国内，对于听障儿童的语畅障碍治疗方面的研究相对较少，对于促进治疗法、重读治疗法、快速用力呼气法、语音切换及轮替法等治疗方法在听障儿童不流畅问题中的应用暂缺大样本的随机对照实验证实其在听障儿童语畅治疗中的有效性和针对性。

4.2 听障儿童语言治疗现状分析

相对于言语治疗，语言治疗的范畴更为广阔。语言表达是表达一种思维、理论、行动和需要的交流方式［16］。除口语外，还包括书面语、手势和表情等表达形式。包括对符号（sign）的接受（理解）和运用（表达）的能力。对于听障儿童来说，在其口语表达能力因构音障碍、嗓音障碍或流畅度等原因存在不足的情况下，可运用一些代偿方式帮助其表达。下面介绍一些具有代表性的语言治疗方法。

4.2.1 听觉口语法

听觉口语法（AVT）［15］指的是在助听设备等科学技术的协助下，教导听障儿童学习听声音、听懂口语并开口说话，成为一个听觉的学习者，最终成功融入社会的教学法。该方法在国内近年来的实践和研究显示其成果较显著，是稳定性较高的方法之一［15］。宋彩凤［28］指出

0—2岁的听障婴幼儿使用听觉口语法越早，干预效果越好。在康复训练中，前0—6个月听觉训练重点应建立婴幼儿对声音的察觉、分辨能力；言语训练应关注理解性语言积累；后6—12个月听觉训练应加强声音的辨识和理解能力。言语发展起步阶段应鼓励婴幼儿积极运用口语进行沟通，不断提升综合运用口语的能力。不过，该方法目前涉及面还相对较窄，在以听障儿童家庭为中心的相关研究较少［23］。

该方法也是听障儿童常用的早期干预方法之一［9］。早期干预对听障儿童成功康复至关重要［30］。早期干预包括“三早”，即早发现、早使用助听设备和早进行系统的言语语言康复［16］。郗昕［31］认为，耳外科专家与听力学专家应携起手来，审慎、稳妥、积极地开展低龄儿童耳蜗植入的循证医学研究。相比之下，言语语言方面的康复往往更容易被忽略。所以在给听障儿童适配助听设备之后，听力师需要让家长关注孩子言语理解和表达的能力，如果发现异常，需早期介入言语语言方面的相关干预。

4.2.2 综合沟通法

综合沟通法［12］（total communication）又称为全面交流法或同步沟通法。该方法并非倾向于某种特定的交流方法，而是综合运用手语法、声音扩大、口语法、手指法、读唇法等方法进行沟通训练，其目的主要是为其与家人、教师及同伴建立一个简单且高效的沟通模式［35］。该方法强调，为了利于听障儿童进行交流，可同时运用手语和口语中的一种或两种方式进行沟通。但其对家长有较高的要求，该模式提倡家庭成员中至少有一人但最好是全员均应接受一种视觉语言系统（如手语）的培训，并鼓励听障儿童坚持佩戴助听设备，家人在日常生活中与其交流时最好同步配以较为流畅的手语，为听障儿童建立一个更加良好的沟通环境。所以，在听障儿童的康复过程中，家长扮演着不可或缺的角色［33］。临床上，有些家长对于听障患儿的康复存在参与度不够及认知不足的问题。如在听障儿童年龄较大的情况下才介入言语语言康复，此时听障儿童已形成错误的构音方式，或伴随社交障碍，康复难度也会相应增大。有的家长由于经济因素或心态上急于求成，仅做了短期的康复后，见收效甚微就放弃治疗。所以，在对患儿进行言语康复治疗之外，对家长的宣教指导至关重要。

4.2.3 辅助与替代沟通系统

辅助与替代沟通系统（Augmentative and Alternative Communication，AAC）指任何能够帮助一个人提高沟通能力和效率的设备、系统或方式［21］。包括肢体动作、表情、图片和平板电脑等。它能帮助有言语表达障碍的人表达自己的需求、情绪、意见等，并且提高语言和阅读能力。许多听障儿童在言语语言发展方面表现出与同龄人明显的差距，这可能直接影响他们的社会互动。所以，辅助与替代沟通系统不失为一种可以帮助不同程度听障儿童提升语言理解与表达的有效方式。

Meinzen-Derra 和 Sheldon［4］介绍了一项将 AAC 策略纳入传统的言语语言治疗模型的实验，其研究结果表明，通过平板技术的 AAC 核心词汇语言策略可以支持学龄听障儿童持续和快速的口语技能增长。通过借助 AAC 技术，研究人员正在开拓一种结构化和动态的语言学习方法，为听障儿童的概念和语法奠定有效基础。

但是，由于 AAC 技术的运用需要患儿具备一定的认知及手功能（指认）操作能力，对于有认知障碍或无法指认的听障儿童，其效果有待进一步研究。

另外，AAC 的运用也需要多学科团队的支持［7］。比如指认等精细运动的操作及手眼协调能力就需要作业治疗师（OT）的协助。有些听障儿童前庭功能较弱容易引起身体平衡和姿势控制的问题，此时就需要物理治疗师（PT）的帮助。另外，患儿家长对 AAC 的了解程度也会影响听障儿童对其的使用效率。综上，多学科团队合作模式的运用对 AAC 的使用十分重要。

4.2.4 其他

（1）手型提示法［20］（Cued Speech）

手型提示法是一种以手型（Hand Shapes）线索来辅助呈现不同口语发音的

视觉沟通策略。听障儿童借助手型辅助线索可以更加全面且准确地了解沟通对象所传递的信息（如辨识相同唇形的语音）。此方法的主要目的之一是使听障儿童能更好地融入听力社会，并促进其沟通技巧的发展［20］。但其对家长有较高的要求，该模式提倡听障儿童父母双方或至少一方应学会手型提示法且流畅地运用于日常生活中，为其提供良好的示范，从而促进听障儿童沟通能力的发展［16］。

（2）针灸疗法

针灸疗法是以中医理论为指导，运用针刺和艾灸防治疾病的一种方法。但国内将其应用在听障儿童上的个案少之又少。Min［9］的个案研究介绍了一名15岁女孩，由于感冒引发感音性听力障碍，在发病后93—135天运用鼓室内类固醇无效的情况下，运用针刺、经皮电神经刺激和艾灸疗法后，平均纯音、语音识别阈值和单词识别分数有所提升。该作者认为针灸疗法可在使用类固醇或错过早期治疗无显著改善的情况下，作为治疗突发性感音神经性听力损失的一种选择。作为针灸疗法的发源国，这篇文章值得我们思考。针对一些听障儿童，在传统方法无明显效果的情况下，怎样融合祖国传统医学进行治疗方法创新需要我们深入探究。

5. 总结和展望

经听障儿童言语语言治疗的现状分析，笔者认为：

首先，针对听障儿童言语语言障碍的评估，由于国内听障言语语言康复起步相对较晚，全国统一的标准化评估工具相对较少［16］。所以，加强各地区学术交流合作，形成全国层面的听障儿童言语语言康复学术组，开发全国统一、汉语特色的听障儿童言语语言标准化评估工具是当前需要进行的任务。

其次，对于听障儿童言语障碍的康复治疗，在语音发展上应遵守由易而难，循序渐进的原则。传统治疗法和构音PCT法是解决听障儿童构音异常问题的首选方案，呼吸训练和声带放松训练用于治疗听障儿童的嗓音障碍。对于语畅问题，常采用促进治疗法、重读治疗法、快速用力呼吸法和语音切换轮替法。这些方法对于有口语能力的听障儿童来说，可以有效提升其言语清晰度、流畅度，让他人更好地理解听障儿童言语表达的内容，改善其沟通与社交能力。只是，以上方法在听障儿童言语治疗方面的研究仍较少，且以个案研究居多。

另外，在听障儿童语言障碍的康复治疗方面，常采用听觉口语法、手型提示法、综合沟通法、辅助与替代沟通系统（AAC）和针灸疗法进行干预。这些方法或借助视觉提示，或借助高科技设备，在语言理解方面，为听障儿童提供了除语音输入外其他的信息输入大脑的方式，是对听力障碍的代偿。在语言表达方面，针对无口语表达能力的听障儿童，手形提示或AAC等都是良好的语音代偿方式。而针对有口语表达能力但口语清晰、流畅度较差的听障儿童，这些方法可以为其言语表达提供补偿，使他人更好地理解听障儿童所传达的内容。不过这几种方法专业性较强，听障儿童家庭是否能灵活运用有一定挑战。所以，治疗师对家长专业、系统的家庭指导和培训势在必行。

与此同时，笔者认为早期康复、持续康复和家长参与等康复模式的运用对听障儿童家庭也很重要。

当然，临床上患儿的情况比较复杂，需要我们结合患儿的情况具体问题具体分析，根据患儿的临床表现、性格特点以及家庭的配合程度，选择高效有针对性的治疗方法。目前，我国听障患儿的言语治疗早期引进借鉴了国外的成熟经验，与此同时，我们要思考这些方法是否可以更好地适应本土，更符合中国儿童的语言特点和文化习惯。因为针对言语及语言障碍，不同语种的语法构成及语音特点各不相同。相对其他外语，汉语在语音学上有阴平、阳平、上声、去声四个不同声调，同一音节不同声调有截然不同的含义。汉语在听觉感受上更加抑扬顿挫，需要大脑对不同声调更高的辨别能力。

在音素组成上，绝大多数外文是拼音

文字，每个单词由不同音节组合而成，而中文由汉字组成。基本上汉字与音节是一一对应的关系，且由特定的声母、韵母构成。所以汉语构音错误的类型（音素省略、添加、歪曲、置换的方式）相较于其他语系也会有所不同，值得进一步探究。

综上所述，当下我们可以在借鉴国外听障患儿言语语言康复成功经验的基础上，制定更符合汉语特点的介入方案以及家庭宣教方案，提高社会对听障儿童的关注度，发展中国特色、汉语特色的听障儿童言语语言介入计划，更好地造福听障儿童，帮助其更好地适应环境、适应社会。

参考文献

[1] Sorkin, D. L., Gates-Ulanet, P., Mellon, N. K. 2015. Psychosocial Aspects of Hearing Loss in Children, *Otolaryngol Clin. N. Am.* 1 – 8.

[2] Weir, F. W., Hatch, J. L., McRackan, T. R., Wallace, S. A., Meyer, T. A. 2017. Hearing Loss in Pediatric Patients With Cerebral Palsy. *Otology & Neurotology* 39, 59 – 64.

[3] Roth, F. P., Worthington, C. K. 2016. *Treatment Resource Manual for Speech-Language Pathology 5th Edition.* Clifton Park: Cengage Learning.

[4] Meinzen-Derra, J., Sheldon, R. M. 2019. Enhancing language in children who are deaf/hard-of-hearing using augmentative and alternative communication technology strategies. *International Journal of Pediatric Otorhinolaryngology* 125, 23 – 31.

[5] Yang, J., Vadlamudi, J., Yin, Z., Lee, C. Y., Xu, L. 2016. Production of word-initial fricatives of Mandarin Chinese in prelingually deafened children with cochlear implants. *International Journal of Speech-Language Pathology* 19, 153 – 164.

[6] Yang, J., Xu, L. 2017. Mandarin compound vowels produced by prelingually deafened children with cochlear implants. *International Journal of Pediatric Otorhinolaryngology* 97, 143 – 149.

[7] Hawley, K., Goldberg, D., Anne, S. 2017. Utility of a multidisciplinary approach to pediatric hearing loss. *American Journal of Otolaryngology* 1 – 4.

[8] Rissatto-Lago, M. R., da Cruz Fernandes, L., Lyra, I. M., Terse-Ramos, R., Teixeira, R., Salles, C., Ladeia, A. M. T. 2019. Hidden hearing loss in children and adolescents with sickle cell anemia. *International Journal of Pediatric Otorhinolaryngology* 116, 186 – 191.

[9] Kim, M. H., Kim, B. H., Kang, M., Choi, I. 2018. Delayed recovery of pediatric sudden sensorineural hearing loss treated with acupuncture. *Medicine* 97(51), 1 – 3.

[10] Pham, N. S. 2017. The management of pediatric hearing loss caused by auditory neuropathy spectrum disorder. *Current Opinion in Otolaryngology & Head and Neck Surgery* 25, 1 – 4.

[11] Kerr, R., Kang, E., Hopkins, B., Anne, S. 2017. Pediatric tinnitus: Incidence of imaging anomalies and the impact of hearing loss. *International Journal of Pediatric Otorhinolaryngology* 103, 147 – 149.

[12] Owen, R. E., Dale, J., Metz, E., Farinella, K. A. 2018. *Introduction to Communication Disorders: A Lifespan Evidence-Based Perspective, 5th Edition.* New York: Pearson.

[13] Wilson, B. S. 2019. The remarkable cochlear implant and possibilities for the next large step forward. *Acoustics Today* 15(1), 53 – 61.

[14] Zheng Y, Soli SD, Wang K, et al. 2009. Development of the Mandarin pediatric speech intelligibility (MPSI) test. *International Journal of Audiology*, 718 – 728.

[15]陈军兰：《听觉口语教学理论与实操》，北京出版社2018年版。

[16] 刀维洁：《听觉口语法在我国推广应用的现状与展望》，《中国听力语言康复科学杂志》2020年第18期。

[17] 高墨梅、尹德佩、窦训武等：《儿童单侧听力损失的临床常见病因及听力学表现》，《临床耳鼻咽喉头颈外科杂志》2020年第5期。

[18] 高晓慧、万勤、惠芬芬等：《对听障儿童言语不流畅问题的干预研究》，《中国特殊教育》2016年第12期。

[19] 黄昭鸣、万勤、张蕾：《言语功能评估标准及方法》，华东师范大学出版社2007年版。

[20] 胡向阳：《听障儿童全面康复》，北京科学技术出版社2012年版。

[21] 李欢、杨爱佳、李登钰等：《循证理念视域下听障儿童言语康复方法研究》，《中国特殊教育》2016年第3期。

[22] 李明华：《乐调匹配训练法对听障儿童音调异常的个案研究》，《科教导刊》2013年11月上。

[23] 林桂如：《以家庭为中心的听觉障碍早期疗愈—听觉口语法理论与实务》，心理出版社2014年版。
[24] 刘巧云、候梅：《康复治疗师临床工作指南—儿童语言康复治疗技术》，人民卫生出版社2019年版。
[25] 刘莎、郗昕：《我国儿童言语测听的现状与发展》，《听力学及言语疾病杂志》2013年第3期。
[26] 马晶、徐芬、万浪等：《学龄前儿童听力损失的原因及干预效果分析》，《听力学及言语疾病杂志》2019年第6期。
[27] 马琪琪、刘艳玲、朱晓丹等：《社会生态系统理论视角下听力障碍儿童照顾者照顾感受的质性研究》，《护理学杂志》2019年第20期。
[28] 宋彩凤：《0～2岁听障婴幼儿听觉口语法教学策略研究》，《中国听力语言康复科学杂志》2020年第5期。
[29] 汪梅梅、刘晋宣、万勤等：《不同视听提示方式对学龄前听障儿童嗓音基频的影响》，《听力学及言语疾病杂志》2018年第6期。
[30] 郗昕：《儿童人工耳蜗植入年龄下限降至9月龄的启示与应对》，《中国耳鼻咽喉颅底外科杂志》2020年第6期。
[31] 郗昕：《人工耳蜗相关的中文言语测听材料十年发展巡礼》，《中华耳科学杂志》2013年第3期。
[32] 杨影、孙喜斌、王丽燕：《先天性重度及以上程度听力损失婴幼儿语言能力康复效果观察》，《听力学及言语疾病杂志》2015年第23期。
[33] 杨影、孙喜斌：《听力障碍婴幼儿家庭早期干预研究进展》，《中国康复理论与实践》2013年第7期。
[34] 张宁、盛玉麒、刘莎等：《普通话儿童词汇相邻性单音节词表的编制》，《听力学及言语疾病杂志》2009年第4期。
[35] 张宁生、胡雅梅：《听觉障碍者的综合交流法》，《心理科学》2002年第6期。
[36] 张青允：《基于PCT法的听障儿童舌根音g的构音个案》，《山东农业工程学院学报》2016年第2期。
[37] 张奕雯、唐俊、金星等：《听障儿童嗓音问题的康复治疗研究进展》，《临床耳鼻咽喉头颈外科杂志》2016年第17期。

倪佳伶 目前为同济大学附属养志康复医院儿童言语治疗师，硕士，研究兴趣包括听障儿童构音训练。
E－mail：1565445320@qq.com

陈伟民 目前为同济大学附属养志康复医院儿童言语治疗师，本科，研究兴趣包括听障儿童语言训练。
E－mail：1076309056@qq.com

张蓓华 目前为同济大学附属养志康复医院儿童康复治疗师，硕士，主要研究领域为儿童康复及脑科学研究。
E－mail：helley－007@163.com

PERCEPTION OF VELARIZED /l/ AND VOWEL /ɔ/ CONTRAST BY CHINESE LEARNERS OF ENGLISH

LIAO Sishi, DING Hongwei

Abstract This paper aims to examine the second language (L2) phonetic categorical perception (CP) pattern by Chinese learners of English, regarding the contrast of dark /l/ and vowel /ɔ/. Three perception experiments were carried out progressively: a simple identification task, an AXB identification task, and a revised AX discrimination task. The study discovered a significant difference in vowel contexts in the perception of dark /l/ and vowel /ɔ/, in which high vowels stand out, and demonstrated that English proficiency evaluated by standard examinations cannot be reflected in L2 phonetic discrimination. The study also proved the validity of adding reference stimuli in enhancing CP performance, but this improvement only benefits the identification tasks. The study helps to fill in the current knowledge gap concerning Chinese L2 learners' difficulty in distinguishing dark /l/ and vowel /ɔ/. The new finding contributes to a deeper understanding of the vowel-context effect on CP performance, as well as implications in second language teaching in exploring the connections between L2 speech perception and production.
Key Words L2 speech perception, Velarized /l/, Categorical perception

1. INTRODUCTION

It is known that late learners of the second language (L2) tend to have a foreign accent that is resulted from the imperfect acquisition of L2 phonology and phonetics [9]. L2 English production presents various characteristics by English language learners (ELLs) at both segmental [5] and suprasegmental levels [16]. Segmental inequivalence induces more severe problems to comprehensibility, thus bears more relative studies [21].

Even so, not as much attention has been paid to the acquisition of L2 liquid consonants, especially an allophone of English /l/— velarized /l/ (i. e. dark /l/). Dark /l/ commonly locates in syllable coda. Few studies have explored the perception of /l/ vocalization, similar to the /w/-like sound [22].

Phoneme /l/ in the Mandarin Chinese phonological system is similar to /l/ in Received Pronunciation (RP), in which no velarized dark /l/ exists. As for the dark /l/ in syllable coda, Mandarin Chinese speakers have different ways of realization. According to the study of He [6], Chinese speakers usually adopt three strategies to modify syllable-final /l/, i. e. vocalization, deletion, and retroflection. Among all these strategies, vocalization is the most common method for all vowel contexts. As the apical gesture is lost and the dorsal gesture is maintained, vowels that share the features of [+back, +round] would mostly fit the substitution [10]. Between /ɔ/ and /u: /, /ɔ/ appears more frequently in our pilot study. Therefore, we would like to answer this question: What is the perception pattern of dark /l/ and /ɔ/, among native speakers of Mandarin in the current study?

Categorical perception (CP) in speech refers to the action of perceiving the continuous sound stimuli as discrete and limited categories. It requires the ability to find a clear-cut boundary between two categories of phonemes. Stimuli between categories are easier to discriminate than those within one category.

Opposite to CP, continuous perception refers to a failure to find a clear-cut boundary between two categories of phonemes. Also, another perception pattern called quasi-categorical perception, which suggests that there is a gradient of categoricity in the perception of the various types of linguistic speech elements [13], and a distinction of categoricity between consonants and vowels [18]. When it comes to this kind of perception, a boundary occurs between two categories but is not clear-cut and extends across a wider range.

Identification and discrimination tasks have similarities as well as differences: (1) simple identification tasks focus more on strong features, while discrimination tasks emphasize more on the holistic shapes [20]; (2) simple identification and discrimination tasks are processed in different stages in language acquisition [14]; (3) discrimination tasks are more powerful in determining sounds that are between categories [7] (as in this case, dark /l/ and vowel /ɔ/ belong to different phoneme categories).

To answer our research question, we conducted experiments to examine the following issues: (1) the existence of CP between /ɔ/ and dark /l/; (2) the different CP patterns in different vowel contexts (i. e. in syllables like /hVl/ with different vowels); (3) the different CP patterns among learners with different English proficiencies; (4) the differences among experimental paradigms.

2. METHOD

2.1 Participants

All the participants were from Shanghai Jiao Tong University with Mandarin as their native language, without listening or oral deficiency. According to self-report and observation, all the participants had normal vision and hearing.

2.1.1 Grouping of participants

The participants were divided into two groups with respect to their English proficiency levels through their scores in standardized English tests: College English Test Band 4 (CET-4) and Band 6 (CET-6), Test for English Majors Band 8 (TEM-8), and TOEFL or IELTS.

Group 1 (G1) included participants who were English majored masters and above and had scored more than 600 in CET. Group 2 (G2) included participants who were from intermediate English level and had scored less than 500 in the College English Test (CET).

2.1.2 Age

The distribution of age in G1 and G2 were both in Gaussian distribution. The mean values were $\mu_{G1} = 23.3$ and $\mu_{G2} = 22.4$, and the standard deviations were $\sigma_{G1} = 2.48$ and $\sigma_{G2} = 2.42$. There was no significant difference between the ages of the two groups, using the ANOVA analysis.

2.2 Years of learning English

The distribution of years in learning English in G1 and G2 were both in Gaussian distribution, the mean values were $\mu_{G1} = 14.43$ and $\mu_{G2} = 12.26$, and the standard deviations were $\sigma_{G1} = 3.441$ and $\sigma_{G1} = 3.129$. There was a significant difference in years of learning English between the two groups ($p < 0.01$).

2.3 Onset age of learning English

Although controversially criticized, according to the Critical Period Hypothesis [11], the onset age of learning a foreign language is also regarded as an important factor in determining one's English proficiency. The distributions of onset year in learning English in G1 and G2 were both Gaussian distributed, the mean values were $\mu_{G1} = 8.87$ and $\mu_{G2} = 10.13$, and the standard deviations were $\sigma_{G1} = 2.60$ and $\sigma_{G1} = 2.43$. By grouping the participants according to their certificates of English, no significant difference was found in the same group for their onset age.

2.4 Stimuli

2.4.1 Recording of stimuli

The audio stimuli were recorded in a studio in Shanghai Jiao Tong University. The speaker was a native American speaker who had grown up in Chicago in the United States. The speech stimuli were collected with *Praat* [3]. Audios were recorded in monochannel, with a sampling frequency of 44.1 kHz, bit depth of 16 bit, and in .wav format.

The texts were syllables in /hVl/ and /hVɔ/ pattern with seven different English vowels (i.e. /ɑː/, /æ/, /ɔ/, /e/, /ɜː/, /iː/, /uː/). /h/ was chosen as the syllable initial consonant to eliminate the undesired influences caused by the preceding consonant. Among the fourteen syllables, six were real words: Hal /hæl/, hall /hɔːl/, hell /hel/, heal /hiːl/, hurl /hɜːl/, hool /huːl/, while all the words ending with /ɔ/ were pseudowords or nonwords. This should not contribute to the bias of perception [1].

2.4.2 Manipulation of stimuli

Normalization is requisite for simple identification and discrimination tasks. Some scholars [4] use synthetic stimuli throughout the continuum to control variables; but in this study, natural recordings were used and manipulated to control variables, which could generate more natural-sounding speech stimuli. The "calibration sounds" were then normalized using *Praat* [3], and the processes included three aspects of manipulation, i.e. duration, intensity, and pitch. All these three parameters were normalized according to stimulus A, i.e. the word ends with /l/.

Firstly, duration modification was executed. After the manipulation with *Praat* scripting, we achieved the modified sound of /hVɔ/ in each pair, which had the same duration for each phoneme as their /hVl/ counterpart.

Secondly, as an acoustic feature, the pitch is also important. We adopted the *resynthesis* function to keep the overall word pitch the same.

We adopted the synthesis algorithm in *Straight* [12] to make a natural and smooth continuum between two "calibration sounds". After getting the seven pairs of "calibration sounds", the stimuli continuum was generated.

Finally, we obtained 77 continuum stimuli: 11 continua for each pair, and 7 pairs in all.

2.5 Procedure

2.5.1 Instructions

Instructions were given to the participants after they arrived at the lab. In the experiment, audios were played by PC, through Sennheiser headphones. Participants conducted the task with the Numpad on the keyboard, using "1" key for /hVl/ and '3' key for /hVɔ/.

The overall presentation of the three tasks included two phases: a training phase and an experiment phase. Seven sections were included in the experiment phase, with each section containing words in /hVl/ and /hVɔ/ patterns with different vowel contexts /ɑː, æ, ɔ, e, ɜː, iː, uː/.

For each participant, the order of the three experiments was in a random manner, which excluded the possibility that participants' experiences in earlier tasks facilitated their performances in later ones.

2.5.2 Task 1

Task 1 was a simple identification task. In this task, participates were presented with one stimulus each time, and were instructed to make a forced choice between two contrasting labels.

In this task, the stimulus appeared once

in a trial, so the Inter-Stimulus Interval (ISI) was the same as the Inter-Trial Interval (ITI) -400 ms. ISI was the amount of time between separate stimuli in psychological experiments, as illustrated in [15] (see Fig. 1):

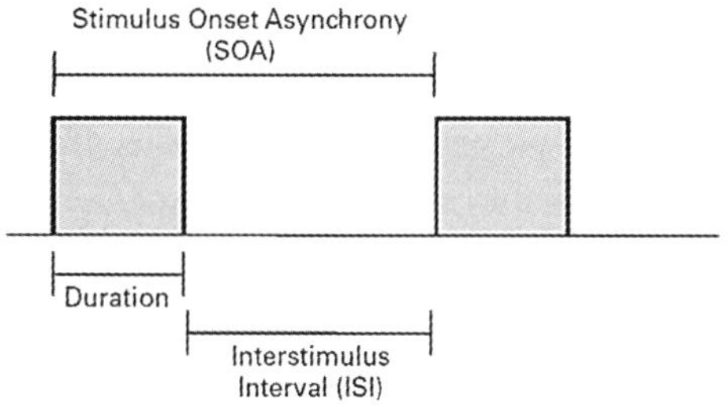

Figure 1 Duration of stimulus, ISI, and SOA

2.5.3 Task 2

Task 2 was an AXB identification task. ABX discrimination task was the prototype of a CP experiment [13]. However, a seemingly similar but inherently different paradigm was adopted in this task. AXB identification tasks differed in the endpoint stimuli from AXB discrimination tasks. A and B were end stimuli; X was either identical to A or B. This revised experiment was conducted, as we intended to compare it with the result of the simple identification task. This revision alleviated the exclusive use of memory of auditory traces and labeling.

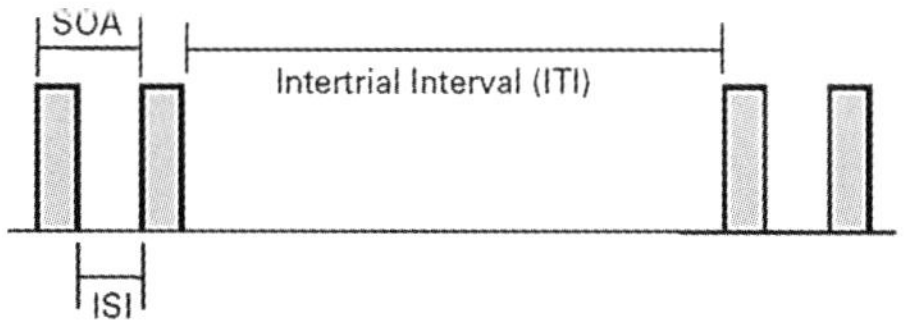

Figure 2 The relationship between stimulus duration, SOA, ISI, and ITI

In the previous simple identification experiment, there was only one stimulus per trial, so the ISI equaled ITI. However, in this AXB identification experiment (see Fig. 2), there were three stimuli in each trial, with different duration values in each part, thus the ITI was no longer the same as ISI.

In this task, there was an inequality between ISI and ITI. This was because the SOA should be kept as 1000 ms, despite the different duration values of audio files.

2.5.4 Task 3

Task 3 was a revised AX discrimination task. In the original AX discrimination experiment, the subject should decide whether the two stimuli in a trial were the same or different. A disadvantage of this paradigm lies in the different ways of perceiving as "different". Some participants might decide to respond with "different" once a very slight difference was observed; others might only respond with "different" only to those stimuli broadly across the boundary. This means that AX may be strongly biased: a subject's response could be completely dominated by a subjective criterion.

So we modified the task paradigm in such a manner: in each trial, there were four sounds, the first and the last were the same stimuli (either s01 or s11). Take s01 as the end stimulus, for example, the two stimuli in between would be s01 and s04, s02 and s05, s03 and s06, s04 and s07, or vice versa.

Such as: *s01 s01 s04 s01*,

or: *s01 s04 s01 s01.*

For every vowel context as a separate section, the arrangement of stimuli—a row as a trial-repeated for three times, for a more accurate outcome.

Different from the traditional AX discrimination task, this experiment changed the classical paradigm in two ways: one was the stripping of "same" pairs for time limit reason, the other was that we appended calibration stimuli on both sides of the central stimuli as reference.

3. RESULTS

3.1 Task 1

3.1.1 Differences among vowels

● *Analysis: boundary position*

In CP, we defined the boundary position as the 50% crossover point along the rising continua [4, 17]. From the different perceptual boundary among vowels, we assumed that L2 learners of English had different abilities in distinguish dark /l/ and /ɔ/ with different vowel contexts. To testify our assumption, we adopted a set of *linear mixed effect regressions* ("lmer" package in R [2]). We set boundary position as the dependent variable and the vowel contexts as the independent variables. After seven rounds of regressions, each with a different vowel as its baseline, we concluded vowel pairs that had significantly different perceptual boundaries: /ɑː/ and /iː/ ($p < 0.1$), /ɑː/ and /uː/ ($p < 0.01$), /æ/ and /ɔ/ ($p < 0.05$), /æ/ and /iː/ ($p < 0.01$), /æ/ and /uː/ ($p < 0.001$), /ɔ/ and /e/ ($p < 0.1$), /e/ and /iː/ ($p < 0.01$), /e/ and /uː/ ($p < 0.001$), /ɜ/ and /iː/ ($p < 0.05$), /ɜ/ and /uː/ ($p < 0.01$).

It is clear that among the seven vowel contexts, the high vowels /iː/ and /uː/ stood out. In a lenient standard, there was a significant difference in high vowels (/iː/ and /uː/) compared to /ɑː/, /æ/, /e/, /ɜ/. This result provided a concrete basis for the assumption that L2 learners of English had different abilities in distinguishing dark /l/ and /ɔ/ with different vowel contexts.

● *Analysis: boundary width*

In CP, boundary width is commonly defined as the linear distance between two percentiles along the continua, which is assessed by probit analysis of every single curve [8]. In this experiment, the boundary width was defined as the linear distance between the 25th and 75th percentiles [4, 17].

We found a great difference in boundary width among all the vowels, among which /iː/ and /uː/ stood out in their boundary width. The mean perceptual boundary width ranged from 2.73 to 7.22. We assumed that L2 learners of English tended to have different abilities to distinguish dark /l/ and /ɔ/ in different vowel contexts. Using the same function [2], we set boundary width as the dependent variable and the vowel contexts as the independent variables. After seven rounds of regressions, each with a different vowel as its baseline, we found the vowel pairs that have significantly different perceptual boundary widths: /ɑː/ and /ɜ/ ($p < 0.05$), /iː/ ($p < 0.001$), /uː/ ($p < 0.05$); /æ/ and /e/ ($p < 0.05$), /ɜ/ ($p < 0.001$), /iː/ ($p < 0.001$), /uː/ ($p < 0.001$); /ɔ/ and /iː/ ($p < 0.01$), /uː/ ($p < 0.1$); /e/ and /ɜ/ ($p < 0.1$), /iː/ ($p < 0.001$), /uː/ ($p < 0.05$), /ɜ/ and /iː/ ($p < 0.1$).

3.1.2 Differences between groups

Differences occurred not only among vowels but also between groups of participants. From the raw data, participants in G2 seemed to have better performances than those in G1, therefore the same calculation was conducted as in 3.1.1.

● *Analysis: boundary position and boundary width*

We conducted t-tests to investigate the significance of differences between groups. There turned out to be no significant difference in the performance between the two groups in any vowel context.

3.2 Task 2

3.2.1 Differences among vowels

The situation that boundary position differed in each vowel also existed in this AXB identification task. The mean perceptual boundary ranged from 5.75 to 6.48, although not as obvious as it in simple identification tasks – 4.40 to 6.85. We adopted a set of *linear mixed-effects regressions* [2], in which we set boundary position as the dependent variable and the vowels as the independent variables. After seven rounds of regressions, each with a different vowel as its baseline, we obtained the vowel pairs that had significantly different perceptual boundaries: /ɑː/ and /æ/ ($p<0.05$), /ɔ/ ($p<0.001$), /e/ ($p<0.05$), /æ/ and /ɔ/ ($p<0.001$), /ɜ/ ($p<0.001$), /iː/ ($p<0.001$), /ɔ/ and /e/ ($p<0.001$), /ɜ/ ($p<0.001$), /iː/ ($p<0.001$), /uː/ ($p<0.001$), /e/ and /ɜ/ ($p<0.05$), /iː/ ($p<0.05$). There was significant CP in all vowel contexts.

On the difference of boundary width, similar conclusions could be drawn with the last experiment. We noticed a legible difference in perceptual boundary width can be noticed among vowels, with a distinguishable median value and Q1/Q3.

3.2.2 Differences between groups

The obscure boundary in CP appeared more frequently in participants from G2 than G1, which caused the clearness of boundary position to vary between groups.

- *Analysis: boundary position and width*

For each vowel context, the boundary position and width differed between the two groups. T-tests were conducted for each vowel context, concerning boundary position and width to testify whether there was a significant difference between groups of participants in different vowels. The results turned out to be not significant either in the performance between groups or in the performance between groups in any vowel contexts.

3.2.3 Differences between tasks

We found significant differences not only in the interaction between vowels and groups but also between the two tasks (see Fig. 3).

In order to testify whether there was a significant difference in boundary position and width between tasks, one-way ANOVA was conducted in each vowel context. The results showed that participants performed significantly better in task 2 than in task 1, with: (1) the number of valid cases doubled in task 2 (364) than in task 1 (186); (2) the p value stated the significance: for boundary position, $p<0.05$ in /ɑː/, /e/, and /ɜ/; in boundary width, $p<0.001$ in /æ/, $p<0.01$ in /e/, and $p<0.05$ in /uː/.

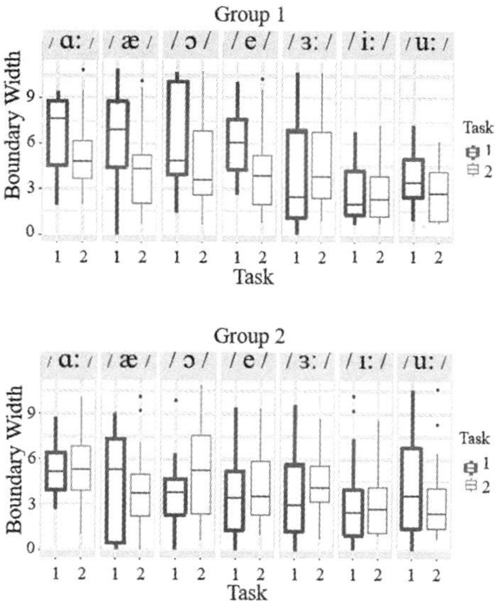

Figure 3 The comparison of boundary width between tasks among each vowel

3.3 Task 3

The percentage of correctness for different groups of participants was plotted with the stimuli pairs as the x-axis (see Fig. 4). In the figure, G1 slightly outperformed G2, but the difference was not significant. A peak may appear between stimuli belonging to two categories [4]. The peaks in most vowels (/ɑ/, /æ/, /e/, /ɛ/) were left-skewed, while that in vowel /ɔ/ was right-skewed. Participants' performances in vowel contexts of /iː/ and /uː/ were much better than the other vowels.

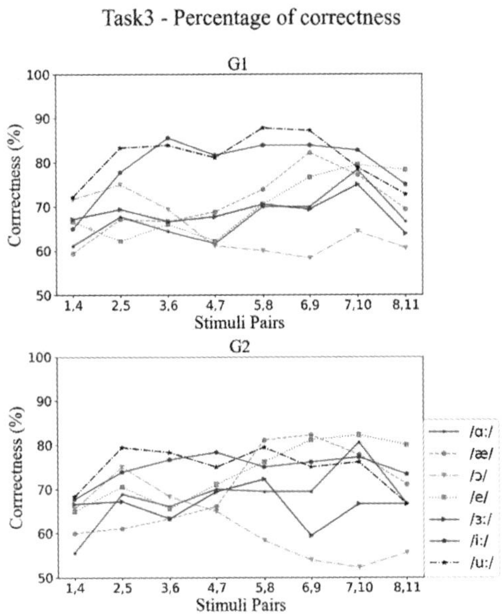

Figure 4 The comparison in accuracy between group one and group two in their performance in the revised AX discrimination tasks

4. DISCUSSION

4.1 Task 1

The results of this simple identification experiment provided evidence for two of our research questions.

Firstly, there was only CP in certain vowel contexts (i. e. /iː/ and /uː/). Participants had better performances in high vowel contexts, which gives us a clue on the influence of formants in the perception pattern of dark /l/ and /ɔ/.

Secondly, English proficiency was not a determinant in the CP of dark /l/ and /ɔ/ contrast. The participants from the two groups did not have a significant difference in the perception tasks, from two signs (boundary position and width). This phenomenon testifies that this task takes place in the phonetic stage of speech perception, see illustrations in [19]. High-level L2 speakers are more likely to concentrate on other aspects (such as vocabulary, grammar), instead of phonetics. The indistinguishable performances between the two groups of participants suggest that the current L2 education rarely focuses on phonetics or speech training, and that only very well-designed or multi-model practices could stimulate the L2 learners' abilities in speech perception and learning.

We conclude that in the analysis of boundary position and width, high vowels (/iː/ and /uː/) stand out, which confirmed our assumption that L2 learners of English have different abilities in distinguishing dark /l/ and /ɔ/ with different vowel contexts.

4.2 Task 2

The results of this AXB identification task confirmed different perceptual patterns in different experimental paradigms.

There was a significant difference in the CP in all vowel contexts. Different from the results in the simple identification task, in which only high-vowel contexts contributed to the significance, this AXB identification task made every monophthong context significant in boundary position/width. One-to-one lmer test was conducted for each pair of vowel contexts. A significant difference between vowels was detected, resulting in a similar conclusion: as vowel contexts, all the seven monophthongs can be regarded as a factor influencing the coda's perception, except for the vowel /ɔ/.

There was no significant difference between groups of participants with different English proficiencies. This finding suggests that L2 proficiency does not influence the perceptual results in any task type.

From the two perspectives including boundary position and width regarding CP, this AXB identification task presented a significantly better performance than the simple identification task, showing a task effect

[6]. We here conclude from the comparison between the two identification tasks, that adding reference stimuli to each side of the stimulus could enhance the participants' ability in identifying dark /l/ and /ɔ/.

4.3 Task 3

In the previous experiments, we concluded that adding reference stimuli to each side of the stimulus could enhance the participants' ability in identifying dark /l/ and /ɔ/. This experiment used a revised AX discrimination task to test the validity of the "adding reference stimuli enhances perception" hypothesis.

There was categorical perception in certain vowel-contexts, while nearly no CP in others. Between groups of participants, the performance turned out to be different only in high vowels. However, the performance of the revised task was not as good as expected, for only two vowel contexts' accuracy reached above 80%. This suggests that adding a reference to each side of the testing stimuli enhances the performance of identification tasks more than discrimination tasks.

4.4 Limitations and implications

There were also some limitations in this study: for example, there were more female participants than their male counterparts, which prevented us from comparing gender differences in the perception tasks. Moreover, it would be better if we could recruit native speakers as well, so as to investigate the differences in the perception patterns by native vs. non-native speakers.

Despite the limitations, this study supplies a great many implications for future research.

Firstly, because of the bias of different methods, complementary experiments can be conducted to compare the perceptual inequivalence between native and L2 learners in distinguishing dark /l/. Secondly, more could be explored on the relationship between two elements in categorical perception, according to their distance to specific vowel context in the F1-F2 coordinate. Thirdly, more realizations (vocalization, deletion, retroflection) of dark /l/ could be investigated, which could be compared to /ɔ/-substitution in CP performance as well. Also, the conduction of a set of perception experiments between dark /l/ and other substitutions could give rise to a scale of vowel contexts in dark /l/ perceptual accuracy.

5. CONCLUSION

There was CP only in certain vowel contexts (/iː/ and /uː/) in the simple identification task; but in the AXB identification task, CP existed in all vowel contexts, which shows a task effect in categorical perception. No matter in simple or AXB identification tasks, the two high vowels' overwhelming performance gives us a clue on the formant's influence on the distinction of dark /l/ and /ɔ/.

There was no significant difference between students with different English proficiencies. English proficiency, as a determinant in perceiving linguistic-level difference, did not play a role in CP performances, which could only be addressed by that dark /l/-vowel /ɔ/ contrast depends more on acoustic processing rather than merely phonetic processing.

There was a task effect in perceiving the contrast. In this study, the validity of enhancing perceptual performance by adding a reference stimulus was explored. From the two perspectives including boundary position and width, the AXB identification task presented a significantly better performance than the simple identification task, showing a task effect [6]. In task 1, there was no significant difference between any two vowel contexts; in task 2, there was a significant difference between some pairs of vowel contexts. This suggests that adding reference stimuli reduces the difficulty of speech perception.

Vowel context seemed to be an influential factor in the perceptual tasks for Chinese learners of English, which was also true for native speakers of English. In this case, high vowels had a better performance. Adding reference stimuli was helpful for the identification tasks but had little influence on discrimination tasks. Neither the identification task nor the discrimination task showed an outcome with a significant difference between participants from two-level English proficiency, which illustrates the processing stage in perceiving the dark /l/-vowel vs. /ɔ/ contrast is still in the acoustic level.

6. ACKNOWLEDGEMENTS

The work was supported by the Shanghai Social Science Project (2018BYY003), the Major Program of National Social Science Foundation of China (No. 15ZDB103), and China Scholarship Council.

REFERENCES

[1] Arndt, J., Lee, K., Flora, D. B. 2008. Recognition without identification for words, pseudowords and nonwords. *Journal of Memory and Language* 59, 346 – 360.

[2] Bates, D., Maechler, M., Bolker, B., Walker, B. 2015. Fitting linear mixed-effects models using lme4. *Journal of Statistical Software* 67, 1 – 48.

[3] Boersma, P., Weenink, D. 2007. Praat: Doing phonetics by computer (Version 4.5.) [Computer program]. Retrieved from http://www.praat.org/.

[4] Chen, F., Yan, N., Wang, N., Yang, T., Wu, J., Zhao, H., Peng, G. 2015. The development of categorical perception of lexical tones in Mandarin-speaking preschoolers. *Proceedings of Interspeech*, 3130 – 3134.

[5] Deterding, D. 2006. The pronunciation of English by speakers from China. *English World-Wide* 27, 175 – 198.

[6] Edwards, J. G. H., Zampini, M. L. 2008. *Phonology and Second Language Acquisition.* Amsterdam: John Benjamins Publishing Company.

[7] Eimas, P. D. 1963. The relation between identification and discrimination along speech and non-speech continua. *Language and Speech* 6, 206 – 217.

[8] Finney, D. J. 1971. *Probit Analysis.* 3rd ed. New York: Cambridge University Press.

[9] Flege, J. E. 1981. The phonological basis of foreign accent: A hypothesis. *TESOL Quarterly* 15, 443 – 455.

[10] He, Y. 2014. Production of English syllable final /l/ by Mandarin Chinese speakers. *Journal of Language Teaching and Research* 5, 742 – 750.

[11] Johnson, J. S., Newport, E. L. 1989. Critical period effects in second language learning: The influence of maturational state on the acquisition of English as a second language. *Cognitive Psychology* 21, 60 – 99.

[12] Kawahara, H. 2006. STRAIGHT, exploitation of the other aspect of VOCODER: Perceptually isomorphic decomposition of speech sounds. *Acoustical Science and Technology* 27, 349 – 353.

[13] Liberman, A. M., Harris, K. S., Hoffman, H. S., Griffith, B. C. 1957. The discrimination of speech sounds within and across phoneme boundaries. *Journal of Experimental Psychology* 54, 358 – 368.

[14] Ling, D. 1990. *Foundations of Spoken Language for Hearing-impaired Children.* Washington, D. C: Alexander Graham Bell Association for Deaf.

[15] Luck, S. J. 2005. *An Introduction to the Event-related Potential Technique.* 2nd ed. Cambridge, Massachusetts: The MIT Press.

[16] Meng, H., Tseng, C., Kondo, M., Harrison, A., Viscelgia, T. 2009. Studying L2 suprasegmental features in Asian Englishes. *Proceedings of Interspeech*, 1715 – 1718.

[17] Peng, G., Zheng, H. Y., Gong, T., Yang, R. X., Kong, J. P., Wang, W. S. Y. 2010. The influence of language experience on categorical perception of pitch contours. *Journal of Phonetics* 38, 616 – 624.

[18] Schouten, M. E. H., Hessen, A. J. 1998. Modeling phoneme perception. I: Categorical perception. *Journal of the Acoustical Society of America* 92, 1841 – 1855.

[19] Studdert-Kennedy, M., Shankweiler, D., Pisoni, D. 1972. Auditory and phonetic processes in

speech perception: Evidence from a dichotic study. *Cognitive Psychology* 3, 455 – 466.

[20] Taniguchi, K., Tayama, T. 2010. Comparison between discrimination and identification processes using line-drawing stimuli. *Journal of Vision* 10, 991.

[21] Thomson, R. I., Derwing, T. M. 2014. The effectiveness of L2 pronunciation instruction: A narrative review. *Applied Linguistics* 36, 326 – 344.

[22] Wong, N. 2013. The perception of /l/ vocalization by listeners with speech therapy as children. *Studies in the Linguistic Sciences: Illinois Working Papers* 5, 184 – 196.

LIAO Sishi She is a PhD student at the Institute of Phonetics and Speech Processing, University of Munich. Her research interests include phonetics, speech perception, acoustic analysis, etc.
E-mail: sishi. liao@ phonetik. uni-muenchen. de

DING Hongwei PhD Correspondence Author. She is a professor at the School of Foreign Languages, Shanghai Jiao Tong University. She mainly works on phonetics, prosody, and speech synthesis.
E-mail: hwding@ sjtu. edu. cn

汉语官话方言区英语学习者元音的声学特征和语音偏误

徐 亮 王 宇

摘 要 本文基于二语习得中的语言迁移假说，针对英语学习者元音产出中的系统偏误，采用语音声学实验的方法，从四个典型官话方言区发音人语料中提取核心元音的相关声学参数，对比母语、中介语和目标语元音在空间和时间层面的表现，透视语际迁移的影响力和学习者目标语音范畴的构建策略。实验发现：（1）学习者的元音分布空间与英语母语者间存在系统差异，前者呈现相对集中且向下的系统偏移；（2）学习者目标元音的产出受其母语相似元音的影响显著，中介语与官话方言顶点元音/i，u，ɑ/构成的元音三角呈现出更好的重合度；（3）松紧元音的时长对立表现出类型化的结构特征，北京—西安、济南—哈尔滨方言组被试分别呈现出更为相近的结构类型。同时，与英语母语发音人相比，学习者在区分英语松紧元音时更为依赖时长的推断受到了挑战。

关键词 元音，官话方言，英语学习者，语音偏误

An Experimental Study of Vowel Acoustic Features and Speech Errors by Chinese Mandarin-Speaking EFL Learners

XU Liang WANG Yu

Abstract Focusing on the acoustic features of EFL learners' vowel production and their typical speech errors, by extracting vowel formants and duration data from the speech corpora of Mandarin speakers from Beijing, Xi'an, Ji'nan and Ha'erbin, We conducted a cross-linguistic analysis of the vowels in order to see the power of inter-language transfer and EFL learners' strategies in forming phonetic categories of L2. The results indicate that a centralized, descending trend in tongue position makes the spatial distribution of EFL learner's basic vowels systematically different from that of the English native speakers. The overlapping degree of formant-based vowel plots respectively formed by the boundary vowels suggests remarkable influence of Mandarin vowels in second language acquisition. Besides, study on the tense/lax vowel pairs from both L1 and L2 also reports typological significances, with two different patterns of their relative durations being roughly identified.

Key words Vowel production, Mandarin, EFL learners, Speech errors

1. 引言

国内二语习得研究始于20世纪80年代，历经初期的理论推介、研究综述和初步应用，随着研究视角的拓展、层次的深入和技术的更新，已逐步演进成为一门系统的边缘交叉学科。然而，对二语习得过程中语音意识培养和语音能力发展的关注，因功能与形式的理念之争，特别是英语学习者身份构建和自我认同的局限性，相对于其他层面的语言发展研究，一直表现得相对小众和滞后。

语言迁移假说从学习者母语和目的语之间的相互影响出发，预测和解释二语习得者语言能力的发展模式。其发展经历了20世纪50—60年代通过语际差异预测二语学习错误和难点的对比分析假说、60—70年代认知主义对经典理论提出的挑战、70年代末、80年代“过渡语”对两种观念的融合以及90年代以来对语言迁移在二语习得中地位的迅速承认。认知心理学的“平行分布加工”甚至为语言迁移提供了类神经网络的模式：母语知识贮存在由相互联通的节点构成的网络上，大脑在习得二语时通过搜索和对比寻求建立新旧知

识之间的连接，母语的知识和特征得以被激活并进入第二语言［5］。

虽然迁移在表面上只是关系到学习者的母语与目标语体系间的相互作用，但在真实、自然的语境中，语言的接触往往更为复杂。例如，以汉语为母语的中国英语学习者来自不同的方言片区，对其母语使用的评价不仅需要包括具有独特语音体系和语调特征的方言方音的先验知识，还要涉及他们对标准体母语，即汉语普通话的认知和掌握程度。因此对语言的迁移考量往往需要涵盖多语（L1，L2，L3）间的互动，聚焦语言的共性限制和变异模式，描述和解释第二语言习得中的各种现象；亦可根据语言类型的标记性为预测学习难点提供新的视角和参项，从而提高二语习得和中介语研究的理论高度［6］。因此，本文以英语母语者为对照组，提取北京、西安、济南和哈尔滨四个官话方言区英语学习者产出的英汉基本元音的声学数据，从空间和时间层面描述学习者语音实现的典型声学特征，检验实验结果是否支持迁移假说对学习者元音产出偏误的预判。

2. 研究方法

所谓“官话”，指汉语方言中具有最为广泛分布的官话方言，可分为北京、东北、冀鲁、胶辽、江淮、中原、兰银和西南八个官话方言区［1］。各官话方言的演化既反映出其历史继承性，也受到社会人文因素的影响。本文选取的方言语料分别来自北京方言、西安方言（隶属中原官话）、济南方言（隶属冀鲁官话）和哈尔滨方言（隶属东北官话）发音人。四种方言作为次方言既具有相对的独立性，又同时隶属于秦淮以北相互毗邻续接的官话方言区，在基本元音系统上具有较强的可比度，对方言区二语语音习得和偏误研究具有类型学意义。

2.1 文本设计

实验语料以在音段层面反映英语学习者“方言英语发音的特征”［6］为目标。对应 10 个目标元音测试项（/i，ɪ，ɛ，æ，ɜ，ʌ，u，ʊ，ɔ，ɑ/），每个元音最多甄选 10 个音节结构为 CVC 英语单音节词，同时对词首和词尾辅音类型加以限定，以控制不同辅音对数据的影响。词条总量为 87 个（见附录）。为了考察学习者母语在二语习得中的迁移效应，实验还设计了对官话方言中相似元音的观察。因篇幅限制，主要观测目标被限定为可以反映元音系统总体分布态势的三个顶点元音/i，u，ɑ/，备选词来自中国社会科学院语言研究所提供的协录员手册，各官话方言均衡选取声母为阻塞音的 30 个单音节测试词。

2.2 被试

实验被试为 24 名英语专业在校大学生，来自四个官话方言区，每个方言区男女被试各 3 人。被试在该方言区出生和成长，无言语和听力障碍的相关报告，在日常交际中能够在普通话和官话方言之间进行熟练地转换。为了进一步控制被试的二语语言背景，实验筛选的语料均来自专业一、二年级学生。被试的英语学习时间在 10 年以上，具备一定的材料阅读和口语表达能力，此前没有在英语国家学习的经历。此外，实验还选取了 6 名无地方口音的标准美语本族语发音人（男女各 3 人）作为对照组。

2.3 录音和标注

被试朗读文本中的词项并在具有特殊隔音效果的语音室中完成录音。通过内置声卡的头戴式耳机，连接安装有 Cool Edit 音频处理软件的手提式电脑，存储语音文档。录音采样频率为 16000Hz，精度 16 bit。基于计算机程序对音段的自动切分和对齐，标注员结合语料的声学线索和听感印象完成对音段边界的手工调整和对音段的标注。

2.4 数据处理

实验提取元音共振峰频率和音长的核心数据。为了提高被试语音产出的可比性，抑制年龄、性别、语速、发音习惯及语境因素造成的数据波动，实验对 Praat 提取的共振峰频率进行了归一化处理，将

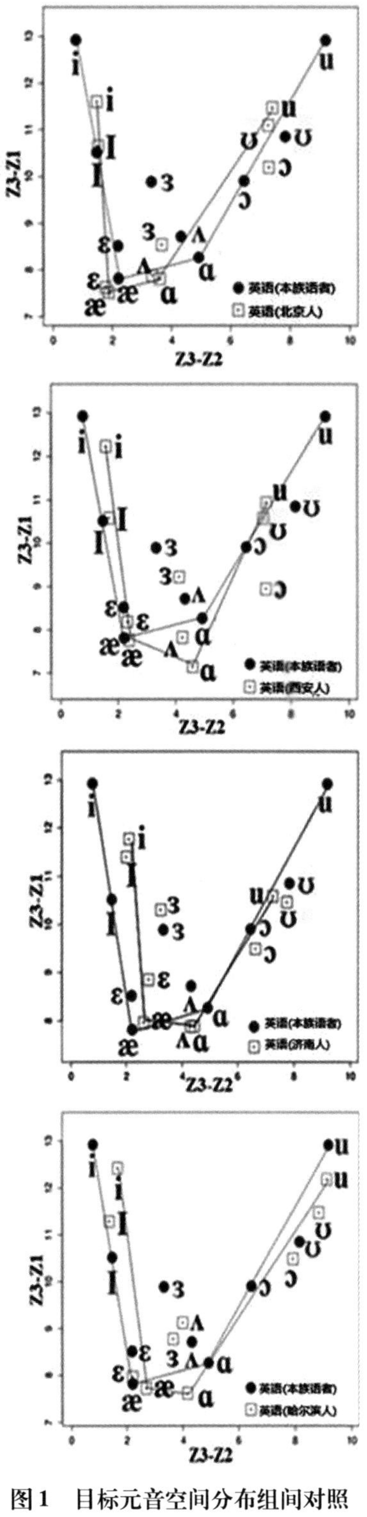

图1 目标元音空间分布组间对照

承载目标元音稳定段特殊信息的共振峰频率值转化为对应的临界频带率，即单位为 Bark 的 Z 值，其公式为：

$$Z_i = 26.81/(1 + 1960/F_i) - 0.53 \quad (1)$$

其中，Fi（i = 1，2，3...）代表元音各采样点共振峰的频率值，Zi 为共振峰频率对应的 Bark 值。根据 Sydral 和 Gopal［3］的归一算法，以度量差值 Z3—Z2，Z3—Z1 为坐标，构建目标元音在元音四边形中相对的前后和高低空间维度关系。

对元音时长数据的标准化处理则通过计算目标元音的相对时长 RD［4］来完成，即获取某元音全部样本绝对时长的平均值，再除以其所在组别中绝对时长最大的平均值所得的数据。

3. 发现

元音共振峰频率数据的提取和观测呈现了各方言组别发音人与英语母语者语音产出空间分布的共性和差异。通过计算英语—中介语—官话方言相似元音的空间距离，可量化系统间的相似度，反推发音人母语和目标语对中介语的影响力，检验语音迁移假说对语音偏误的预判效度；而借助被试与对照组发音人间松紧元音实现时长的结构性对比，则可以透视学习者目标元音辨识策略的组间趋势和异同。

3.1 共振峰频率与元音的空间分布

使用 Praat 脚本，基于共振峰频率数据绘制的声学元音图反映了各官话组别发音人与对照组间目标元音的空间分布关系：首先，发音人产出的目标元音基本分布在其各自语音系统顶点元音/i/、/u/、/æ/、/ɑ/构成的元音四边形内，由样本语料提取的数据偏离度小，奇异度较低；其次，在等比的坐标矩阵内，各方言组别发音人目标元音的分布空间均小于英语本族语者，系统呈现相对“内敛”和“下移”的态势。与作为本族语产出的目标元音比较，方言组被试二语顶点元音在空间上与其母语中的相似元音（/i，u，ɑ/）更为接近，两者构成的元音三角也更为契合。

以北京方言发音人产出的英语单元音

为例（见图 1），高元音/i/、/u/的舌位明显低于对照组的母语发音人。前元音/ɛ/、/æ/，央元音/ɜ/、/ʌ/和后元音/ɑ/的取位也都分别低于母语者。在水平位置关系上，被试/ɛ/、/æ/、/ʌ/、/u/、/ʊ/、/ɑ/舌位较母语者均相对靠前。元音共振峰频率数据对比的 t 检验结果显示：发音人/i，ɛ，ɜ，u，ʌ，ɑ/的 F1 频率组间差异显著（$p<0.05$），其中三个后元音/u、ʌ、ɑ/的 F2 频率差异亦相对显著（$p<0.05$），而包括/ɪ，æ，ɔ，ʊ/在内的其他元音的共振峰则未表现出具有统计学意义的差距。

对西安、济南和哈尔滨方言组的实验调查显示，被试与对照组发音人的元音空间分布存在类似的系统差异：除了元音四边形整体向下偏移指示了目标元音相对较低的舌位，方言区学习者产出的英语前元音趋后，后元音则相对靠前，导致其元音分布因空间相对收窄，较英语母语者更为集中。

基于图 1 的另一项重要发现是学习者目标元音产出中音质相近的松紧元音对立弱化。说北京话的英语学习者产出的前高元音/i/和/ɪ/与后高元音/u/和/ʊ/在第二共振峰 F2 频率数据上均未体现出显著差异（$p>0.05$）。这一趋势同样可见于其他三个方言组别，比较西安方言发音人产出的二语目标元音/u/和/ʊ/，其第一、二共振峰均无显著差异（$p_{F1}>0.05$，$p_{F2}>0.05$）；济南方言发音人/i/－/ɪ/、/u/－/ʊ/共振峰 F1，F2 的差别也均不如英语母语者明显（$p_{F1}>0.05$，$p_{F2}>0.05$）。相对于各方言区的被试，英语母语发音人则表现出对松紧元音对立更高的敏感度：两个前高元音和两个后高元音第一、二共振峰（传统上被认为与发音人的舌位高低呈负相关）频率都表现出极为显著的差异（$p_{F1}<0.01$，$p_{F2}<0.01$）。英语本族语发音人前高元音/i/－/ɪ/和后高元音/u/－/ʊ/的产出结合了舌位高低和前后位置（一般认为与第二共振峰 F2 频率值的变化呈现正相关）的控制，使它们之间的差异较英语学习者更为显著。

3.2 时长表现

发音时长是除共振峰频率之外元音声学特征描述的另一重要参数。图 2 分别呈现了英语母语发音人和英语学习者产出的前高元音/i/－/ɪ/、后高元音/u/－/ʊ/、后中元音/ɔ/和后低元音/ɑ/以及各官话方言组中存在的相似元音的时长均值比较。

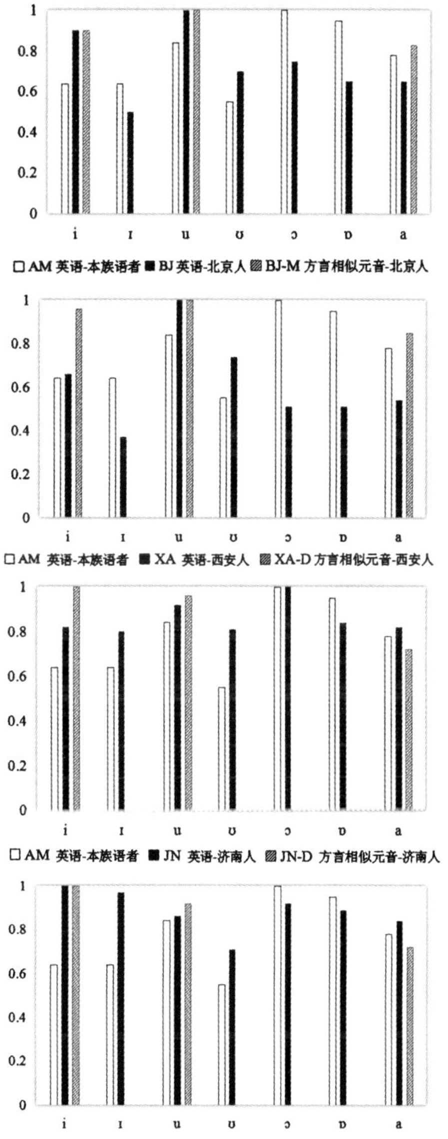

图 2 目标元音/i，ɪ，u，ʊ，ɔ，ɑ/与官话方言相似元音的相对时长比较

如上文所述，为了消除元音产出过程中人际和语际因素对时长分析的干扰，实验选择计算并比较元音的“相对时长”，也就是用某元音（如北京方言的元音/i/）绝对时长的平均值除以该元音所在组别（即北京方言）中最大的元音绝对时长平均值所得的数据［4］。

表 1　发音人元音相对时长的组间比较

（北京—西安组）

	北京组			西安组		
	英语母语	中介语	北京方言	英语母语	中介语	西安方言
i	0.64 <0.90 <1.00			0.64 <0.66 <0.96		
ɪ	0.64 <0.50			0.64 >0.37		
u	0.84 <1.00 >0.83			0.84 <1.00 =1.00		
ʊ	0.55 <0.70			0.55 <0.74		
ɔ	1.00 >0.75			1.00 >0.51		
ɑ	0.78 >0.65 <0.90			0.78 >0.54 <0.85		

（济南—哈尔滨组）

	济南组			哈尔滨组		
	英语母语	中介语	济南方言	英语母语	中介语	哈尔滨方言
i	0.64 <0.82 <1.00			0.64 <1.00 =1.00		
ɪ	0.64 <0.80			0.64 <0.97		
u	0.84 <0.92 <0.96			0.84 <0.86 <0.92		
ʊ	0.55 <0.81			0.55 <0.71		
ɔ	1.00 =1.00 >0.54			1.00 >0.92		
ɑ	0.78 <0.82 >0.72			0.78 <0.84 >0.72		

3.2.1　前高元音/i/和/ɪ/

各方言区三个语料组别（英语本族语者产出的母语元音、方言区发音人产出的二语目标元音和方言相似元音）中前高元音/i/相对时长数据显示了统一的趋势：即官话方言相似元音时长 > 学习者 L2 目标元音时长 > 作为 L1 的英语元音时长。以北京组为例，英语本族语发音人（AM）产出的前高元音/i/相对时长为 0.64，北京方言（BJ - M）相似元音时长为 1.00，而官话方言区英语学习者（BJ）实现的 L2 目标元音的相对时长则介于两者之间（0.90），并明显长于母语者。

官话方言的元音体系不存在松紧对立，在前高元音位置没有对应的松元音/ɪ/。英语母语者和方言区英语学习者产出的前高元音/ɪ/相对时长呈现出两种不同的趋势：在北京组和西安组中，英语母语发音人/ɪ/的相对时长（0.64）长于英语学习者（BJ：0.50/XA：0.37），而济南组和哈尔滨组的结果刚好相反（0.64 vs 0.80/0.97）。

此外，实验测得英语母语者两个前高元音的相对时长均为 0.64，而英语学习者产出的松紧元音是存在时长差异的，紧元音较长。其中以北京组和西安组更为明显，松紧元音相对时长差分别为 0.40 和 0.27。

3.2.2　后高元音/u/和/ʊ/

后高元音在各官话方言组别呈现的时长趋势与前高元音基本一致，且相对更为规整：方言中相似元音的相对时长 > 被试 L2 目标元音时长 > 英语母语者后高元音时长。以济南组为例，官话方言后高元音/u/的相对时长均值为 0.96，被试产出的英语后高元音相对时长为 0.92，均长于对照组英语母语者的发音。但北京和西安组的数据没有完全呈现这一趋势，其中北京方言（BJ - M）后高元音/u/的相对时长为 0.83，与英语母语发音人（AM）后高元音时长 0.84 差别甚微，均短于被试 L2 目标元音（BJ）时长 1.00。而实验测得西安方言（XA - M）/u/的相对时长则与该组被试 L2 目标元音（XA）时长是相等的，都是 1.00。

官话方言在后高元音位置也不存在松紧对立。各方言组被试产出的 L2 目标元音/ʊ/（BJ：0.70，XA：0.74，JN：0.81，HEB：0.71）都长于英语母语者（AM：0.55）。后者松紧元音相对时长差为 0.29，四个方言组别被试二语松紧元音时长差在 0.11—0.30 之间。北京和西安组时长差相对更明显。

3.2.3　后中元音/ɔ/和后低元音/ɑ/

后中元音/ɔ/和后低元音/ɑ/的时长数

据反映出的趋势比较复杂，但仍具有类型学上的意义。首先，四个官话方言组中只有济南方言有对应的后中元音/ɔ/，其相对时长的平均值为0.54，该组被试产出的L2目标元音与英语母语者等长，为1.00。而北京、西安和哈尔滨组中，英语母语发音人的/ɔ/都长于二语学习者，与前高元音和后高元音时长呈相反趋势。其次，后低元音/ɑ/的时长表现为两种趋势：北京组和西安组被试产出的L2目标音时长（BJ：0.65，XA：0.54）都短于英语母语者（AM：0.78），其官话方言相似元音时长最长（BJ－M：0.90，XA－M：0.85）；济南组和哈尔滨组被试的L2后低元音（JN：0.84，HEB：0.84）则较英语母语者更长，其方言相似元音的相对音长反而最短（JN－M：0.72，HEB：0.72）。

4. 讨论

本文的元音声学实验聚焦方言区学习者中介语的元音实现。通过提取和观察元音共振峰频率和音长数据，尝试描述和分析四个官话方言组别发音人产出的L2目标元音音征及方音迁移的影响。基于顶点元音/i，u，ɑ/的共振峰数据绘制的元音分布空间显示，被试实现的二语目标元音较英语母语发音人的产出发生了空间上的偏移。其中前高元音/i/位置下移后退，后高元音/u/和后低元音/ɑ/下移前出，在相对低位形成更为内敛的元音三角，整体空间位于英语母语元音和官话方言相似元音之间，且与对应的官话方言（特别是北京方言、西安方言和济南方言）元音的分布空间更为接近，具有较明显的"重合度"。

单因素方差分析的结果进一步显示，北京方言区被试作为中介语产出的目标元音/ɑ/与方言中的相似元音实现没有显著的差异（$p>0.05$），而两组对应的高元音/i/和/u/则分别在舌位的高低（$p_{F1}>0.05$）和前后（$p_{F2}>0.05$）上呈现相似性，由此可以推断官话方言元音音征对目标元音习得的影响。类似的语际迁移同样作用于西安方言区和济南方言区的二语习得者，各被试组产出的目标

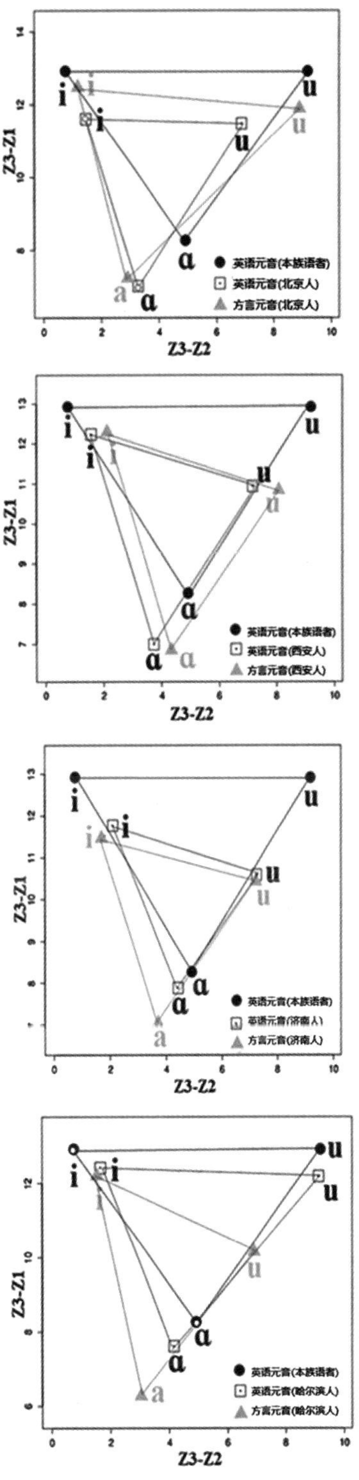

图3　英语母语者与官话方言区发音人（L1& L2）元音分布空间对照

元音/i, ʊ, ɑ/的第一、二共振峰频率与其官话方言中的相似元音均未表现出统计学意义上的显著差别，从而预示了形成语音迁移和语音偏误的可能性。济南方言区英语学习者的中介语后低元音/ɑ/在空间关系上更接近英语母语发音人，说明发生语音偏误“风险”相对较低。而对哈尔滨方言发音人中介语和官话方言元音的比较发现，由顶点元音构成的元音三角的空间契合度在实验的四个被试组别中相对最差，方言相似元音未对中介语产生明显的迁移。

为了明确语音迁移的效度，实验基于标准化的共振峰频率数据计算了各组相似元音之间的欧式距离（Euclidean Distance）：

$$ED = \sqrt{(x_2 - x_1)^2 + (y_2 - y_1)^2} \quad (2)$$

其中 x 和 y 分别代表某对元音第一、第二共振峰频率的标准值。当学习者 L2 某个目标元音与其方言相似元音的欧式距离小于它与英语母语发音人产出的该元音之间的欧式距离时，即作出因负向迁移而导致的语音偏误发生概率较高的推断；如果相反，则二语产出受到方言元音音征的影响的可能性较小。

表2　被试组L2目标元音与官话方言元音欧式距离

	BJ	XA	JN	HEB
i	0.91	0.55	0.51	0.25
u	0.42	0.63	1.10	1.76
ɑ	2.07	1.01	0.16	3.01

表3　被试组L2目标元音与控制组英语母语元音欧式距离

	BJ	XA	JN	HEB
i	1.49	1.06	1.76	1.02
u	2.09	1.74	0.62	1.00
ɑ	2.72	3.17	3.03	0.73

对比表1、表2的实验数据，北京、西安和济南方言组（除后高元音/u/外）发音人中介语三个顶点元音与其方言中对应的相似元音的欧式距离更近，或者说目标元音共振峰特性上与方言更为相近，受到方言音征的迁移；而哈尔滨方言组中介语元音/u/、/ɑ/与其官话方言相似元音的欧式距离大于它们与英语母语发音人产出之间的差别，也就是说，被试 L2 目标元音明显与对照组英语母语者的发音产出更为相近（EDu = 1.00；ED ɑ = 0.73），这一结果与其他组别反映出语音迁移的态势相背离，有待在更大规模数据基础上的进一步观察。总体而言，英语学习者基本元音共振峰数据分析的结果在产出层面支持了迁移假说的语音学习模型：即 L1 和 L2 音素相似性较大时，L1 的音素会阻隔学习者建立 L2 的语音范畴［7］，形成语音偏误。

对元音时长的关注聚焦英语母语、学习者二语和官话方言之间的比较以及松紧对立呈现出的时长差异。核心元音的时长数据表现出类型化的结构趋向。

各方言组别元音时长数据比较显示，顶点元音中前高元音/i/和后高元音/u/音长模式比较齐整：官话方言相似元音 > 学习者产出的 L2 目标元音 > 英语母语者发音，英语学习者中介语目标元音音长可以为官话方言的负向迁移做出有利推断。后低元音/ɑ/的两种音长模式都没有为 L2 元音音长表现提供合理的线索，当前数据不支持官话方言对二语习得的影响。但北京与西安方言组被试表现出更多类型上的一致性，济南和哈尔滨方言区学习者中介元音产出则相对趋近。非顶点元音情况相对复杂，其中北京和西安方言组发音人产出的 L2 前高元音/ɪ/相对音长大于英语母语者，而济南和哈尔滨方言组却与此相反，语间差异也更为显著。再次呈现出类型化的差别。此外，四个官话方言组别发音人 L2 后高元音/ʊ/音长均大于英语母语者，后中元音/ɔ/的音长又都小于英语母语者。这种非顶点元音的非一致性表现可能是由于学习者官话方言体系中可以作为参照的相似元音的缺失而造成的。在元音松紧对立的时长表现上，英语母语发音人并未将音长作为区别性特征。而各方言组被试产出的中介语前高元音/i/和/ɪ/的相对时长差异在 0.02—0.40 之间。其中北京、西安组差别明显，济南、哈尔滨组差别细微。后高元音/u/ - /ʊ/的时长差在西安、济南和哈尔滨组都没有英语母语者（0.29）明显，仅北京方言发音人对该目标元音的时长差（0.30）微弱地大于英语母语者。英语学习者并非依赖音长区分元音的松紧对立。时长差异的组间对比显示，济南—哈尔滨、北京—西安方言组数据表现分别更为接近。

5. 结论

基于以上讨论,被试发音人L2目标元音空间偏移的统一趋势支持了关于英语学习者二语元音产出典型特征的假设。学习者二语核心元音和与之对应的官话方言元音空间吻合度的计算支持了语音相似性的语际影响和对语音学习困难的预判（这一点可在后续的范畴感知实验中予以进一步的验证）。

在时间层面，英语学习者与英语母语者产出的元音时长呈现出类型化的组间差异，官话方言对L2高元音的语际影响更为显著，后者多表现出相对“拉长”的趋势。非边界位置的目标元音产出中未见明显的语音迁移证据，推测是由于缺乏与之对应的官话相似元音。

对松紧对立元音相关实验数据的观测显示，学习者紧元音的相对时长长于松元音，而英语母语者并不完全依赖音长来区别两者，该结论对语音教学在产出和感知层面都具有重要的指导意义。

6. 致谢

本文研究为宁波大学教学科研项目“英语语音教学中学习者音调感知与产出互动的发展研究”（编号：JYXMYB2020）的一部分，其中的实验部分得到了国家社科基金重大项目“中国方言区英语学习者语音习得机制的跨学科研究”（编号：15ZDB103）的支持。

参考文献

[1] Jia, Y., et al. 2017. Typology of convergences and divergences of English monophthongs by EFL learners from Guanhua regions. *Proceedings of the 14th National Conference on Man – Machine Speech Communication*. Lianyungang.

[2] Reetz, H., Jongman, A. 2009. *Phonetics: Transcription, Production, Acoustics and Perception*. Wiley – Blackwell.

[3] Sydral, A. K., Gopal, H. S. 1986. A perceptual model of vowel recognition based on the auditory representation of American English vowels. *Journal of the Acoustical Society of America* 79, 1086 – 1100.

[4] 贝先明、向柠：《实验语音学的基本原理与Praat软件操作》，湖南师范大学出版社2016年版。

[5] 黄怀飞：《二语习得中的语言迁移及其理论阐释》，《泉州师范学院学报》（社会科学版）2010年第3期。

[6] 贾媛、李爱军、郑秋豫：《中国方言区英语学习者语音库构建》，《中国语音学》2014年第4辑。

[7] 孙文访：《基于语言类型学的第二语言习得研究》，《语言教学与研究》2012年第2期。

[8] 王韫佳：《跨语言语音对比与L2语音习得》，《第8届中国语音学学术会议暨庆贺吴宗济先生百岁华诞语音科学前沿问题国际研讨会论文》，2008年，北京。

徐 亮 宁波大学外国语学院副教授，硕士，研究方向：语音学，二语习得。
Email：xuliang@nbu.edu.cn

王 宇 郑州商学院外国语学院助教，硕士，研究方向：英语教育。
Email：1275341457@qq.com

附录　用于提取发音人元音数据的英语单音节词词表

	塞音 + 元音 + 塞音	擦音 + 元音 + 塞音/擦音/塞擦	塞擦 + 元音 + 塞音/擦音	鼻音 + 元音 + 塞音/擦音	其他
i	bead deed deep	feat feast heap heat		meat neat need	
ɪ	pit pick bick dig kip kick	hip hit hid	chick		
ɛ	dep kep keck gep	feck head zep	chep check	net	
æ	bad dad tap cab gap		chap	nap	
ɜ	pert perk	turf curse	fern	merge	burn hurl word wordy
ʌ	pus bud tug	sup shap thud		muck nut	rut rub
u	dupe		choose	moose mute move	true who shoe new use
ʊ	bush good			nook	look
ɔ	bought corpse	ford forge			bald four whore ward quart raw
ɑ	barb start	chart	jad jat		wat

普通话和“台湾国语”在语流中的节奏特征
——以《还珠格格》为例

张　凌

摘　要　本文采用自然语料，截取电视剧《还珠格格》大陆和台湾演员的录音文档，通过 Praat 软件进行声学语音测量，研究普通话和“台湾国语”在语流中的节奏特征。实验数据显示，“台湾国语”比普通话有更强的句末延长效应。普通话和“台湾国语”在轻声音节时长方面也有差别，这与在句子里的位置有关。在句中，普通话和“台湾国语”相若，轻声皆“轻”，即轻声音节时长皆明显短于非轻声音节。在句末，普通话的轻声也较短，是“真轻”；而“台湾国语”的轻声发得较长，轻声“不轻”。
关键词　普通话，“台湾国语”，节奏，句末延长，轻声

Rhythmic Features of Putonghua and Taiwan Mandarin in Continuous Speech

A Study of TV Episodes “My Fair Princess”

ZHANG Ling

Abstract This study collected the original audio clips of Mainland speakers Jie Zhou and Wei Zhao, Taiwan Mandarin speakers Alec Su and Ruby Lin from TV Episodes “My Fair Princess” and conducted acoustic measurements of syllable duration through Praat, which provided evidence for the rhythmic features of Putonghua (PTH) and “Taiwan Mandarin” (“TWM”). The experimental results showed that sentence-final lengthening effect existed in both PTH and “TWM”, but the effect in “TWM” was stronger. The durations of neutral tones at different positions showed very interesting patterns in PTH and “TWM”. In the middle of sentences, neutral tones in both PTH and “TWM” were similar, as “unstressed” with a short duration of a syllable compared with the full tones. At the end of sentences, neutral tones of PTH were also short and “unstressed”. However, neutral tones of “TWM” were actually long and not really “unstressed”.
Key words Putonghua, “Taiwan Mandarin”, Rhythm, Sentence-final lengthening, Neutral tone

1. 引言

普通话和“台湾国语”同根同源［10］。过往也有不少研究比较普通话和“台湾国语”语音上的异同，较多是印象式的描写和总结［8，14］。也有一些是语音实验的研究，如［7，12］等，则多是在实验室的条件下进行，并且是对单音节的语音特性进行研究。在现今的技术条件下，语音的声学测量比以往更为简便，且能提供更客观、精确的数据，用以进行更为深入的研究。实验室条件下的语音研究确实能避免一些干扰因素，但可能会受实验设计者主观因素的影响，也可能会过滤一些自然语境下的语音特点。Harrington 等的研究［5］取材于连续的自然语料，纵向追踪英女王伊丽莎白二世历年的圣诞演讲，从而研究女王口音的历时变化。本研究借鉴于此，取材于客观而真实的自然语料，即电视剧《还珠格格》（第一部）中的台词录音。我们研究的不是理想状态下的单音节，而是自然连续语流的节奏韵律特征，更好地揭示普通话和“台湾国

语”在常态下的细微差异。

2. 研究材料和方法

2.1 研究的语料

本文的研究从电视剧《还珠格格》中截取数段台词录音作为分析的语料。该剧在1997年拍摄，1998年播出，当时火遍大江南北，至今仍被奉为电视剧的经典之作。《还珠格格》中的两位大陆演员周杰及赵薇，分别从北京电影学院与上海戏剧学院的戏剧专业毕业，不仅台词演绎方面经过训练，且普通话的发音标准上有所保证，可作为普通话的发音人代表。而两位台湾演员林心如与苏有朋，都是来自台北，从小在台湾长大及生活，能作为“台湾国语”的发音人代表。需要特别说明的是，《还珠格格》在大多数情况下，周杰和赵薇都使用的是他们的原声，而苏有朋和林心如则使用配音，就是因为当时的剧组认为苏有朋和林心如有“台湾腔”，为了这部电视剧的整体感，所以另外使用了配音。只有少数片段中用的是林心如和苏有朋的原声，我们特地甄别使用他们的原声录音作为研究素材。每位演员分别截取30句台词，四个人共120句台词，台词有长有短，但每个人的台词音节数总和接近，其中苏有朋356个音节，林心如362个音节，周杰321个音节，赵薇348个音节，合计1387个音节。

2.2 实验方法

我们使用Praat软件［3］，对所选取语料的录音（wav格式音档）进行音节时长的测量。我们先使用Textgrid功能对音节开始和结束的边界做好标注，再使用自行设计的脚本程序进行音节时长的测量，并把各音节的数据导出到Excel文档中，进行后续的数据分析。

2.3 数据分析方法

本文的研究，注重的是语流中的节奏韵律特征。因此在获得各音节的相对时长数据之后，我们的数据分析注重以下几个方面的特点。

第一，音节的等时性。过往对世界各语言的节奏韵律特征研究，认为各语言中存在等时单位，即语言的产出应该符合一定的节拍，按照等时单位的不同，大致把各语言分作音节等长（syllable-timed）和重音等长（stress-timed）两大类［1］。然而，等时性在不同语言里存在程度上的差异。Grabe & Low定义了成对相异系数（Pairwise Variability Index，PVI 4）来衡量语言的等时性，具体又分为原始成对相异系数（raw PVI，*rPVI*）和归一化成对相异系数（normalized PVI，*nPVI*），计算公式如下：

$$rPVI = \left[\sum_{k=1}^{m-1} \left| d_k - d_{k+1} \right| / (m-1) \right] \quad (1)$$

$$nPVI = 100 \times \left[\sum_{k=1}^{m-1} \left| \frac{d_k - d_{k+1}}{(d_k + d_{k+1})/2} \right| / (m-1) \right] \quad (2)$$

其中d_k是第k个音段的时长，d_{k+1}是第$k+1$个音段的时长，m是句子总音节数。*rPVI*和*nPVI*这两项系数越大，则音段之间的时长差异越大，等时性越弱；反之则等时性越强。在Grabe & Low［4］的研究中，此公式主要用于计算不同音段（interval）的时长差异，包括元音（vocalic）音段或元音间（intervocalic）的音段。在本文的研究中，我们计算的则是整个音节的时长差异。另外，如下面所提及的，因为句末音节很可能存在延长效应，因此我们把句末音节排除在外，只计算非句末音节的*rPVI*和*nPVI*，以此观察在音节等时性方面普通话和“台湾国语”是否有明显区别。

第二，句末音节的延长效应。过往的研究显示，普通话的句末音节有延长效应［6，9，13］，即在句子最后一个音节明显比非句末的音节要长，这也是句子韵律边界的显著特征。在我们的研究当中，为避免不同语速的影响，我们不仅看音节的绝对时长，而是先对音节时长数据进行归一化处理。处理的方式为，先计算句子中所有非句末音节的时长平均值a，再把每个音节的时长除以a，得出的比值即为这个音节的相对时长。例如，一个句子里有6个音节，我们会先把前5个音节的时长取平均值，即可得出 a。若第一个音节的绝对时长是 d_1，则第一个音节的相对时长则是 d_1/a，相应地第2个音节的相对时长是 d_2/a，……，依此类推，最后的第六个音节的相对时长是 d_6/a。若句子有句末延长效应，则句末的 d_{final}/a 大于1。句末延长效应越强，则 d_{final}/a 越大。

第三，轻声音节的时长特点。传统来说，“调值”更强调的是声调在音高（pitch）方面的特性，即声调的高、低、升、降、曲、直等具体的变化。“调类”则指的是声调的类别。魏钢强的研究［11］指出，汉语的轻声可以从调类和调值两方面来认识，北京话调值上来说是“读得很短”，调类上来说是“失去了原来的声调”。这里，轻声的“调值”主要指音节时长（duration）很短的语音性质，轻声的“调类”的概念则指的是失去原来的声调类别，而中和化为独立的类别。本文的研究关注的是时长方面的特征，暂不探讨音高方面的特点，因此下文中谈及“调值”和“调类”，采用的是魏钢强［11］的概念。

郑良伟的研究［15］揭示了北京话和台湾话（实际上是台湾闽语）轻声出现的异同，“台湾国语”受台湾闽语的影响，轻声的特点也很可能与普通话不同。因此，在本文的研究中，我们也会特地把语料中的轻声音节标记出来，比较分析“台湾国语”和普通话的轻声音节在句中和句末的时长。

3. 时长数据的初步观察

3.1 音节等时性

从绝对时长（单位：ms）的数据看来，《还珠格格》中四位主角的音节平均时长和标准偏差分别是：苏有朋 133 ± 51ms，林心如 153 ± 62ms，周杰 136 ± 59ms，赵薇 136 ± 47ms。可见林心如的语速稍慢一点，其他几位演员的语速相近。从各演员的音节时长变化幅度来看，苏有朋和赵薇的变化稍小，林心如和周杰的变化稍大。

而这四位主角的平均 *rPVI* 数据分别是：苏有朋 45.43，林心如 59.14，周杰 56.88，赵薇 59.58。他们的 *nPVI* 数据分别是：苏有朋 37.26，林心如 40.86，周杰 42.16，赵薇 33.95。初步看来并不能看到普通话和“台湾国语”在这两项系数上有截然的区别，我们会在第四部分通过进一步的统计检验分析来验证这一点。

3.2 句末延长效应

图1的柱状图显示的是《还珠格格》四位主角的轻声及非轻声音节在句子不同位置的相对时长数据。我们把语流位置（句中/句末）和音节类型（轻声/非轻声）统称为语境类型。因此，图中的语境类型有四组，分别是句中轻声、句中非轻声、句末轻声和句末非轻声，在每组中并置了苏有朋、林心如、周杰和赵薇的平均值数据，还用误差杆标出正负一个标准差。数据柱下部的阿拉伯数字标出的是各发音人在各语境类型中参与统计的音节数目。例如图1最左边的数据柱下部标出“24”，表示在句中轻声的语境中，苏有朋的音节数为24个。

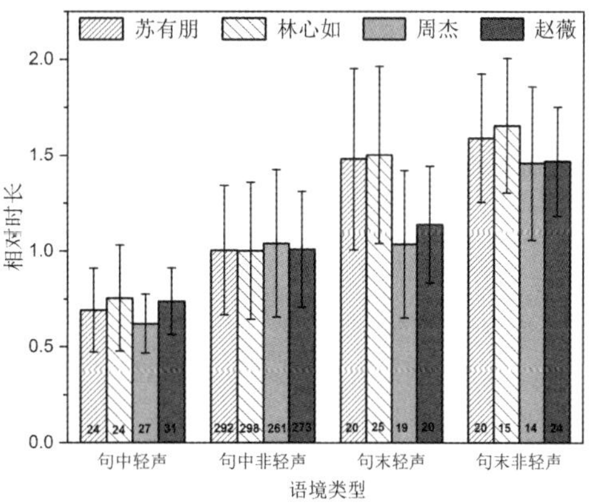

图1 《还珠格格》四位主角在不同语境类型中音节的相对时长

从图1可看出，句中和句末轻声组相比，以及句中和句末非轻声组相比，句中的长度都只有句末的1/2—2/3，即句末都比句中音节明显更长，可见无论是普通话还是“台湾国语”，都存在着明显的句末延长效应。

若只看句末位置的数据，苏有朋和林心如无论是在轻声还是在非轻声的条件下，句末音节都比周杰和赵薇长，也就是整体来看，“台湾国语”的句末延长效应都要比普通话强。

3.3 轻声音节

图1的数据显示在句中的位置，四位主角的轻声都明显比非轻声音节短，普通话和“台湾国语”未见明显差别；在句末的位置，虽然整体来说轻声音节还是要比非轻声音节短，但苏有朋和林心如轻声音节和非轻声音节的时长差别似乎不大，而周杰和赵薇轻声音节和非轻声音节的时长则有较明显区别。由此看来，要比较普通话和“台湾国语”在轻声音节时长方面的差异，不能简单地一概而论，还必须关注这些轻声音节在句子的不同位置。

4. 进一步的统计检验分析

在这一节中，我们把数据从 Excel 导入 IBM SPSS Statistics，通过进一步的统计检验来验证第三部分初步观察揭示的各种差异是否显著。

4.1 音节等时性 *rPVI* 和 *nPVI* 不同发音人的差别

为了检验 *rPVI* 和 *nPVI* 这两项系数不同发音人的差别是否具有统计检验意义上的显著区别，我们进行了单因素方差分析（One-way ANOVA），因变量分别是 *rPVI* 和 *nPVI*，因子则是不同的发音人（苏有朋、林心如、周杰和赵薇）。结果显示，*rPVI* 的 $F(3, 116) = 1.208$，$p = 0.310$，即各发音人的数据无显著差别；*nPVI* 的 $F(3, 116) = 1.208$，$p = 0.0306 < 0.05$，即发音人之间至少有一组彼此有显著差别，需要通过进一步的事后多重比较分析（Post hoc）。进一步的 LSD 检验显示，只有林心如和赵薇之间（$p = 0.025$）、周杰和赵薇之间（$p = 0.008$）有显著差异，其他各组皆无显著差异。结合前面3.1中所列的数据，可见赵薇的 *nPVI* 要明显比林心如和周杰小，她的等时性要明显更强，这反映了赵薇在语流中节奏韵律的个人特征。

因此，从 *rPVI* 和 *nPVI* 这两项系数的统计检验分析结果来看，普通话和“台湾国语”在音节等时性方面并无明显的区别。

4.2 同一发音人在不同语境类型的音节时长差别

我们分别对各位发音人在不同语境类型中的音节时长比较进行单因素方差分析，因变量为音节的相对时长，因子为语境类型（句中轻声、句中非轻声、句末轻声和句末非轻声）。结果显示各发音人在不同语境类型下的时长差异皆显著，p 值皆小于0.05：苏有朋 $F(3, 352) = 38.233$，$p < 0.001$；林心如 $F(3, 358) = 34.387$，$p < 0.001$；周杰 $F(3, 317) = 17.122$，$p < 0.001$；赵薇 $F(3, 344) = 29.725$，$p < 0.001$。我们还分别进行了事后多重比较分析的 LSD 检验，结果如表1所列，其中“＊＊＊”表示显著性系数 $p < 0.001$。

表1的结果显示，苏有朋和林心如皆是在句末位置的轻声与非轻声音节时长无显著差异，p 值皆大于0.05，而其他各组的比较皆有显著差异。周杰和赵薇皆是句中非轻声与句末轻声音节时长无显著差异，p 值皆大于0.05，而其他各组的比较皆有显著差异。结合图1显示的数据，我们可以推断，苏有朋和林心如代表的“台湾国语”，在句中位置，轻声音节与非轻声音节有显著的时长差别，只是在句末的情况下，句末延长效应很强，轻声音节与非轻声音节的时长差别消失了。而周杰和赵薇代表的普通话，无论是在句中位置还是在句末位置，轻声音节和非轻声音节之间的时长差异都很显著，轻声音节都明显比非轻声音节短。普通话在句末的轻声音节，虽然也受句末延长效应的影响，和在句中的轻声音节相比明显更长，但是它比句末非轻声音节明显要短，最后它的长度与句中非轻声音节相若，因此普通话的这两类音节时长在不同语境的单因素分析中无显著差异。

表1 各发音人在不同位置和不同音节类型下时长比较的事后多重比较分析

发音人		句中非轻声	句末轻声	句末非轻声
苏有朋	句中轻声	* * *	* * *	* * *
	句中非轻声		* * *	* * *
	句末轻声			0.306
林心如	句中轻声	* * *	* * *	* * *
	句中非轻声		* * *	* * *
	句末轻声			0.197
周杰	句中轻声	* * *	* * *	* * *
	句中非轻声		0.677	* * *
	句末轻声			* * *
赵薇	句中轻声	* * *	* * *	* * *
	句中非轻声		0.129	* * *
	句末轻声			* * *

4.3 同一语境类型中不同发音人的音节时长差别

我们也对各语境类型中不同发音人的差异进行了单因素方差分析，因变量是音节的相对时长，因子是不同的发音人（苏有朋、林心如、周杰和赵薇），统计结果为：句中轻声 $F(3, 102) = 2.181$，$p = 0.095$；句中非轻声 $F(3, 1120) = 0.714$，$p = 0.544$；句末轻声 $F(3, 80) = 6.819$，$p < 0.001$；句末非轻声 $F(3, 69) = 1.373$，$p = 0.258$。除了句末轻声音节之外，其他语境类型下，各发音人的时长无显著差异。

表2 句末轻声音节时长的事后多重比较分析

	林心如	周杰	赵薇
苏有朋	0.857	* * *	*
林心如		* * *	* *
周杰			0.444

我们进而对句末轻声音节进行了事后多重比较分析（Post hoc）的 LSD 检验，结果如表2所列，其中“* * *”表示显著性系数 $p < 0.001$，“* *”表示 $p < 0.01$，“*”表示 $p < 0.05$。有趣的是，苏有朋和林心如之间无显著差异（$p > 0.05$），周杰和赵薇之间也无显著差异（$p > 0.05$），但其他的配对之间则有显著差异，也就是说明“台湾国语”和普通话之间有显著差异，而“台湾国语”内部无显著差异，普通话内部也无显著差异。因此，句末轻声音节的时长的区别，是普通话和“台湾国语”在语流中的节奏韵律特征的重要区别，普通话句末轻声音节短而“台湾国语”句末轻声音节长。

4.4 发音人、语流位置和音节类型的多因素方差分析

在以上4.2和4.3的分析中使用的皆是单因素方差分析，分别从语境类型和发音人的角度分析数据。除了逐个因素地观察，我们还进行了多因素方差分析，以更好地观察这些不同因素的主效应及交互作用。在多因素方差分析中，因变量是音节的相对时长，因子是语流位置（句中/句末）、音节类型（轻声/非轻声）以及语言变体（普通话/“台湾国语”）。表3中列出此多因素方差分析的结果。

另外，图2可直观显示语流位置、音节类型、语言变体这三个因素两两之间的交互关系。其中图2a是音节类型和语流位置的均值分布图，图2b是语言变体和语流位置的均值分布图，图2c是语言变体和音节类型的均值分布图。表3和图2可一起使用，观察这三个因素之间的交互作用。

表3 语流位置、音节类型和语言变体的多因素方差分析结果

比较的因素	第Ⅲ类平方和	*df*	*F*	*p*
语流位置（句中/句末）	34.359	1	295.558	< 0.001
音节类型（轻声/非轻声）	8.707	1	74.897	< 0.001

续表

比较的因素	第Ⅲ类平方和	*df*	*F*	*p*
语言变体（普通话/“台湾国语”）	2.299	1	19.775	< 0.001
语流位置 × 音节类型	0.098	1	0.844	0.358
语流位置 × 语言变体	2.016	1	17.339	< 0.001
音节类型×语言变体	0.672	1	5.782	0.016
语流位置 × 音节类型 × 语言变体	0.251	1	2.156	0.142

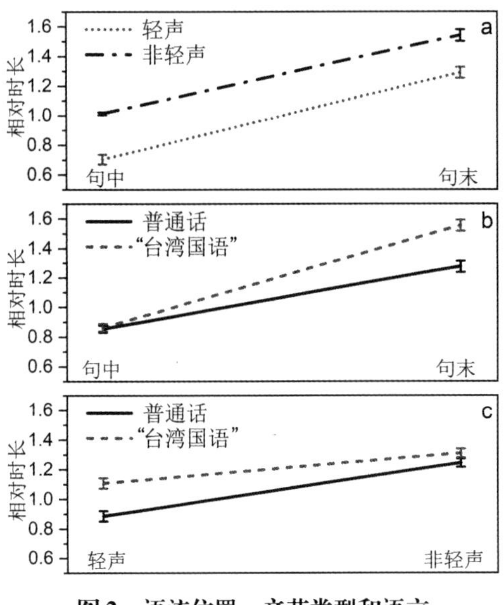

图2　语流位置、音节类型和语言变体相互对照的均值分布

从表3的结果可看出，单看语流位置（句中/句末）、音节类型（轻声/非轻声）及语言变体（普通话/“台湾国语”）这三项因素的主效应皆十分显著，p 值均小于0.001。

再看不同因素的交互作用。第一，语流位置和音节类型的交互作用不显著（$F=0.844$，$p=0.358 > 0.05$）。在图2a中，无论在句中还是在句末，非轻声数据皆高于轻声数据，并且两组数据接近平行，同样反映语流位置和音节类型的交互作用不显著。

第二，语流位置和语言变体的交互作用非常显著（$F=17.339$，$p < 0.001$）。图2b显示普通话和“台湾国语”在句中位置数据很接近；而在句末位置的数据相差较大，“台湾国语”的句末音节要明显长于普通话。

第三，音节类型和语言变体的交互作用显著（$F=0.844$，$p=0.016 < 0.05$）。图2c显示普通话和“台湾国语”在轻声音节的数据相差较大，普通话轻声音节明显短于“台湾国语”；而在非轻声音节则两者的数据较接近。

第四，语流位置、音节类型和语言变体这三者总体的交互作用不显著（$F=1.156$，$p=0.142 > 0.05$）。可能由于语流位置效应最大，其他两个因素并未体现显著的交互作用。

5. 讨论和总结

本文的研究，取材于电视剧《还珠格格》中的台词片段，皆为苏有朋、林心如、周杰和赵薇的自然语流的原声录音资料，其中苏有朋和林心如代表了“台湾国语”，而周杰和赵薇代表了普通话，可让我们管窥普通话和“台湾国语”的异同。我们通过Praat软件测量语料中各音节的时长，进行量化分析，再辅以统计检验分析以验证差异是否显著，使研究更精确和客观。

从上述的数据分析可见，在音节等时性方面，我们以 *rPVI* 和 *nPVI* 作为参数，“台湾国语”和普通话并无截然的区分，只是发音人之间可能有个性化差异（赵薇的 *nPVI* 明显比周杰和林心如的小）。在句末延长效应和轻声音节时长方面，“台湾国语”和普通话则呈现系统的差异。

就句末延长效应而言，普通话和“台湾国语”中皆存在句末延长效应，无论是轻声组还是非轻声组，相应的句末音节皆明显长于句中音节。“台湾国语”和普通话相比，句末延长效应要更强，无论句末音节是轻声或者非轻声，其延长的幅度都比普通话大，尤其当句末是轻声音节时，“台湾国语”和普通话具有统计检验意义上的显著性差异。

就轻声音节的时长特征而言，普通话里的轻声音节无论是在句中还是在句末都明显比非轻声音节短，也就是无论句子位置，普通话里的轻声都能同时体现轻声的“调类”和“调值”。“台湾国语”的轻声音节则不然，要分开句中和句末两种情况讨论：在句中轻声音节也显著比非轻声音节短，能同时体现轻声的“调类”和“调值”，但是在句末，只是略比非轻声音节短，在统计检验意义而言，“台湾国语”句末的轻声与非轻声音节的时长已趋同，也就是说“台湾国语”句末的轻声只剩下轻声的“调类”而无轻声的“调值”。

音节等时性、句末延长效应和轻声音节的时长特征都是在语流中节奏韵律特征的要素，而我们比较和分析普通话和“台湾国语”的异同，也必须留意这些要素之间的交互作用。本文的数据显示，普通话和“台湾国语”总体而言在音节等时性方面并没有截然不同的区别。如前所述，研究者留意到语言中有等时性，但等时性更多是一个感知概念［2］，是理想的状态或整体的趋势，在实际语言产出中，即使是在所谓具有“音节等时性”的语言里，每个音节并不会完全等长，而是会受到各种因素的影响，如我们探讨的句末延长效应和轻声调值之缩短效应，都是与“音节等时性”相悖的，而且正好是方向相反的两种效应。在普通话和“台湾国语”里，同时存在句末延长效应和轻声调值之缩短效应，只是这两种效应的强度和优先级不同。从4.4的多因素方差分析结果来看，句末延长效应比轻声调值之缩短效应更强，并且在普通话和“台湾国语”中也有效应强弱的差异。

就普通话而言，轻声调值之缩短效应更强，因此位于句末的轻声音节，虽也受句末延长效应影响，比句中的轻声音节长，但它更受轻声调值缩短效应影响，比句末的非轻声音节明显要短，两方面效应共同作用之下，普通话句末轻声与句中非轻声时长相若，其相对时长都约在1上下，而没有远大于1（若句末延长效应明显，句末音节的相对时长应该远大于1）。

就“台湾国语”而言，句末延长效应更强，即使调值本应“很短”的轻声，在句末的位置也变得很长，只是比非轻声音节稍短一点点，句末轻声与句末非轻声并无统计意义上的显著差异，也就是说，“台湾国语”因为很强的句末延长效应使句末的轻声音节牺牲了其“短”调值，并非真“轻”。另外，如果因为句末轻声不“轻”而认为“台湾国语”没有真正的轻声，这样的看法也是片面的：在句中位置时，轻声音节也是明显比非轻声音节短，可见“台湾国语”在句中还是能真正实现轻声的“短”调值的。也就是说，“台湾国语”有真正的轻声能实现“短”调值，只是它们必须满足一个条件，即要处于非句末的位置上。

本文的研究为普通话和“台湾国语”语音上的细微差别提供了量化的实证证据。根据［16］，普通话说得非常流利、发音比较标准的人其实并不多，只有20.42%。一般人的普通话往往带着汉语地方方言的特征，这样的普通话被称为“地方普通话”。“地方普通话”和标准普通话往往也存在着节奏韵律上的差别，本研究也为今后更大规模的地方普通话的研究提供了参考。

6. 致谢

本文的研究受香港教育大学内部研究基金（RG88/2018－2019R）资助，张钧琳女士在资料的收集和数据的测量时提供了大量的帮助。两位匿名评审专家提供了很有用的意见和建议，在此一并致谢。当然，文中若有任何错漏，皆为作者的责任，与他们无关。

参考文献

［1］Abercrombie, D. 1967. *Elements of General Phonetics*. Edinburgh: Edinburgh University Press.
［2］Beckman, M. E. 1992. Evidence for speech

rhythms across languages. In Tohura, Y., Vatikiotis - Bateson, E., Sagisaka, Y. (eds.), *Speech Perception, Production and Linguistic Structure*. Tokyo: IOS Press, 457 - 463.

[3] Boersma, P., Weenink, D. 2018. *Praat: Doing phonetics by computer* [computer program], Version 6.0.37, retrieved from http://www.praat.org/.

[4] Grabe, E., Low, E. L. 2002. Durational variability in speech and the rhythm class hypothesis. In Gussenhoven, C., Warner, N. (eds.), *Laboratory Phonology VII*. Berlin: Mouton de Gruyter, 515 - 546.

[5] Harrington, J., Palethorpe, S., Watson, C. I. 2000. Does the Queen speak the Queen's English? *Nature* 408(6815), 927.

[6] 曹剑芬:《语速特征及其变化》,《第六届全国现代语音学学术会议论文集》,2007 年,第 143—148 页。

[7] 邓丹、石锋、吕士楠:《普通话与台湾国语声调的对比分析》,《声学学报》2006 年第 6 期。

[8] 李青梅:《海峡两岸字音比较》,《语言文字应用》1992 年第 3 期。

[9] 王蓓、杨玉芳、吕士楠:《汉语韵律层级结构边界的声学分析》,《声学学报》2004 年第 1 期。

[10] 王理嘉:《从官话到国语和普通话——现代汉民族共同语的形成及其发展》,《集思广益(第三辑):普通话学与教的实践与探讨》,1999 年。

[11] 魏钢强:《调值的轻声和调类的轻声》,《方言》2000 年第 1 期。

[12] 严菡波、Allard Jongman:《普通话及台湾国语舌尖音与卷舌音的声学比较分析》,《语言研究集刊》(第 20 辑),2018 年。

[13] 杨玉芳:《句法边界的韵律学表现》,《声学学报》1997 年第 5 期。

[14] 张岚:《海峡两岸现代汉语通用语语音差异对比研究》,博士学位论文,华东师范大学,2009 年。

[15] 郑良伟:《北京话和台湾话轻声出现的异同、历史由来和台湾新生代国语的形成》,《语言研究》1987 年第 12 期。

[16] 中国语言文字使用情况调查资料领导小组办公室:《中国语言文字使用情况调查》,语文出版社 2006 年版。

张 凌 香港教育大学中国语言学系,博士,助理教授,主要研究领域为汉语语音学、社会语言学、汉语作为第二语言教学等。
Email:zhangl@eduhk.hk

普通话阴平—上声听感边界的再测试

王大佐

摘　要　本文以二字组真词为听辨材料，依据大样本数据将参照字的音高设定为自然语言音高，对普通话阴平—上声听感边界进行再测试。实验结果显示，参照字音高越贴近自然语言，声调范畴感知越向理想模式靠近，表明范畴感知程度加深；听感边界、边界宽度和区分峰离散程度减小，组间数据更趋规整，感知稳定性增强。参照字音高对听感边界影响显著，变动后参照字若更能凸显刺激音听感“低”特征，上声听感范围相应扩大。依据实验结果，本文也对普通话声调听感原理进行了检验和修正。

关键词　声调，听感边界，声调听感原理

Retesting the Categorical Boundary between Mandarin Tone 1 and Tone 3

WANG Dazuo

Abstract This paper retests the categorical boundary between Tone 1 and Tone 3 in Mandarin using disyllabic words as experiment materials. The pitch of the reference syllable is reset in accordance to that of natural speech based on big data. The results show that the closer the pitch of the reference syllable is to natural speech, the closer the perception performance is to the ideal model of Categorical Perception(CP), indicating that the degree of CP deepens. The reduction of the degree of dispersion of the three crucial parameters, categorical doundary position, width and discrimination peak, will increase the stability of perception. The main effect of the reference syllable pitch on the perception of the categorical boundary is significant. If the resetting of the reference syllable can better highlight the “low” characteristics of the stimuli, the perceptual category of Tone 3 will be expanded accordingly. Based on the results, this paper verifies and revises the principles of Mandarin tone perception.

Key words Tone, Categorical boundary, Principles of Mandarin tone perception

1. 引言

范畴感知是认知科学研究的重要课题，是指我们倾向于依据大脑已建立的范畴来感知世界。范畴感知效应使不同范畴的个体间差异在感知中更凸显，而同一范畴内的个体差异则弱化甚至不被察觉。

视觉和听觉是人类感知世界最直接的方式，范畴感知现象在这两个模态中均有发现，如色彩感知［2］和语音感知［8，15，20］。不仅是人类，有相关研究表明，毛丝鼠［7］和猕猴［10］对人类语音也展现出范畴感知特点。Liberman 等［8］最早运用语音合成技术开展语音范畴感知实验研究，并开创性地提出了范畴感知的经典实验范式。他们合成了一系列等差异音节，构成英语三个浊塞音/b/、/d/、/g/音位范畴连续统，音节的元音均为/e/，请听音人进行辨认和区分实验。研究关注的问题是：音位辨认和区分关系如何？若听音人将连续统刺激音听辨到三个离散的音位范畴中，辨认函数上的范畴边界处，区分函数是否有明显曲折与之对应？听音人对同一范畴内和范畴边界两端的两个等差异音节的区分表现是否一致？结果表明，听音人将连续的音节感知到三个离散的音位范畴中；听音人对范畴间两音节的区分很容易，对同一范畴内的则难以分辨。这种语音的感知现象和结果模式被称为语音的范畴感知。Studdert - Kennedy 等［14］进一步提出了判断范畴感知的

实验结果标准：(1) 辨认率突然改变，表现在辨认函数的陡降/陡升；(2) 区分函数在范畴边界位置处有显著区分峰；(3) 范畴内区分率处于或接近50%；(4) 区分函数可以通过辨认概率得到良好预测。

Studdert－Kennedy 等［14］提出的是理想范畴感知的标准，然而实际实验结果总会有偏离，范畴感知和其另一端连续感知的二分法已不能准确描述其间存在的中间状态。由此他也提出了范畴感知程度（degrees of categorical perception）的概念。Repp［13］认为可把范畴感知看作三种变量：任务变量、刺激变量和被试变量综合作用的函数。变量值的改变会影响范畴感知的程度。以上观念在语音知觉研究中一定程度得到证实［12，25，38］。

声调感知是否为范畴感知，仍有争议，尚无定论。Wang［15］研究表明，普通话母语者对阴平和阳平的感知具有明显范畴感知特点，几项研究的实验结果均支持这一结论［11，20，27，36，38］。孔江平［24］对藏语拉萨话声调进行感知测试，结果表明拉萨话的声调无论在音高及调型，还是在长短上，都属范畴感知。Abramson［1］则得出泰语母语者对泰语三个平调的感知为连续感知的结论，依据是区分函数整体区分率较高，在范畴边界处并无区分峰。Francis 等［5］在广州话中同时考察两种对立类型的声调间的感知模式，结果表明呈调阶对立的平调感知更像连续感知，而调型对立的声调感知更具范畴感知的特点。然而，金健［23］在负载句中进行声调听辨，发现广州话平调感知为范畴感知或类范畴感知。陈曦丹［22］在普通话二字组中发现低平调上声和高平调阴平的感知为范畴感知。后两项研究中负载句或参照字环境，为刺激音的感知提供了环境参照，这似乎是平调范畴感知的原因。

陈曦丹［22］的研究是构建普通话声调听感格局［29］的五种实验之一，其实验材料二字组中非连续统刺激音的参照字音高与其他四种实验进行了统一设定，这种音高设计与自然语言相近，但还存在一定差异。其辨认、区分函数的表现与理想范畴感知标准也有一定偏差，同时在听感边界这一参数上，其不规整性和动态性较大。这也许是参照字的音高设计带来的影响。因此，我们拟参考张妍［39］对北京话二字组较大样本的音高分析，重新设定二字组参照字音高到自然语言音高，考察环境变量对阴平—上声范畴感知程度的影响，同时对两调的听感边界再测试，以进一步精确构建声调听感格局，这是第一个研究目的。

重设参照字的音高涉及环境变动对两调听感边界的影响。以往在二字组中考察声调知觉的相关研究并不多见。林焘、王士元［28］运用合成语音和自然语音重新组合的方法，将北京话双音词中前字 S－A 设定为阴平声，通过逐步提升 S－A 的环境即后字 S－B 的音高，改变两字的音域关系，考察北京人对 S－A 阴平声的听辨是否会有所改变，如果存在改变，是否还受到音节 S－A 本身时长的影响。结果表明，音域关系变化影响了 S－A 的调类判断，总体来说，随着 S－B 音高逐渐提升，S－A 被听辨为阴平声（如：搭的）的比例逐渐降低，阳平（如：答的）的比率逐渐升高，最后出现部分听辨为上声（如：打的）的情况。由此可见，环境产生了对比效应，高音环境中，听音人倾向将 S－A 听辨为低调。这种改变也受到了 S－A 本身音长的影响，当两音节音高差相同时，S－A 音长越长，被听成低平调上声的比例越大。Fox 和 Qi［4］将普通话二字组中的前字设定为阴平或阳平，后字则为阴平到阳平的连续统，考察前字环境对后字的感知影响。结果只发现了边缘效应，方向则是同化的。曹文［21］发现，在普通话双音节词中，平调的感知结果会受到参照调的影响。当参照调居前时，即便是最低的平调也有较大可能被感知为第一声；而当参照调居后时，低平调则有较大的可能被感知为半上。Huang 和 Holt［6］、Moore 和 Jongman［9］、Wong 和 Diehl［17］则通过提升和降低前置负载句的平均 F0 音高，研究声调感知的归一化。结果均发现前置负载句 F0 音高环境对声调辨认的对比效应，即高 F0 音高环境，听音人更倾向于判断为低调；反之则判断为高调。当我们将陈曦丹［22］实验材料二字组中的参照字音高重新设定后，是否会对听感边界产生影响？影响的方向是什么？反映听音人的何种加工调整机制？这是我们研究的第二个问题。

声调听感格局的五种实验：阴平—阳平［27］、阴平—去声［37］、阴平—上声［22］、阳平—上声［35］、去声—上声［26］将实验材料二字组中的参照字设定了不同调类，考察了听感边界在该因素下的表现。石锋、王大佐［32］对这五种实验结果进行了对比，概括归纳出12条普通话声调听感原理。其中基于语言学因素10条：格局、位次、调阶、标记、同调、对折、高降、降阶、邻接、多边原理；基于非语言学因素2条：展示顺序和性别差异原理。重新设定参照字音高后，相关的听感原理是否适用？是否需要修正？这是我们关心的第三个问题。

2. 实验方法

2.1 被试与实验材料

招募了24名在校大学生，男女各半，平均年龄22.08岁（SD = 3.02岁），均为北方方言背景，右利手，非语言学、心理学专业，未受过音乐训练，无视听障碍。

表1 参照字音高合成标准对比

组别		实验词	参照字音高（半音 st）	
			陈曦丹［22］	本实验
前字对比组	阴平组	烟花—眼花	19 - 19st	20 - 20st
	阳平组	梯形—体型	14 - 19st	13 - 18st
	去声组	光大—广大	19 - 9st	20 - 15st
后字对比组	阴平组	天仙—天险	19 - 19st	20 - 20st
	阳平组	图标—图表	14 - 19st	15 - 18st
	去声组	梦乡—梦想	19 - 14st	21 - 14st

实验词沿用陈曦丹［22］所选二字组真词。每对词中，声韵调完全相同的字为参照字，如“花”；声母韵母完全相同；声调存在阴平—上声对立的字为目标字，如“烟”和“眼”。根据参照字调类，分为阴平组、阳平组、去声组（考虑上上相连，前上变读阳平，故暂不考虑上上组合）；根据目标字位置，分为前字对比组和后字对比组。详见表1实验词与组别。

采集原始语料。发音人为一名普通话标准的22岁北京男性。使用 cool edit Pro 2.1 录音，单声道，采样率22050Hz，采样精度16位。采用负载句“我现在读的是＊＊（目标词即表1中的12个词）这个词”，由发音人用自然语速读出，每个句子说3遍。随后在 Praat 中切分基频曲线最为清晰完整、听感最为自然的目标词，作为刺激音合成的原始语料。①

设定参照字和目标字音高、时长和音强合成标准。参照字音高参考张妍［39］普通话双音节词较大样本25位男性北京人发音的平均音高数据进行设置，详见表1。本实验参照字基频曲线与陈曦丹［22］对比见图1。根据上声的本质是低平调的观点［30］，目标字设定为由F0曲线音高相差1半音的11个刺激组成的由上声到阴平的平调连续统。图1为实验刺激音基频曲线合成示意图，其中1号刺激音高为9—9半音，为典型的上声；11号刺激音高为19—19半音，为典型的阴平。阴平、阳平参照字时长为160毫秒，去声参照字为140毫秒；目标字为140毫秒。音强统一设置为65dB。时长与音强均与陈曦丹［22］一致。刺激音合成的母本音节均为原始语料目标字阴平调音节。考虑到感知声调，主要依靠基频和时长［28］，本实验在母本音节基础上只修改这两个参数，保留了其音强曲线。在 Praat 中，参照以上标准，使用自编脚本合成刺激音。对应6组双音节词，共合成连续统6个，共计 6×11 = 66 个刺激音。

① 本实验负载句为无明显语义强调的陈述句，整句音高曲线呈下降趋势。同时，实验词为双音节韵律词，内部也存在音高下倾，实验词后字的调域要低于前字。因此前字对比组和后字对比组的听感边界会受音高下倾作用影响而有所差异。

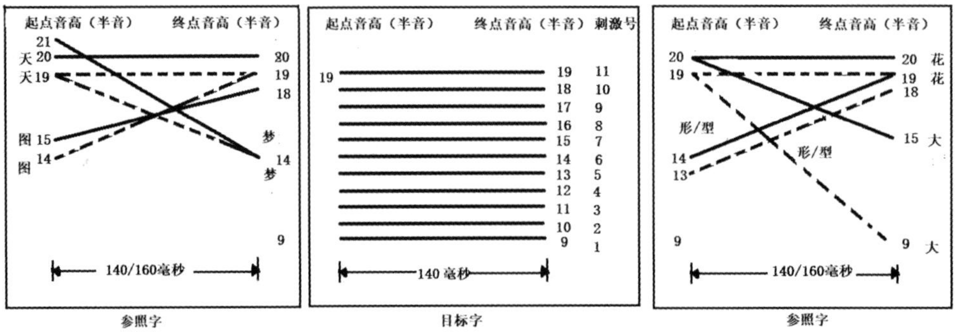

图1　实验刺激音基频曲线合成示意图

2.2　实验过程

实验由辨认实验和区分实验构成。通过E－prime1.1软件进行刺激音播放和被试行为数据采集。实验在南开大学语音实验室进行。被试坐在台式电脑前，佩戴耳机，通过按键对刺激进行反应。一组辨认和区分实验对应一套二字组真词声调连续统，共进行6组，一位被试用时约1小时。

辨认实验中，连续统中刺激音随机呈现给被试，每听到一个刺激音，被试做调类判断，若听辨为阴平（如“烟花”）则按键“1”，上声（如“眼花”）则按键“2”（二选一强迫选择）。一个辨认实验内含4小节，每小节内11个语音刺激重复一次随机呈现，每位被试一个辨认实验做4×11＝44个判断，6个共做44×6＝264个判断。

区分实验采用AX区分任务模式，即对成对出现的刺激判断两者相同还是不同。一个区分实验内含4小节，一小节中共包含29对刺激音，其中18对由来自同一声调连续统中F0音高相差两个半音的刺激音构成，其中顺序9对（刺激号组合为1—3，2—4，3—5，……，8—10，9—11）；逆序9对（刺激号组合为3—1，4—2，5—3，……，10—8，11—9）。另外的11对为相同的刺激音组合（刺激号组合为1—1，2—2，……，10—10，11—11）。若判断为相同则按键“V”，不同则按键“N”。每小节中29个刺激对重复一次随机呈现，每位被试一个区分实验做4×29＝116个判断，6个共做116×6＝696个判断。

2.3 数据分析

2.3.1 辨认实验数据分析

使用概率分析（Probit Analysis）[3]拟合得到每位被试的听感边界和边界宽度。听感边界是指阴平上声辨认函数曲线的交叉点（即辨认率为50%）处所对应的F0曲线音高；边界宽度是指辨认率在50%与75%间的线性距离，该数值由概率分析中的平均偏差与标准差决定[11]。

2.3.2 区分实验数据分析

使用Xu等[20]提出的公式计算每对刺激音的区分正确率。29对刺激音中共包括四种刺激组合类型，即AA，BB，AB，BA，其中A和B相差两个步幅。AA，BB是由相同的刺激音组成，AB，BA是由不同的刺激音组成。相邻的刺激对会包含重叠的AA或BB刺激对，对于每组的区分正确率P的计算公式为：

$$P = P(\text{'S'} \mid S) \cdot P(S) + P(\text{'D'} \mid D) \cdot P(D)$$

其中，P（‘S’｜S）代表被试在听到由相同刺激音组成的刺激对时，做出“相同”判断的百分率，P（‘D’｜D）代表被试在听到不同的刺激音组成的刺激对时，做出“不同”判断的百分率。P（S）代表由相同的刺激音组成的刺激对占所有刺激对的百分率，P（D）代表由不同的刺激音组成的刺激对占所有刺激对的百分率，本实验中，P（S）和P（D）均为50%。

区分正确率 P 中的最大值 Pmax 即为区分峰值。

3. 实验结果

图 2 为本实验与陈曦丹［22］（以下简称前实验）辨认、区分曲线对比图。每个子图中，方形标记曲线为辨认曲线，横轴为连续统中 11 个刺激音，纵轴对应 24 位被试将该刺激音判断为上声的平均百分率；三角标记曲线为区分曲线，横轴对应刺激对 1—3，2—4，……，9—11，纵轴则为 2. 3. 2 中公式算出的 P 值，即区分正确率。

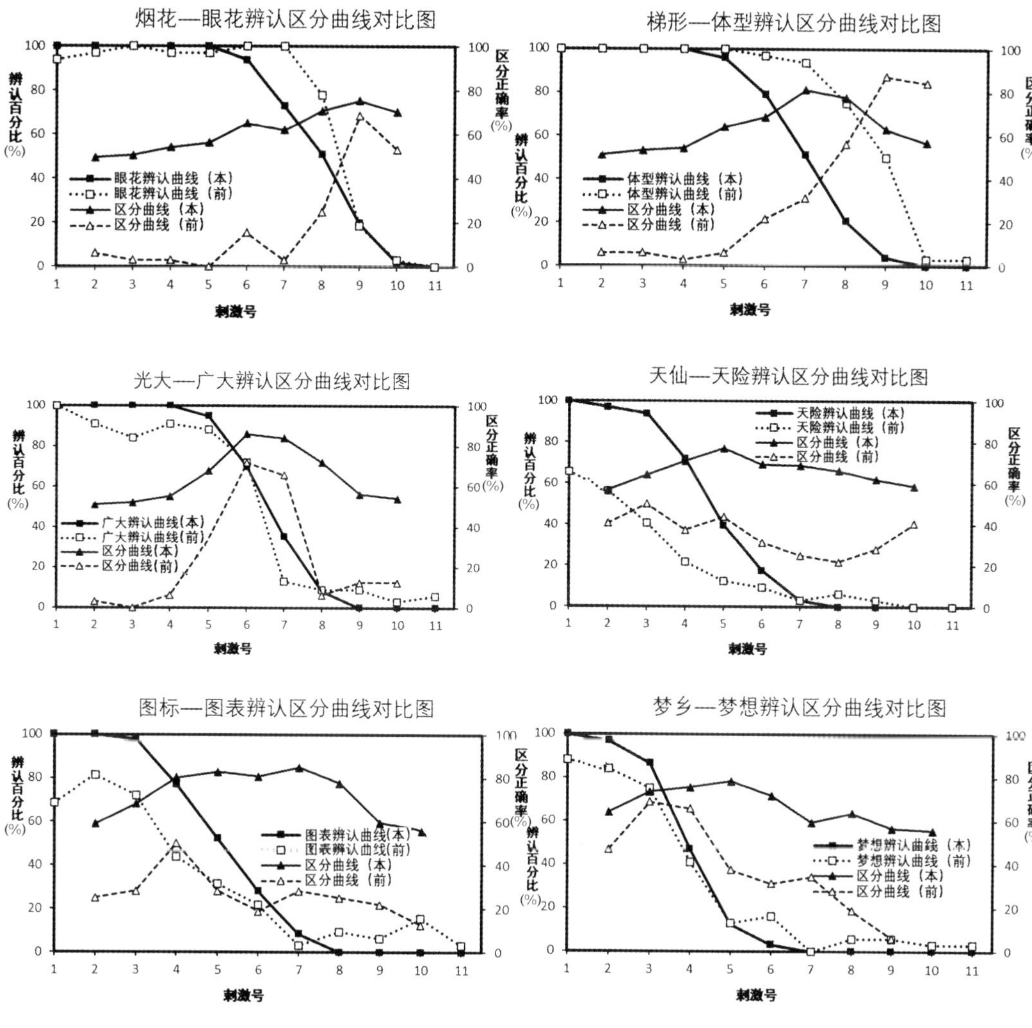

图 2 两实验辨认、区分曲线对比图

3.1 辨认与区分曲线

通过对比明显可见，（1）两实验辨认曲线整体模式基本一致：前几号刺激大概率判断为上声，随后上声辨认率陡降，后几号刺激上声辨认率接近 0。这体现等物理差异连续变化的刺激音，对应心理感知的辨认率并非等差异，连续的语音变化被感知到离散的两个声调范畴中，范畴间的转换是突然的。（2）非陡降部分的辨认曲线，本实验较前实验波动性减小。例如光大—广大组，前 4 个刺激，前实验辨认曲线先降后升，形有波动，而本实验则为稳定直线；图标—图表组后 4 个刺激，前实验被试并未 100% 判断为阴平，而本实验则全部判断为阴平。由 1—11 号刺激，上声典型性由强至弱，阴平的高平特征则逐渐增强。声调辨认率虽不是等差异，但大致应该与这种趋势保持一致。本实验得到的辨认曲线更符合这种一致。(3) 后字对比组的三组辨认曲线，前实验伸展不完整，尤其是天仙—天险和图标—图表两组，第 1 号刺激上声辨认率分别为 64%、65%，而本实验则均达到 100%。被试在听感上完全认同目标字声调为上声。并且，本实验 6 组辨认曲线都充分延展，表现出了规整的一致性。(4) 两实验区分曲线整体模式基本一致：在辨认曲线陡降处，即两声调范畴边界处，出现了区分峰，表明对两声调范畴间的刺激对的区分正确率高于范畴内刺激对区分正确率。(5) 本实验区分曲线，各刺激对辨认率较前实验大幅提升（除梯形—体型组的 8—10、9—11 刺激对）。范畴内刺激对的区分率提升至 50% 左右，例如光大—广大组，前实验 1—3、2—4 对区分正确率为 3%、0；本实验则为 51%、52%。

总结来说，当参照字音高更贴近真实语言，辨认曲线的稳定性和组间一致性得到了明显优化，同时区分正确率也大幅提升了。

表 2 为本实验与陈曦丹［22］的主要考察参数的对比表。

表 2　两实验主要参数对比

组别		实验词	听感边界（半音）		比较		听感边界宽度		比较		区分峰值（%）		比较
			陈曦丹	本实验	差值	p 值	陈曦丹	本实验	差值	p 值	陈曦丹	本实验	差值
前字对比组	阴平组	烟花—眼花	16.4	15.9	−0.5	<0.05	1.70	1.07	−0.63	0.06	68.8	75.5	
	阳平组	梯形—体型	17.0	15.0	−2.0	<0.001	1.01	0.90	−0.11	0.09	87.5	81.2	
	去声组	光大—广大	14.4	14.6	0.2	0.21	1.08	0.83	−0.25	0.21	71.9	85.9	
		平均值	15.9	15.2	−0.7		1.26	0.93	−0.33		76.1	80.9	4.8
		极差	2.6	1.3	−1.3		0.69	0.24	−0.45		18.7	10.4	−8.3
		标准差	1.36	0.67	−0.69		0.38	0.12	−0.26		10.02	5.21	−4.81
后字对比组	阴平组	天仙—天险	10.4	12.7	2.3	<0.001	1.35	0.89	−0.46	0.08	50.0	77.1	
	阳平组	图标—图表	11.8	13.1	1.3	<0.05	1.16	0.67	−0.49	0.61	50.0	84.9	
	去声组	梦乡—梦想	11.7	11.9	0.2	0.17	0.92	0.82	−0.10	0.46	68.8	78.3	
		平均值	11.3	12.6	1.3		1.14	0.79	−0.35		56.3	80.1	23.8
		极差	1.4	1.2	−0.2		0.43	0.22	−0.21		18.8	7.8	−11
		标准差	0.78	0.61	−0.17		0.22	0.11	−0.11		10.85	4.2	−6.65
		总平均值	13.6	13.9	0.3		1.20	0.86	−0.34		66.2	80.5	14.3
		总极差	6.6	4.0	−2.6		0.78	0.40	−0.38		37.5	10.4	−27.1
		总标准差	2.73	1.53	−1.2		0.28	0.13	−0.15		14.31	4.25	−10.06

3.2 听感边界

从两实验各6组实验词间听感边界的离散程度看，较前实验，本实验无论前字组还是后字组，标准差均减小，总标准差减小1.2，听感边界在各组词间集中程度增强，差异减小。前字组与后字组听感边界差（2.6半音）较前实验缩小（4.6半音），但前字组听感边界仍大于后字组，这一趋势在两实验中是一致的。

以参照字音高（前实验、本实验）为自变量，以听感边界为因变量，在每个实验词对中，做单因素方差分析。统计结果显示（见表2），阴平组和阳平组，前后两实验听感边界差异显著；去声组，前后两实验听感边界差异不显著。

在本实验内部，以参照字位置（前、后）、参照字调类（阴平、阳平、去声）、性别（男、女）为自变量，以听感边界为因变量，在SPSS中进行重复测量方差分析。统计结果显示，（1）参照字位置主效应显著［$F(1, 22) = 203.65$，$p < 0.001$］，本实验前字组听感边界（15.2半音）明显大于后字组（12.6半音）。（2）参照字调类主效应显著［$F(2, 44) = 24.26$，$p < 0.001$］，不同参照字调类词组中目标字的听感边界有显著差异。（3）性别主效应不显著［$F(1, 22) = 3.67$，$p = 0.069$］，男女被试的听感边界无显著差异；（4）参照字位置与参照字调类交互作用显著［$F(2, 44) = 8.39$，$p < 0.001$］。简单效应分析显示，在参照字在前水平上，即后字对比组中，参照字调类的简单效应显著［$F(2, 46) = 18.13$，$p < 0.001$］。配对样本t检验结果显示：后字对比组中，阴平组与阳平组差异不显著（$t = -1.719$，$p = 0.099$），阴平组与去声组差异显著（$t = 4.088$，$p < 0.001$），阳平组与去声组差异显著（$t = 7.158$，$p < 0.001$）。去声组梦乡—梦想的听感边界（11.9半音）显著低于天仙—天险组（12.7半音），图标—图表组（13.1半音）。（5）在参照字在后水平上，即前字对比组中，参照字调类的简单效应显著［$F(2, 46) = 15.47$，$p < 0.001$］。配对样本t检验结果显示：前字对比组中，阴平组与阳平组差异显著（$t = 4.160$，$p < 0.001$），阴平组与去声组差异显著（$t = 5.667$，$p < 0.001$），阳平组与去声组差异不显著（$t = 1.551$，$p = 0.134$）。阴平组烟花—眼花的听感边界（15.9半音）要显著大于梯形—体型组（15.0半音）和光大—广大组（14.6半音）。

3.3 听感边界宽度

从两实验各6组实验词间听感边界宽度的离散程度看，较前实验，本实验无论前字组还是后字组，标准差均减小，总标准差减小0.15，听感边界宽度在各组词间集中程度增强，差异减小。

以参照字音高（前实验、本实验）为自变量，以听感边界宽度为因变量，在每个实验词对中，做单因素方差分析。统计结果显示（见表2），6组词前实验和本实验听感边界宽度差异不显著。

在本实验内部，以参照字位置（前、后）、参照字调类（阴平、阳平、去声）、性别（男、女）为自变量，以听感边界宽度为因变量，在SPSS中进行重复测量方差分析。统计结果显示，（1）参照字位置主效应不显著［$F(1, 22) = 0.04$，$p = 0.842$］。（2）参照字调类主效应显著［$F(2, 44) = 6.39$，$p < 0.001$］，表明不同参照字调类对目标字的听感边界宽度有显著影响。（3）性别主效应显著［$F(1, 22) = 4.68$，$p < 0.05$］，女性平均边界宽度（0.98）显著大于男性（0.87）。

3.4 区分峰

从两实验各实验词间区分峰值的离散程度看，较前实验，本实验无论前字组还是后字组，标准差均减小，总标准差减小10.06，区分峰值在各组词间集中程度增强，差异减小。本实验平均区分峰值80.5%，较前实验的66.2%大幅提升14.3%。

4. 讨论

4.1 参照字环境对声调范畴感知程度的影响

本实验第一个研究目的是考察参照字

音高重设至自然语言音高后对阴平和上声感知模式和程度的影响。

从辨认实验结果看，6组词的辨认曲线均出现了陡降，表明等物理差异语音刺激被感知到两个离散的音位范畴中；从区分实验结果看，在对应辨认曲线的陡降处都出现了区分峰（其中图标—图表和梦乡—梦想组呈“平台型”），范畴间刺激区分的正确率高于范畴内刺激。这种结果模式表明在二字组中阴平和上声的感知模式为范畴感知或类范畴感知。这与 Abramson［1］的结果相反，与 Wang［15］、金健［23］、陈曦丹［22］的结果基本一致。

Wang［15］和 Abramson［1］是对孤立音节的听辨，金健［23］、陈曦丹［22］和本实验则是在负载句或二字组中进行。Moore 和 Jongman［9］认为，前置负载句可为刺激音的辨认提供说话人的音高范围信息，这使听音人更容易确定音位范畴的边界位置。Francis 等［5］认为音高范围信息至少有两个来源：一是一个音节本身的 F0 曲线即可提供足够的内部信息，如广州话中的曲拱调；二是这个音节所处的语音环境提供的外部信息，如广州话中的平调更要依靠外部负载句环境。Wang［15］使用的是阴平和阳平的连续统，阳平调可提供说话者的音高范围。Abramson［1］孤立的泰语的平调连续统缺乏负载句提供的外部信息。金健［23］、陈曦丹［22］和本实验则为平调提供了音高范围，提升了听音人对刺激的范畴归类，进而使两调的范畴转换更突然，范畴感知特点更突出。

尽管陈曦丹［22］认为阴平和上声为范畴感知，但其结果与理想标准还有差异。本实验结果与之相比，辨认曲线非陡降部分较前实验波动减小，端点处伸展完整。区分曲线整体较前实验大幅提升，范畴内刺激区分率接近50%。通过对比可见，本实验得到的结果较理想模型更为贴近，这表明自然语言的参照字环境提升了声调范畴感知程度。

另外，本实验6组实验词间听感边界、听感边界宽度和区分峰值数据分布集中，组间平均值差异减小，表明在6组实验词中的感知表现更趋一致。同一种语言的声学语音格局相对稳定，这样才能使不同说话人间能够交流信息［31］。感知作为言语链的重要一环，其听感格局也应与声学格局的性质相对应，具有稳定性。尽管所选的6组词目标字的声母、韵母有所差异，但其声调模式6组均相同，不应在听感边界等参数上存在过大差异，这样才能更利于人们对接收的语音进行分析对比，从而做出正确的理解，使交际顺利进行。

当我们将参照字音高由原实验的统一设置，修改为更贴近自然语言音高后，声调感知得到了明显的优化。一方面，修改后的刺激音，听感自然度得到提升，这排除了原实验人工统一设计带来的干扰，被试能够准确地将其进行范畴归类；另一方面，本实验的参照字音高设计，也使6组实验词刺激音自然度得到均衡，使被试的听感表现在各组中更趋一致。

4.2 参照字环境对听感边界的影响

本实验第二个研究目的是考察参照字音高变动对阴平—上声听感边界的影响。实验结果表明，阴平组和阳平组，本实验与陈曦丹［22］听感边界差异显著，而去声组差异不显著。Wong 和 Diehl［17］表明，平调感知会受环境作用，本实验结果也一定程度上与该结论一致。然而，本实验在6组实验词中并未得到统一的作用方向。

图3为听感边界随参照字音高变化图，其中参照字框中的虚线和实线分别为前实验和本实验的 F0 曲线，箭头表示变动方向。目标字中画出了11个刺激音的 F0 曲线，虚线和加粗实线分别为前实验和本实验的听感边界。去声组：光大—广大；梦乡—梦想，两实验听感边界平均值仅相差0.2半音，且差异不显著，以下主要对阴平组、阳平组进行讨论。

（1）参照字为阴平，目标字在前，参照字音高升高，阴平—上声听感边界下降，阴平听感范围扩大（见图3-a）；目标字在后，参照字音高升高，阴平—上声听感边界上升，阴平听感范围缩小（见图

3 - b)。

我们进行言语加工一般遵循由左至右的顺序，且最后一个音节一般会留下较深刻的听觉印象。Whalen 和 Xu [16] 研究表明，F0 曲线为水平的汉语音节，多被听为高调，除非 F0 曲线绝对音高非常低。Xu [18] 指出，汉语普通话三字组中的第二个音节若为升调阳平或降调去声，其 F0 曲线受到协同发音的影响有时会变为接近水平的 F0 曲线，这时它大多被感知为高平调而非低平调。由此可见，同为平调的阴平和上声，在听感上高平调阴平要占据优势，当 F0 曲线的绝对音高足够低时，才更倾向于判断为低平调上声。

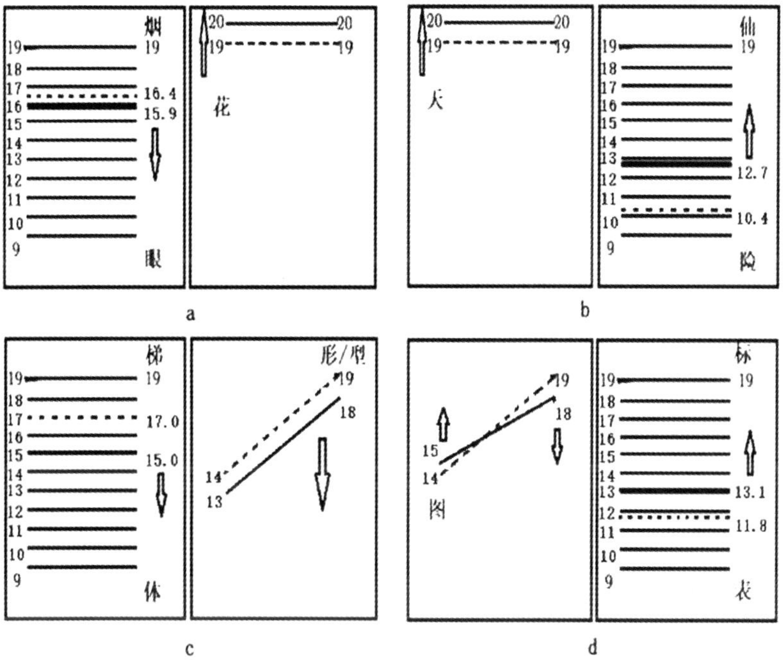

图 3　听感边界变动图

烟花—眼花组，刺激音后接 20—20 半音的高平调“花”，因音高高于刺激音且位置在后，其听感上更为突出，削弱了对刺激音的听觉敏感度。这时被试在听到高平调“花”进行判断时，受到“花”的同化影响，由于阴平调的优势地位，并且边界附近的刺激音本身音高并不低，使被试会认为刺激音也更像阴平“烟”，因此听感边界下降，阴平听感范围扩大了。

天仙—天险组，20—20 半音的高平调“天”后接刺激音，与前实验相比，“天”与后接刺激音的音高差加大。由于左至右的加工顺序，被试更易形成高—低音高对比，且边界附近的刺激音音高较低，因此原实验听起来是阴平的刺激音，现在则被判断为低平调上声“险”，相应听感边界上移，上声的听感范围扩大了。

另一种可能的原因是低平调上声对前字的逆向异化作用。Xu [19] 指出，在发普通话双音节词时，后字若为上声，则对前字音高产生逆向异化作用，使前字 F0 音高提升。本实验中，听音人将参照字“天”音高提升归因为上声的逆向异化，因此较原实验做出更多上声判断。

（2）参照字为阳平，目标字在前，参照字整体音高下降，听感边界下移，阴平听感范围扩大（见图 3 - c）；目标字在后，参照字起点音高上升，终点音高下降，听感边界上升，阴平听感范围缩小（见图 3 - d）。

梯形—体型组，原实验参照字为14—19半音，终点音高较高，使在前刺激音的平调听感上相对具有“低”特征，因此更易判断为上声。当参照字音高整体下降为13—18半音时，在前的刺激音平调听感上“低”特征减弱，因此原来在听感边界附近判断为上声的刺激音现在则倾向于判断为阴平，如第8号刺激16—16半音的平调，原来被听为上声，现在则为阴平。因此听感边界下移，阴平听感范围扩大。

图标—图表组，参照字“图”起点音高上升，听感边界上升，也许是起点音高上升，加大了参照字与目标刺激音的音高落差，被试做出了更多的上声判断，因此听感边界上移，上声听感范围扩大。

（3）参照字为去声，两实验听感边界绝对值仅相差0.2半音，差异不显著。可能的原因是，在普通话声调系统中，去声是唯一具有“降”特征的声调，尽管前后实验去声音高设置不同，但并未显著影响去声的辨识度，未对目标字刺激音的判断产生过多的影响。

4.3 声调听感原理的验证

本实验第三个研究目的是参考自然语言音高环境下的听感结果，尤其是结合统计学分析，来验证初步提出的声调听感原理。与本实验相关的原理共6个，以下分别进行验证。

4.3.1 位次原理

位次原理是指同一个声调在双字组前字中的听感边界通常比在后字中更高更稳定。本实验中，参照字位置对听感边界影响显著，前字组平均听感边界（15.2半音）明显大于后字组（12.6半音），这一趋势与陈曦丹［22］一致（15.9半音 > 11.3半音）。因此，位次原理中关于前、后字组听感边界高低的论述再次得到验证。位次原理发生作用是音高下倾的结果，受到语流中音高普遍呈逐渐下倾的趋势影响，语句中前面的韵律单位的调域普遍高于后面的调域。阴平—上声的听感边界位于后字时，调域要低于位于前字，对应听感，其听感边界也随之下降。

然而，本实验前字组听感边界的标准差要稍大于后字组（0.67 > 0.61），结合我们正在进行的阴平—阳平（前字组0.5 < 后字组1.2）、阴平—去声（前字组0.4 > 后字组0.1）再测试的结果，似乎后字组听感边界通常要更稳定些。由此，位次原理暂可修改为：同一个声调在双字组后字中的听感边界通常比在前字中更低更稳定。

4.3.2 调阶原理

调阶原理是指调阶对立的声调之间的听感边界具有较强的动态性。调阶对立，是指调型相同的两个声调，只在音高上有差别。本实验中阴平和上声都是平调，它们的对立为调阶对立。在本实验中，与陈曦丹［22］相比，前字组听感边界与后字组差距减小，但仍相差2.6半音，这意味着边界动程达26%。我们正在进行的阴平—阳平、阴平—去声听感边界的再测试的结果表明，阴平—阳平前后字两组的听感边界动程为3%，阴平—去声则为8%，与本实验阴平—上声的26%相比，要稳定得多。由此可见，与调型性对立声调相比，调阶性对立的声调间的听感边界显示出很强的动态性。调阶原理在本实验也是同样适用的。

4.3.3 标记原理

标记原理是指标记性强的声调的听感边界具有较大的依赖性。普通话的阴平是无标记的，具有稳定性；上声是有标记的，具有语境依赖性。本实验得到的上声听感范围，前字组为调域的0—62%，而后字组则为调域的0—36%，相差26%。而在阴平—阳平、阴平—去声再测试中，阴平则只相差3%和8%。由此可见，标记性强的上声的感知具有很强的语境依赖性。曹文［21］认为，中平调和低平调的感知均有语境依赖性，本实验与其结论基本一致。沈炯［33］指出，上声基调核心段是低音区平调，上声基调还可能有中音区尾音特征，但只在单说或停顿前才以声调尾音形式出现，以对偶关系支撑上声的低音特征。由此，王萍等［34］认为当目标字在前，后面参照字起到支撑作用，使刺激音更倾向感知为上声；而目标字在后，缺少支撑环境，则更倾向于感知为阴平。

4.3.4 高降原理

高降原理是指当参照字为高降调时，目标字的听感边界会有所下降。本实验中，前字组的光大—广大，后字组的梦乡—梦想，都是组别中听感边界最小、最低的，且在统计意义上，梦乡—梦想组（11.9半音）显著低于参照字为阴平的天仙—天险组（12.7半音）和参照字为阳平的图标—图表组（13.1半音）。这是去声终点低音和高降强烈听感印象的结果。与阴平和阳平相比，虽然去声起点音高达21半音，但其终点14半音较低，且7个半音的音高落差造成了强烈的“降”的听感印象，加强了去声终点的“低”感，这更凸显了后接目标字刺激音的“高”，因此梦乡—梦想组的阴平听感范围显著大于天仙—天险组和图标—图表组，相应梦乡—梦想组的听感边界也是后字对比组中最小最低的。

4.3.5 同调原理

同调原理是指当参照字和目标字之一为同一声调时，这个目标字声调的听感边界会有所减缩。这是基于参照字对目标字的校准效应，有跟目标字声调相同的参照字作为即时对照，使被试者对刺激音的声调判断更为严格，从而造成这个目标字声调的听感边界的压缩。在本实验中，前字组的烟花—眼花和后字组的天仙—天险，参照字为阴平，与目标字之一同调。烟花—眼花组的听感边界（15.9半音）在前字组中显著大于梯形—体型组（15.0半音）和光大—广大组（14.6半音），阴平听感范围最小。后字组中天仙—天险的听感边界（12.7半音）显著大于梦乡—梦想（11.9半音），与图标—图表（13.1半音）无显著差异。同调原理在本实验也是基本适用的。

4.3.6 性别差异原理

性别差异原理，是指男性和女性受试者的反应判断结果具有少量一致性差异，一般在显著水平以下，即不影响交际。本实验中，女性被试总体平均听感边界（14.1半音）略高于男性被试（13.7半音），但性别对听感边界无显著影响。结合我们正在进行的阴平—阳平、阴平—去声听感边界的再测试统计分析，两实验中性别对听感边界的主效应均不显著［$F(1, 22) = 0.723$, $p = 0.404$；$F(1, 22) = 3.250$, $p = 0.085$］。本实验中，女性被试平均听感边界宽度（0.98）显著大于男性（0.87）。同样结合阴平—阳平、阴平—去声的再测试实验统计结果，两实验中性别对听感边界的主效应均不显著［$F(1, 22) = 4.161$, $p = 0.054$；$F(1, 22) = 1.932$, $p = 0.178$］。由此看来，性别差异原理是基本适用的。

5. 结论

普通话二字组中低平调上声和高平调阴平的感知模式为范畴感知或类范畴感知。二字组中的参照字为目标字的判断提供了说话人的音高范围信息，有利于听音人定位两平调之间的范畴边界。

与陈曦丹［22］的研究相比，参照字音高设定为自然语言音高后，阴平—上声范畴感知表现向理想模式靠拢，范畴感知程度相应加深。同时，感知的重要参数：边界位置、边界宽度、区分峰在6组实验词中离散程度减弱，集中趋势增强，数据越加规整，被试在6组实验词中声调感知表现趋同，体现听感格局稳定性这一重要特征。感知表现由原来组间的较为离散优化至本实验的趋向集中，表明了真实语言是最有规则性、系统性的语言。

普通话二字组中阴平—上声的听感边界要受到参照字环境影响。总的来说，变动后的参照字若更能凸显刺激音“低”特征，上声听感范围则随之扩大，相应听感边界上移。

实验结果验证了五个普通话声调原理：调阶原理、标记原理、高降原理、同调原理和性别差异原理的适用性。对于位次原理，综合考虑三个再测试实验，暂可修改为：同一声调在双字组后字中的听感边界通常比在前字中更低更稳定。

本研究再测试得到的阴平—上声的听感边界和听感范围如图4所示。在前字对比组中，阴平—上声的听感边界为调域的

62%，上声听感范围为0—62%，阴平听感范围为62%—100%，较前实验上声听感范围扩大7%；在后字对比组中，阴平—上声的听感边界为调域的36%，上声听感范围为0—36%，阴平听感范围为36%—100%，较前实验上声听感范围缩小了13%。本实验前字组、后字组中两声调的听感边界差达26%，体现了上声听辨的环境依赖性强的特征。

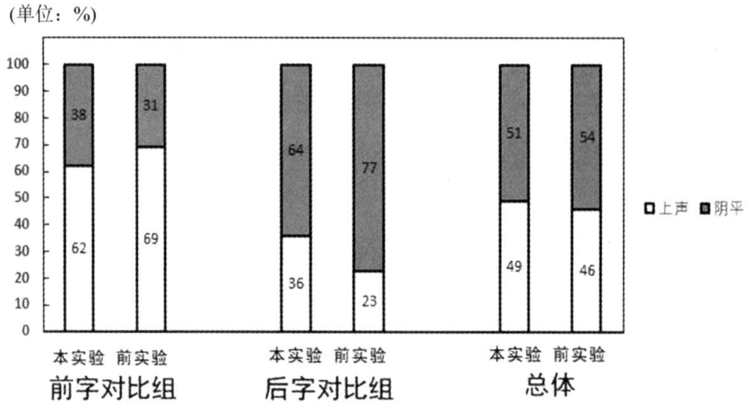

图4 两实验阴平—上声听感范围对比图

6. 致谢

本文在研究和写作过程中还得到了张洪明先生、石锋先生的指导，在此向两位先生表示诚挚的谢意。非常感谢《中国语音学报》编辑部、审稿专家提出的宝贵修改意见。

参考文献

[1] Abramson, A. S. 1979. The noncategorical perception of tone categories in Thai. In: B. Lindblom, S. Ohman (eds.), *Frontiers of Speech Communication*, London: Academic Press, 127 – 134.

[2] Bornstein, M. H., Kessen, W., Weiskopf, S. 1976. Color vision and hue categorization in young human infants. *Journal of Experimental Psychology Human Perception & Performance* 2 (1), 115 – 129.

[3] Finney, D. J. 1971. *Probit Analysis (3rd ed.)*. UK: Cambridge University Press.

[4] Fox, R., Qi, Y. 1990. Context effects in the perception of lexical tone. *Journal of Chinese Linguistics* 18(2), 261 – 283.

[5] Francis, A. L., Ciocca, V., Ng, B. K. C. 2003. On the (non) categorical perception of lexical tones. *Perception & Psychophysics* 65, 1029 – 1044.

[6] Huang, J. Y., Holt, L. L. 2009. General perceptual contributions to lexical tone normalization. *Journal of the Acoustical Society of America* 125 (6), 3983 – 3994.

[7] Kuhl, P., Miller, J. 1975. Speech perception by the chinchilla: voiced-voiceless distinction in alveolar plosive consonants. *Science* 190, 69 – 72.

[8] Liberman, A. M., Harris, K. S., Hoffman, H. S., Griffith, B. C. 1957. The discrimination of speech sounds within and across phoneme boundaries. *Journal of Experimental Psychology* 54, 358 – 368.

[9] Moore, C. B., Jongman, A. 1997. Speaker normalization in the perception of Mandarin Chinese tones. *Journal of the Acoustical Society of America* 102(3), 1864 – 1877.

[10] Morse, P. A., Snowdon, C. T. 1975. An investigation of categorical speech discrimination by rhesus monkeys. *Attention Perception & Psychophysics* 17, 9 – 16.

[11] Peng, G., Zheng, H. Y., Gong, T., Yang, R. X., Kong, J. P., Wang, S. Y. 2010. The influence of language experience on categorical perception of pitch contours. *Journal of Phonetics* 38, 616 – 624.

[12] Repp, B. H., Healy, A. F., Crowder, R. G.

1979. Categories and context in the perception of isolated steady-state vowels. *Journal of Experimental Psychology: Human Perception and Performance* 5, 129 – 145.
[13] Repp, B. H. 1984. Categorical perception: Issues, methods, findings. In: N. J. Lass (eds.), *Speech and language: Advances in Basic Research and Practice* (Vol. 10). New York: Academic Press, 243 – 335.
[14] Studdert-Kennedy, M., Liberman, A. M., Harris, K. S., Cooper, F. S. 1970. Motor theory of speech percepiton: a reply to Lane's critical review. *Psychological Review* 77, 234 – 249.
[15] Wang, W. S.-Y. 1976. Language change. *Annal of the New York Academy of Science* 208, 61 – 72.
[16] Whalen, D. H., Xu, Y. 1992. Information for Mandarin tones in the amplitude contour and in brief segments. *Phonetica* 49, 25 – 47.
[17] Wong, P. C. M., Diehl, R. L. 2003. Perceptual normalization for inter-and intratalker variation in Cantonese level tones. *Journal of Speech Language & Hearing Research* 46(2), 413 – 421.
[18] Xu, Y. 1993. Production and perception of coarticulation tones. *Journal of the Acoustical Society of America* 95, 2240 – 2253.
[19] Xu, Y. 1997. Contextual tonal variations in Mandarin. *Journal of Phonetics* 25, 61 – 83.
[20] Xu, Y., Gandour, J. T., Francis, A. L. 2006. Effects of language experience and stimulus complexity on the categorical perception of pitch direction. *Journal of the Acoustical Society of America* 120, 1063 – 1074.
[21] 曹文:《汉语平调的声调感知研究》,《中国语文》2010年第6期。
[22] 陈曦丹:《阴平和上声的听感分界》,硕士学位论文,南开大学,2012年。
[23] 金健 :《广州方言和东海方言平调的感知研究》,《方言》2010年第2期。
[24] 孔江平:《藏语(拉萨话)声调感知研究》,《民族语文》1995年第3期。
[25] 李晗菲、冯燕、孟亚茹、彭刚:《能量包络和时长对普通话声调感知的影响》,《中国语音学报》2019年第11辑。
[26] 李舒:《上声与去声的听感分界》,硕士学位论文,南开大学,2013年。
[27] 李幸河:《阴平和阳平的听感分界》,硕士学位论文,南开大学,2012年。
[28] 林焘、王士元:《声调感知问题》,《中国语言学报》1984年第2期。
[29] 石锋:《听感格局——汉语语音感知特征初探》,商务印书馆2019年版。
[30] 石锋、冉启斌:《普通话上声的本质是低平调——对〈汉语平调的声调感知研究〉的再分析》,《中国语文》2011年第6期。
[31] 石锋、冉启斌、王萍:《论语音格局》,《南开语言学刊》2010年第1期。
[32] 石锋、王大佐:《普通话声调听感原理》。实验语言学沙龙直播报告,2020年。
[33] 沈炯:《汉语音高载信系统模型》,《中国语言学新进展——庆祝王士元教授六十五华诞》,香港城市大学出版社1999年版。
[34] 王萍、石锋、荣蓉、陈曦丹、李舒、王秀秀:《汉语普通话上声的听感范畴》,《中国语文》2014年第4期。
[35] 王秀秀:《阳平和上声的听感分界》,硕士学位论文,南开大学,2014年。
[36] 王韫佳、李美京:《韩语母语者对普通话阳平和上声的知觉》,《语言教学与研究》2010年第1期。
[37] 薛鑫:《阴平和去声的听感分界》,硕士学位论文,南开大学,2012年。
[38] 张林军:《日本留学生汉语声调的范畴化感知》,《语言教学与研究》2010年第3期。
[39] 张妍:《汉语普通话大样本实验研究》,博士学位论文,北京语言大学,2018年。

王大佐 南开大学文学院,在读博士生。主要研究领域为实验语言学。
E-mail:wangdazuo@163.com

博士学位论文《大规模汉语中介语语音库设计和标注研究》简介

王 玮　张劲松

摘　要　带标注数据的大规模中介语语音库越来越受到学者们的重视，是二语语音习得领域和计算机辅助发音教学技术领域进一步发展的基础数据。但目前以汉语为目的语的中介语音库仍处于发展阶段，对收集到的大规模数据进行高质量、高效率的偏误标注也仍是学界面临的难点之一。博士学位论文《大规模汉语中介语语音库设计和标注研究》，讨论了中介语语音库文本设计，并对语音偏误标注困难的原因进行了系统性探讨。本文将简要介绍这篇博士论文的主要内容。

关键词　中介语，语音库，文本设计，偏误标注

Review of "A Study on Text Design and Annotation for Large Non – native Chinese Speech Corpus"

WANG Wei　ZHANG Jinsong

Abstract Non-native speech corpus with annotated data has attracted more and more attention. It enables researchers of second language acquisition to visualize and analyze the non-native speech, and to train and evaluate articulatory models of language learners. However, non-native speech corpora with Chinese as the target language is scarce, and high-quality error annotation within a short time is still difficult for researchers. Dissertation "A Study on Text Design and Annotation for Large Non-native Chinese Speech Corpus" discussed the design of the text, and explored the reasons for the difficulty of phonetic error annotation. This article briefly introduces the main contents of this doctoral dissertation.

Key words Non-native speech corpus, Text design, Error annotation

《大规模汉语中介语语音库设计和标注研究》，博士学位论文，作者：王玮；导师：张劲松；毕业院校：北京语言大学；论文完成时间：2020 年；全文共七章 162 页。

该论文对汉语中介语语音库的文本设计以及学习者语音偏误标注过程困难的客观原因进行了研究。

在大数据背景下，中介语语音库及其精细标注数据可以为一般语音学研究以及二语语音习得研究提供新的语言描写和研究的范式，同时为计算机辅助发音教学技术的发展提供基础数据资源。目前，以上各领域对中介语语音数据的需求主要体现在：(1) 语音现象覆盖全面；(2) 数据量大，这个量不仅指发音人数量，还指对原始语料的偏误标注数量。实际构建一个语料库的经费和时间成本有限，若同时满足以上需求，我们在构建中介语语音库过程中将主要面临两方面挑战：录音文本和偏误标注。

文本大小影响后期能够收录的发音人数量和标注数据量。文本大，容易覆盖到更多语音现象，但单人收录成本高，不利于收集更多的话者，后期标注工作的压力也会相应增大；文本小，按传统文本设计方法，则很难全面覆盖各类语音现象。由此可见，文本大小和语音现象覆盖面之间存在一定矛盾，在语音库文本设计阶段化解这一矛盾，用最小文本涵盖尽可能多的语音现象，是该研究尝试解决的第一个研究问题。

语音偏误标注目前主要依赖人工，这使得大规模学习者数据的偏误标注将主要面临以下问题：一是效率问题，语音偏误标注需要一定专业背景，能够满足条件的标注群体数量稀少，标注过程费时费力，依靠少数人完成大规模数据标注难度过高；二是质量问题，小样本语音偏误标注已经很难达到较高的标注者间一致性，当数据规模大时，标注质量更不容易控制，而随着数据规模的增大，我们对数据质量的要求也会相应提高。综上，现阶段标注技术很难满足研究者们对标注效率和质量的需求，要更好地解决这一问题，理解和探究问题形成的原因是必要的，因此，该论文引入关系复杂性理论，尝试从认知角度考察中介语语音标注任务一致性低和用时过长的客观原因。

该论文共七章，第一章至第二章是绪论及相关研究综述，第三章阐述文本设计问题，第四章至第六章讨论影响标注效率和质量的客观原因，第七章为综合讨论。下文分别简述各主要章节。

第三章提出了一套文本设计方案，其总体目标是：在控制文本集合大小的前提下，最大限度地涵盖更多语音要素。汉语是声调语言，语流中的声调更是汉语学习者的学习难点，因而这套文本的设计重点在句子层级，句子文本包含一个覆盖音段、声调、调联三音子且文本难度适中的最小句子集合（103 句）。该句子集合由计算机算法从 13 本对外汉语教材中搜索产生。同时还包含一个基于同声调句的同文异焦句集合（35 句）。除句子文本外，还设计了声调齐全的单音节、音韵平衡的双音节文本，同时以《北风和太阳》作为短文文本。依据上述四种录音文本收集了 772 位发音人的语音数据。

第四章探讨影响标注的客观原因。语音偏误标注过程涉及听觉感知、判断、决策等一系列对语音信息进行处理的认知过程。因而，论文首先引入认知心理学领域的“关系复杂性”理论。该理论认为复杂任务背后涉及多种关系变量，带来更高的认知要求，进而导致更高的认知负担。当认知负担过高时，人类的任务表现水平会相应下降。那么，任务隐含的关系复杂程度是否能解释标注结果的表现水平？实验 1 主要回答此问题，考察了关系变量的数量对标注任务完成情况的影响。实验 1 根据关系复杂性理论将传统的中介语音标注任务（四元关系）拆解为由偏误识别和偏误描述两个子任务组成的串行任务（三元关系）。对比标注者完成四元关系任务和三元关系任务的用时及标注正确率，结果显示，三元关系任务虽然包含两个子任务，但平均每句话的标注用时比只包含一个任务的四元关系任务少 20%，标注正确率高 6.4%。此结果说明关系变量数量，也即关系复杂程度，在一定程度上影响标注任务的完成情况，特别是影响标注任务的完成效率。

第五章和第六章分别在偏误识别和偏误描述两个子任务上考察关系变量的特点对标注任务完成情况的影响。

对于偏误识别任务，该文考察了学习者发音与母语标准语音的偏离程度、句子长度、音段种类、单句中错误音段所占比例、错误声调比例、语速，以及句子平均播放次数七类任务特点对任务完成的预测情况，同时考察七类特点在不同经验标注员上的作用是否不同。结果显示，对于熟手，语音偏离程度和句子长度对挑错正确率的共同影响程度为 96%，句子长度和偏误数量对标注时间的贡献率为 95.5%；对于新手，语音偏离程度独自对挑错正确率的贡献达到 90%，句长、偏误数量和声调对标注时间的贡献率为 96.3%。总体上，语音偏离程度对挑错正确率的影响最大，句长对标注时间的影响最大。这表明，偏误发音的偏离程度是影响偏误识别任务准确率的重要因素、句子长度是影响偏误识别任务的标注用时的重要因素，不因标注者标注经验的改变而发生大的变化。偏离程度越高，被标注者成功注意到的可能性越大，句子越长花费的标注时间越长。基于相同实验，还考察了以上任务特点对机器自动标注的影响，结果发现，仅偏误偏离程度一个变量特点可显著预测机器挑错正确率，不过其贡献只达到 12.4%；从任务整体完成情况来看，机器挑错正确率远远高于人类标注员，但同时虚报率较高。这表明偏误偏离程度同样会影响机器的标注性能，但影响程度较低，这可能使得机器的挑错正确率更高，结合机器标注用时短的特点，偏误识别任务由机器自动完成是可行的。

对于偏误描述任务，该文考察了语音偏离程度、偏离方向多重性、句子长度、音节内相邻音段是否正确、错误声调比例、音段类型等任务特点对任务完成的预测情况，同时也考察这些特点在不同经验标注员上的作用是否不同。结果显示，对于熟手，语音偏离方向和程度对标注正确率的共同影响程度为68%，对标注时间的共同影响程度为41.4%；对于新手，偏离方向、音段类型和偏离程度对标注正确率的贡献率为57.1%，对标注时间的贡献率为37.4%，其中音段类型对新手的影响主要表现在韵母的标注正确率低于声母。总体上，不论是对熟手还是新手、对标注正确率还是时间，偏离方向的贡献都是最大的。这表明，在偏误描述任务上，偏离方向多重性是影响偏误描述任务完成情况的重要因素，其次是偏离程度，两者不受标注者经验影响。音段类型主要影响新手标注员，表现在新手声母比韵母标得好。

第七章综合讨论，该研究的文本设计部分有助于语音库构建过程中收集更多发音人样本，同时减少后期标注工作量。标注研究的发现有助于增进我们对于偏误标注困难原因的理解，从而为研究新的标注策略、提升语料库建设质量提供一定的理论支持。

王 玮 新疆大学国际文化交流学院，博士，讲师，主要研究领域为中介语语音库设计和标注、L2语音习得。
E-mail：wangwei_xinjiang@126.com

张劲松 北京语言大学信息科学学院，中国北京语言资源高精尖创新中心，博士，研究员，主要研究领域为语音识别、合成技术、韵律建模、实验语音学、语音习得，以及基于语音识别、合成技术的计算机辅助语音教学技术。
E-mail：jinsong.zhang@blcu.edu.cn